THE HISTORICAL SERIES OF THE REFORMED CHURCH IN AMERICA
IN COOPERATION WITH
ORIGINS STUDIES IN DUTCH-AMERICAN HISTORY
NO. 55

HENRY J. KUIPER

Shaping the
Christian Reformed Church
1907-1962

James A. De Jong

WILLIAM B. EERDMANS PUBLISHING COMPANY
Grand Rapids, MI / Cambridge, U. K.

Wm. B. Eerdmans Publishing Co.
255 Jefferson Ave. S. E., Grand Rapids, Michigan 49503/
P.O. Box 163, Cambridge, CB3 9PU U.K.
www.eerdmans.com

Printed in the United States of America

HENRY J. KUIPER

SHAPING THE
CHRISTIAN REFORMED CHURCH
1907-1962

To James Wyngaarden,

With deep appreciation and
thanks for your generous
support of Calvin Seminary
in honouring your father.
You'll find a few familial
ghosts haunting these pages!
With best regards always.

James A. De ____

*To my former colleagues and students
at Calvin Theological Seminary*

In gratitude for their dedication, gifts, and insight

The Historical Series of the Reformed Church in America

The series was inaugurated in 1968 by the General Synod of the Reformed Church in America acting through the Commission on History to communicate the church's heritage and collective memory and to reflect on our identity and mission, encouraging historical scholarship which informs both church and academy.

General Editor,
　　　The Rev. Donald J. Bruggink, Ph.D, D.D.
　　　Western Theological Seminary
　　　Van Raalte Institute, Hope College

　　　Laurie Baron, copy editor
　　　Russell L. Gasero, production editor

Commission on History
　　　James Hart Brumm, M.Div., Blooming Grove, New York
　　　Lynn Japinga, Ph.D., Hope College, Holland, Michigan
　　　Mary L. Kansfield, M.A., New Brunswick, New Jersey
　　　Hartmut Kramer-Mills, M.Div., Th.D, New Brunswick, New Jersey
　　　Jeffrey Tyler, Ph.D., Hope College, Holland, Michigan
　　　Lori Witt, Ph.D., Central College, Pella, Iowa

Contents

Illustrations

Acknowledgments

The appearance of this book acknowledges substantial debts.

Henry J. Kuiper's daughter Claire and her husband, Edsko Hekman, were generous patrons who donated the fifth floor of The Hekman Library at Calvin College and Seminary, thereby reclaiming for it the Hekman name so prominent on the former Calvin campus. They also established the H.J. Kuiper chair in the Calvin Seminary doctoral program. I am deeply grateful for their support and friendship.

Help in writing and revising this book came from many sources, and I thank them all profoundly. Student James Honeyford mapped H.J. Kuiper sources at the project's outset, his summer research funded by a grant from the Calvin Seminary Faculty Heritage Fund. The administrations of Calvin College, Calvin Theological Seminary, Reformed Bible College (now Kuyper College), and CRC Publications, as well as the councils of the five congregations (or their offspring) served by Kuiper, all graciously entrusted me with permission to read and cite official, restricted minutes. The theological librarians and the staff of the Calvin archives were always responsive and encouraging. Richard Harms, an enormous and winsome font of insight on Christian Reformed history and its important sources, was an engaging conversationalist who taught me much in our frequent interchanges. The Calvin Seminary board generously made research time available for this endeavor toward the end of my faculty tenure. The Historical Committee of the Christian Reformed Church contributed generous encouragement and support. Students in my last several Christian Reformed Church history classes produced stimulating papers on facets of Kuiper's life and work. My former secretary, Geraldine Kuiper (no relation to H.J.), facilitated technical matters for several drafts. Clarence Boomsma, P.Y. De Jong, Lester De Koster, John B. Hulst, Andrew Kuyvenhoven, and Henry Zwaanstra offered encouragement and helpful insights, anecdotes, and correctives at various stages.

Particularly important are the approval and suggestions of the Commission on History of the Reformed Church in America. This project interfaces with the history of the Reformed Church at a number of points, leading to its publication in The Historical Series of the Reformed Church in America. General editor Donald Bruggink's counsel and encouragement are especially appreciated. So is the superb copy editing of Laurie Baron.

Without the help of all of these people and organizations, this book would not have been completed.

–James A. De Jong

Introduction

Historians of the Christian Reformed Church have given Henry J. Kuiper a place of unparalleled influence in the denomination he served. The latest, James C. Schaap, in his popular and anecdotal review, *Our Family Album: The Unfinished Story of the Christian Reformed Church*, states: "No single individual may ever again come to speak so much both for and with the mind of the CRC as did longtime *Banner* editor Henry J. Kuiper. Today it is inconceivable that any single person could lead the denomination so completely. Many looked to Kuiper's words as if they were Holy Writ."[1] Accordingly, Kuiper assumed prominence in Schaap's narrative.

In the trade edition of his Ph.D. dissertation, James D. Bratt offers an arresting observation concerning Kuiper the editor: "Indeed, as his tenure lengthened it became increasingly difficult to distinguish between the man, the periodical, and the group they served." He amplifies: "In his years of greatest power, Kuiper made the *Banner* stronger than it had ever been or ever would be—*the* authority on all matters of truth and morals, a voice whose every word was to be eagerly awaited, treasured, and—most of all—heeded"[2] (italics Bratt's). The solidly defensible first part of the latter quotation quickens interest in Kuiper.

[1] Grand Rapids: CRC Publications, 1998, 273.
[2] James D. Bratt, *Dutch Calvinism in Modern America: A History of a Conservative Subculture* (Grand Rapids: Eerdmans, 1984), 125.

John H. Kromminga sat under Kuiper's preaching weekly in his youth and adolescence, was catechized in the faith by Kuiper, and made profession of that faith during Kuiper's ministry at the Neland Avenue Christian Reformed Church. Years later, as president of Calvin Theological Seminary and resident denominational historian, Kromminga wrote his former pastor's tribute for the denominational record. Kromminga said, "No man in our time has left a deeper imprint on the Christian Reformed Church than Henry J. Kuiper. . . . Any future historian of this period of the denomination will find his name the one he can least afford to ignore."[3] His opinion carries the added weight of careful historical research for his doctorate and the balanced judgment expressed in his published history of the denomination.[4]

These assessments alone compel an in-depth study of Kuiper. They also suggest that understanding Kuiper more fully will yield deeper, more solid insight into the church he served than presently exists. Since the 1950s, historians of the denomination have endeavored to represent its dynamics in terms of identifiable groups that were sometimes embroiled in theological and cultural tension and even combat.[5] This study suggests that such spiritual profiling, while helpful

[3] John H. Kromminga, "1962 In Retrospect," *1963 Yearbook of the Christian Reformed Church* (Grand Rapids: Christian Reformed Publishing House, 1964), 338.

[4] John H. Kromminga, *The Christian Reformed Church: A Study in Orthodoxy* (Grand Rapids: Baker, 1949). Kromminga provides fine summaries of many of the issues with which Kuiper was involved.

[5] The *Afscheiding* ("separation") in 1834 and the *Doleantie* ("sorrowing") in 1888 were both movements of people and leaders out of the reorganized, state-controlled, and doctrinally tolerant church in the Netherlands; they joined forces in 1892 in the new, Reformed confessional denomination known as *De Gereformeerde Kerken in Nederland*. Christian Reformed historians before 1970 recognized the existence of the "A" or pietistic tradition of 1834 and the socially engaged and intellectually accomplished "B" or *Doleantie* tradition led by Abraham Kuyper, and they charted the dynamic interplay of the two in the immigrants who shaped the denomination in its formative years. Henry Zwaanstra, *Reformed Thought and Experience in a New World* (Kampen: J.H. Kok, B.V., 1973), in chapter 3, "Proceeding on the Basis of Principle," 68-131, nuanced this view by developing portraits of "the Confessional Reformed," "Separatist Calvinists," and "American Calvinists" in the church prior to 1918. Bratt, *Dutch Calvinism*, 47, in an expanded chart, profiles two groups of 1834 Seceders (outgoing and introverted) and two sorts of Kuyperians (positive and antithetical) in the Dutch Reformed subculture. Schaap's labels of "Inward," "Upward," and "Outward" believers in *Our Family Album*, 275, imposed a misreading of

to a point in clarifying operative accents and themes, may be more of an imposition on the record than a completely accurate interpretation of it. Kuiper himself, seen up close, defies easy categorization. He was both a product and proponent of 1834 *Afscheiding* spirituality and of turn-of-the-century Kuyperian social and cultural engagement.[6] He led Americanization on some fronts but pointedly resisted it on others. He was simultaneously a progressive agent of change and a conservator of traditions. He courted evangelical contacts but warned readers about becoming like them. Like many of his contemporaries, he was part of different coalitions on different issues. Religious genes were sometimes dominant and sometimes recessive in each church leader, often depending on the issue, but everyone in the church was defined by the same pool. They knew it, and they valued and respected their familial identity during Kuiper's era more than they did their shifting, differing emphases. Recovering that deeper, complex unity for the historical record seems more important and necessary now than a generation ago, when it was more clearly understood and appreciated by leaders and church members than is the case today. Furthermore, Kuiper's time in denominational life needs the comprehensive, systematic historical examination that to date it has not received. This study endeavors to make a contribution toward that end. By paying close attention to the original sources, it also attempts to construct a balanced and accurate

a Kuiper editorial on the record by asserting that what the editor warned might develop was his perceived state of affairs. See *Banner*, 75/2227 [the *Banner* followed a practice of numbering the volumes in every year and also continued sequential numbering from year to year —Ed.] (1/12/1940), 29, and 275. Both Dutch movements that exited the state church also affected the western, nineteenth-century immigrant wing of the Reformed Church in America, as Bratt's study shows.

6   Concerning similar classifications he developed, George Marsden appropriately observed, "These categories are useful if one recognizes that the outlook of each of the three groups includes something of the main emphases of the other two," in "Our Present Task in the American Setting," *Reformed Journal* 31 (September, 1981), 15. The *Afscheiding* was a somewhat disparate movement, whose leaders assumed differing postures on the controlled religious establishment imposed in 1816 after the Napoleanic era in their shared desire to reassert biblically Reformed polity, vitality, and orthodoxy. Abraham Kuyper's Neo-Calvinism in frequent religious newspaper articles and books like *Ons Programm* (*Our Program*) articulated a program for re-Christianizing Dutch national life and culture. Both streams flowed into the Christian Reformed Church and blended with varying degrees of ease and comfort.

presentation of a man who has been both inappropriately revered and ungraciously caricatured, as strong leaders often are.

Until the end of the twentieth century, the Christian Reformed Church was organizationally uncomfortable with the mainline ecumenical movement as well as with American evangelicalism. While it displayed features of both, it had compatibility with neither. Understanding Kuiper is a window on understanding why. This study might also serve, therefore, as a forthright testimony to interested observers of the denomination in both the mainline and evangelical communities, of whom there are any number, on why this communion has seemed so reticent about wider and more enthusiastic ecclesiastical fellowship.

On all these counts, the life and work of H.J. Kuiper deserves a close look. He contributed substantially to the era of the Christian Reformed Church's greatest cohesiveness and many of its most remarkable accomplishments. Probably before and certainly since Kuiper's ministry—before 1910 and after 1962—the church was considerably less unified and less committed to joint endeavors. The claim of this study is not that Kuiper deserves primary credit for what the denomination came to be on his watch. Standing shoulder to shoulder with him in significance are men of his generation like Henry Beets, Louis Berkhof, R.B. Kuiper, Samuel Volbeda, and Clarence Bouma,[7] all of whom we will meet in this study. These were supported and complemented by a dozen or two remarkable educators and ministers who collectively formed a Maginot Line of confessional Reformed orthodoxy and who inspired a burst of world-and-life-view service that created and sustained a remarkably broad spectrum of Christian ministries and institutions. H.J. Kuiper, who edited the denomination's official weekly magazine and sounding board, the *Banner*, from 1929 until August of 1956—the church's middle years—simply affords a singularly comprehensive and

---

[7]   Beets was Kuiper's predecessor as editor of the *Banner*, the Christian Reformed Church's first full-time director of missions, its stated clerk, and an early historian of its life and work. Berkhof served for four decades on the seminary faculty, toward the end as president, and was a widely published systematic theologian. R.B. Kuiper was successively president of Calvin College, Westminster Seminary, and Calvin Seminary. Volbeda was professor of practical theology at Calvin Seminary and served as president between the tenures of Berkhof and R.B. Kuiper. Bouma edited the influential *Calvin Forum* for two decades and was Calvin Seminary's professor of ethics. Each man made substantial contributions to the denomination and is worthy of in-depth study.

accessible point of entry into an understanding of the church of his day.

H.J. Kuiper is the chosen subject of this study also because, as editor of the *Banner*, he articulated with clarity and passion the Reformed faith and life weekly for the entire constituency. He was the middle man without whose contribution the denomination would not have become a movement, which to a large extent it was on his watch. To what degree the *Banner* became such a powerful force because of Kuiper's industry and genius, and to what degree it became so because in his day it was still part of a largely print, pre-electronic culture, this study does not presume to answer. But that is a subject worth contemplating.

If the shaping of the Christian Reformed ethos in Kuiper's day is remarkable, its indebtedness to its Dutch progenitors needs to be acknowledged. The clear social vision, the single-minded and sacrificial commitment, the organizational genius, the confessional articulateness and theological passion, the spiritual superiority complex, the disciplined and imposed solidarity, the *angst* over being culturally assimilated and compromised, and the pattern of ecclesiastical division were all Dutch ecclesiastical features that helped define the Christian Reformed Church. Thoroughly bilingual, Kuiper and his peers rode the crest of that immigrant wave in North America. As energetic and gifted as they were, they were debtors to Herman Bavinck, Abraham Kuyper, and their immense and gifted cast of supporters in the Netherlands. Most of them also brought to the *Doleantie's* Neo-Calvinist themes and emphases the perceptive piety of the 1834 *Afscheiding,* with its spiritual warmth and tenderness, its unswerving commitment to the Word written and preached, its deeply experiential knowledge of sin and grace, its reverence for the church and its offices, and its disciplined devotion and sweet communion with the Almighty. These sources gave them all, including H.J. Kuiper, a discerning point from which to critique their American context and later Christian Reformed developments. For five or more decades they fed on the Dutch sources, and the spiritual muscle developed from this hearty menu carried their sons and students for a generation beyond the Second World War. One of H.J. Kuiper's deepest worries was that loss of the Dutch language in the 1930s would cut the church off at its spiritual knees. To a significant degree, his concern was prophetic, although the denomination's changing self-perception by the end of the twentieth century can be attributed as much, possibly more, to its gradual American evangelical homogenization as to its linguistic loss of contact with Dutch sources. Kuiper and his generation were remarkable leaders because they followed remarkable theological progenitors, whose ideas and energy they brokered and filtered in their new context.

This study is organized into three parts. The first reviews Kuiper's early life and his pastorates, including his wider involvement in ecclesiastical service during those years. Here a complete reading of the consistorial, classical, and synodical minutes and records forms the basis for my interpretation. Personal papers and family records are disappointingly thin, which significantly reduces the biographical value of this book. I suspect that Kuiper intentionally engineered this outcome, although I cannot verify that suspicion.

The second section is devoted to the extradenominational projects in which H.J. Kuiper was involved. These are remarkably broad and visionary. Here official minutes were not always existent or available, and several projects—like the federation of congregationally based young men's societies for study and fellowship— in which he played a less formative role, are not included. This second section of the book overlaps chronologically with the first and third sections. Segregating Kuiper's service to the organized church, including its assemblies, from his involvement in Christian projects not directly belonging to or controlled by the institutional church will be understood and appreciated by readers with Kuyperian sensitivities. It affords a way of managing a rather substantial amount of material as well as honoring the distinction between the church as institute (organization) and the church as organism (followers of Christ in corporate solidarity in all other endeavors). Because his roles in these enterprises were not equally significant, the chapters on them are not all of equal length.

The third section is dedicated entirely to Kuiper's service as editor of the *Banner*, which by the end of his tenure was being read in the overwhelming majority of Christian Reformed homes. This section of the study is based on a complete reading of all his editorials and articles, as well as an extensive reading of committee and board minutes and reports. Secondary sources and a rereading of several years of seminary student papers on H.J. Kuiper were only fully and systematically examined after research in the primary sources and writing the preliminary drafts had been completed.

CHAPTER 1

Early Life and Education

Religious Context

Henry J. Kuiper was born December 22, 1885. His family belonged to the Spring Street Holland Christian Reformed Church, as the denomination was then known. The church building was located a block south of Fulton Street on what today is Commerce Street in Grand Rapids, Michigan. Its pastor was the Reverend J.H. Vos, father of the brilliant young theological student, Geerhardus Vos, who had already served as an instructor in the preparatory program of the denomination's theological school, had attended Princeton Seminary the year before Kuiper's birth, and had just left on a Princeton fellowship to pursue Old Testament studies in Berlin.[1]

By 1885, the church's membership stood at 390 families and 1,550 souls; it was then easily the largest of the 65 congregations in the young denomination that had its beginnings in an 1857 departure from the Reformed Church in America. That the church reported only 310 confessing members indicates that it was characterized by the religious practice in the more experiential churches of the Netherlands of tolerating adult members who, lacking full assurance or conviction,

---

[1] On the Vos father and son, see George Harinck, "Geerhardus Vos as Introducer of Kuyper in America," in *The Dutch- American Experience: Essays in Honor of Robert P. Swierenga*, ed. Hans Krabbendam and Larry J. Wagenaar, VU Studies on Protestant History, no. 5 (Amsterdam: VU Uitgeverij, 2000), 243-61.

did not make public profession of their faith but still might have their children baptized.[2] Only three other congregations that year showed fewer professing members than families, which rendered the Spring Street congregation among the most experiential and subjectivistic in the denomination. This feature of the church's spirituality certainly influenced the young Kuiper.

Vos had come to the Spring Street church in August 1881, after having served five congregations in Germany and the Netherlands. In his 1913 obituary tribute, J.W. Brink, a son of the congregation who became a successful pastor and missionary to the Navajos, regarded Vos as his "spiritual father in Christ." Brink characterized Vos's preaching as "especially devout and unctuous. How he could pour out his soul speaking of the love of Christ, exhorting to love and holy living."[3] Vos undoubtedly encouraged H.J. Kuiper to consider ministry, prayed that he would be led by the Spirit into theological training, and spoke to his parents about the young man's abilities—as he had done with Brink and his parents. Several revivals broke out in the congregation during Vos's nineteen-year ministry. The complacent were awakened by the Spirit, the church would fill for evening services, and at those times young people—some of them weeping under conviction or in joy—would occupy the front benches of the church.

Vos had studied at the Secession or *Afscheiding* seminary in Kampen in its earliest years. He had graduated in 1858. There the Reverend Jan Bavinck, father of the renowned theologian Herman Bavinck, had been his teacher and had a substantial influence on him. By the time Vos emigrated, he was an experienced and respected minister. Two years after his arrival in America, he was chosen president of the 1883 synod of the Holland Christian Reformed Church. As a denominational leader, he held a variety of assignments: secretary of the synodical committee, secretary of the board of heathen missions, member of the theological school's *curatorium* or board, member of the

---

[2]   This practice had synodical sanction and required parents to attend an adult catechism class. Known as the *doopledenstelsel* (baptized members' system), it was terminated by the synod of 1898, although it continued in some churches for a time thereafter.

[3]   J.W. Brink, "Personal Reminiscences of the Late Rev. J.H. Vos," *Banner* 48/ 856 (3/16/1913), 155. Material for this paragraph was also found in the "Christian Reformed Ministers Database" and in the J.H. Vos file, Archives of the Christian Reformed Church, located at Heritage Hall, Calvin College, Grand Rapids, Michigan. (Hereafter, Archives, CRC.)

home missions committee. On the *curatorium*, he exerted a significant level of influence on the seminary, where he even taught for a year in the 1890s when his son Geerhardus accepted a permanent appointment to the faculty of Princeton Seminary. He also contributed articles to several church papers and had theological connections. He was married to Aaltje Beuker, sister of Henricus Beuker, who for years edited *De Vrije Kerk* (*The Free Church*), the Secession's leading theological magazine, and who immigrated in 1893 and taught theology at the Christian Reformed seminary from 1894 until his untimely death in 1900.[4] That same year, at age seventy-four, Vos retired. By then he had been H.J. Kuiper's pastor for all of his fifteen years and had had both a spiritual and a theological influence on him.

At the time of Kuiper's birth, the total membership of the denomination stood at 21,156. It was by then divided into five districts or classes: Grand Rapids, Holland, Hudson, Illinois, and Iowa. Classes Holland, with 17 congregations, and Classis Grand Rapids, with 20, together reported 15,592 members or 73.7 percent of the denomination's total membership and 57 percent of its congregations. The denomination was then served by 32 active and three retired ministers.[5] It was just beginning to realize a huge infusion of new immigrants that would not subside until the outbreak of World War I, by which time it boasted 223 congregations, 13 classes, 154 ministers, and 86,779 souls.[6]

The new immigrants flooded Holland Christian Reformed congregations and schools, bringing with them the several nuances of the *Afscheiding* temperament and the vision and energy of Abraham Kuyper's emerging movement, dubbed the *Doleantie* (meaning literally "lamentation," "mourning," or "grieving") a few years after H.J. Kuiper's birth. The term denoted the heavy-heartedness with which Kuyper and his following left the substantially apostate, in their opinion, state church. The new immigrants were attracted to the Holland Christian Reformed Church because of its cultural compatibility as well as at

---

[4]   See James A. De Jong, "Henricus Beuker and *De Vrije Kerk* on Abraham Kuyper and the Free University," in *Building the House: Essays on Christian Education*, ed. James A. De Jong and Louis Y. Van Dyke (Sioux Center, Iowa: Dordt College Press, 1981), 27-46.

[5]   Statistics in this paragraph are taken from the *Jaarboekje voor de Hollandsche Chr. Ger. Kerk, in Noord Amerika, voor het Jaar 1885* (Grand Rapids: D. J. Doornink, 1884).

[6]   *Jaarboekje 1915* , 31.

the counsel of their spiritual leaders in the homeland, who a few years earlier had shifted their preference away from the Reformed Church in America because of its toleration of Free Masonry.

But the newcomers did not always blend easily with the earlier immigrants in the denomination, whose leaders reflected the traits and emphases of the more rigidly conservative northern wing of the *Afscheiding*. The new mix did produce dynamic church life, a flurry of local and national papers in the Dutch language and intense, prolonged, and rarified theological debates. Young Kuiper was raised at the height of the intense controversy over supra- and infralapsarianism, an esoteric and speculative Calvinistic debate over the order of God's eternal decrees.

The Spring Street congregation had met initially in several rented locations in downtown Grand Rapids. Within a year it had erected a two-story, wood-frame building on the corner of Ionia and Weston, where it worshiped for the next decade. In 1868 it had built its handsome church on Spring Street, to which it added a majestic, high steeple in 1888 and which it occupied until it moved to its massive fortress on Bates Street in 1912 and was thenceforth known as the First or Bates Street Christian Reformed Church. The congregation's membership peaked at four hundred families the year after Kuiper's birth. By then it had already produced five daughter churches. The Christian Reformed churches in Kelloggsville and Jenison were organized in February and July of 1875, respectively. Exercised over issues of election and assurance, a small group left to form the Netherlands Reformed congregation, the runaway child, in 1877. Two years later, in 1879, the Eastern Avenue, and four years later, in 1881, the Alpine Avenue, churches were planted on the eastern and western edges of the expanding city.[7]

Half a mile north of the mother church, the Coldbrook Holland Christian Reformed Church was wearing its new name comfortably. Under the leadership of its competent, respected pastor, the Reverend L.J. Hulst, it had left the Reformed Church in America in 1881 over the lodge issue. Coldbrook was the fourth congregation within the Grand Rapids city limits; Kelloggsville and Jenison were beyond them. Coldbrook was the third largest in the denomination in 1885, listing 246 families and 1,129 members. Hulst was a wise and mature pastor who had written a complete Reformed dogmatics during his

[7]   For the best material on this congregation see *Centennial, 1857-1957: First Christian Reformed Church, Grand Rapids, Michigan* (Grand Rapids: First Christian Reformed Church, 1957).

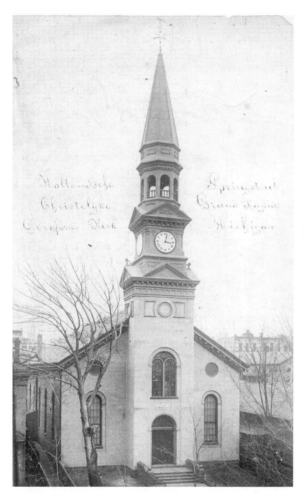

The Spring Street
*Hollandse Christelijke
Gereformeerde Kerk*
(Holland Christian
Reformed Church) as
it appeared in Kuiper's
youth.

twenty-five years of service in the Netherlands and who had assumed prominence in the western Reformed Church as a frequent contributor to its leading Dutch-language religious weekly, *De Hope*.[8] Ordained in 1849, he served in active ministry in both denominations for another thirty-six years after coming to America—until he retired at age eighty-five, in 1910. The fifth and sixth Grand Rapids congregations appeared

[8]   Elton Bruins calls Hulst's leaving "the greatest loss" to the Reformed Church in the early 1880s. Robert P. Swierenga and Elton J. Bruins, *Family Quarrels in the Dutch Reformed Churches of the 19th Century*, The Historical Series of the Reformed Church in America, no. 32 (Grand Rapids: Eerdmans, 1999), 132. Also see James D. Bratt, "Lambert J. Hulst: The Pastor as Leader in an Immigrant Community," in *The Dutch- American Experience*, 209-21.

in 1887: La Grave Avenue in February and Franklin Street in March. La Grave was formed as the denomination's first English-speaking congregation—a harbinger of Americanization, the most monumental adjustment made by the immigrant church in its entire history. Its birth had been stressful, opposed by Vos and the Spring Street consistory, who thought the transition to the English language should be gradual and should occur in existing congregations. As annual statistics testify, the membership of both new congregations came substantially from Spring Street, which never again reached the size it achieved shortly after H.J. Kuiper was sprinkled at its font.

The year Kuiper was born the denomination supported only six Christian grammar schools, all of them under the direct ownership and control of a congregation's consistory, or governing body, as had been the Dutch custom for three hundred years. One of the six belonged to the Spring Street congregation. The school began in the winter of 1855-1856, founded by the Second Reformed Church in Grand Rapids. It was appropriated by the Spring Street church in 1857, after the Reverend H. Klyn was physically blocked from his pulpit at Second Church on a January Sunday morning because of his public criticism of the state of the Reformed Church and his reported plans to leave it. He protested this consistorial obstruction dramatically by marching out of the building, followed by half of the church's one hundred families. They joined a group of dissidents already meeting separately, formed the Spring Street congregation in March, and the next month joined others in creating the new denomination. They also appropriated the school. Klyn soon returned to the Reformed Church, but the school did not. In the 1870s, the church erected the school building attended by Kuiper in the 1890s; it was located two blocks south of the church, on the corner of Spring and Williams streets. By the time Kuiper was born, the second floor of the Williams Street School had been rented out to the synod of the Holland Christian Reformed Church for nine years—since 1876—for use by its fledgling theological school. The seminary met in those quarters until 1892, when it moved into the first building of its own, on the corner of Madison and Franklin. The first year or two that Kuiper attended Williams Street Christian School, theological education was still underway upstairs.

If Kuiper entered this life a scant generation after the Christian Reformed Church was born, he was only two generations removed from the incorporation of the city of Grand Rapids in 1838. The city's population had not yet reached 45,000 by 1885. Electric lights had only been introduced four years earlier. The year of his birth the city charter was adjusted to give women the right to vote in school elections. The city's only high school, not yet twenty years old, was situated up Heritage Hill, on Fountain Street, among the mansions of the affluent. It would be six years before John Ball Zoo was created, and seven years before the Holland Home for aged immigrants opened on East Fulton Street.[9] But the four blocks on Spring Street between Fulton and Wealthy were the geographic center of the Holland Christian Reformed Church in Grand Rapids and the spiritual hub of the flourishing young denomination. This was the neighborhood, geographic and spiritual, in which Henry J. Kuiper was formed. He was quite literally raised in the bosom of the Christian Reformed Church.

Family

The Kuiper family lived a few blocks west and several blocks south of their church, at 18 King Street, a short cul-de-sac west off Grandville Avenue, a half block south of Wealthy Street. It was just around the corner from father Jacob's blacksmith business at 92 Grandville Avenue. Henry Kuiper, a furniture finisher at the Phoenix Furniture Company, lived at 29 King Street. Boarding with him was John Kuiper, a blacksmith employed with the J.O. Fitch Company.[10] Henry was undoubtedly Jacob's father and H.J.'s namesake; John was Jacob's single brother, eight years his junior. The next year an Albert Kuiper, possibly another younger brother or an uncle of Jacob, was also living at 29 King Street and was employed as a wood carver at the Berkey and Gay Furniture Company. A decade later Henry had died and his widow, Aafje, was living at 113 King Street. Albert was living at 127 King Street, now presumably married. Jacob had moved his home and business to 141 and 139 Grandville Avenue, respectively. Following typical immigrant patterns, the extended family lived in close proximity and the men plied the same trade.

Jacob had been born in 1855. H.J. Kuiper's mother was Hilligje Franken. She had been born in 1857. The two had arrived in New York together on the *S.S. Schiedam*, a Holland America Line vessel, May 30, 1882, along with Jacob's brother John.[11] Jacob and Hilligje were

9   For a chronology of important civic developments, see Z.Z. Lydens, ed., *A Look at Early Grand Rapids* (Grand Rapids: Kregel, 1976), 189-91.

10   This information is from the *Grand Rapids City Directory, 1885*.

11   This information was obtained from Robert P. Swierenga, "Dutch Immigrants in U.S. Ship Passenger Lists, Port of New York, 1881-1882: an Alphabetical Listing, I, Aalbers—Lefferdink." Photoduplicated.

betrothed, not married. The party traveled in steerage, the lowest and cheapest accommodations available. Within three years the couple had been married and was settled in business and ready to raise a family.

The Jacob Kuiper family had four children, of whom H.J. was the oldest. He was followed by his sister Dena, who later married the Reverend Harry Bultema, the popular Muskegon minister who in 1919 was deposed from the Christian Reformed ministry over his exegetical defense of premillennial eschatology. Two brothers, Frank J. and John, completed the family circle. Frank served in World War I. After the war, H.J. enlisted him to teach on the first faculty of Grand Rapids Christian High School, which he did briefly before returning to school and becoming a successful dentist and a deacon at the family's home church. John became a university professor in Kentucky.

Jacob Kuiper became a leader in the Spring Street church. He was elected deacon for the first time in 1887 and as elder for the first time in 1904. His recurring election to church office is testimony to his exemplary personal and family life. Decades later in his autobiography, Bultema described the Kuiper household as a hospitable and "friendly home."[12] It had taken him, a recently arrived immigrant teenager a year older than H.J., into its circle as he was recovering from a prolonged and almost fatal battle with typhoid fever. He and his brother had joined the Spring Street church in the fall of 1901, and the church had stood beside him during his delirium and months of hospitalization. He remembers H.J., then in his first year at Calvin, standing beside his hospital bed "with tears in his eyes, when he saw me dying."[13] The family welcomed him into its circle later the next summer, and there he first met their daughter Dena, became friends with H.J., and participated in the "almost daily rumpus and some of the finest humor" with the family and Kuiper's fellow students Diedrich Kromminga and George Hylkema.[14] Unfortunately, Bultema's is virtually the only firsthand account we have of the warmth and generosity that characterized Kuiper home life. The children grew and left the home. H.J. assisted in

---

[12]   Harry Bultema, *Valiant and Diligent for Truth: The Autobiography of Harry Bultema*, with a foreword by Daniel C. Bultema (Grand Rapids: Grace Publications, 1986), 45. Written in the 1930s and 1940s and published more than thirty years after Bultema's death, this memoir offers a detailed and sensitive insight into prevailing Christian Reformed piety at the turn of the twentieth century.

[13]   Ibid., 43.

[14]   Ibid., 46.

G. Hornstra   R. Meijering   R. Bolt   J. G. B. Sluyter
Y. Berg   J. Kuiper   Ds. T. VanderArk   A. Mohr   T. Dykstra   W. Hertel
J. Buffenga   H. Drukker   J. B. Hulst   M. Boersma

The church council (consistory) in 1906. Elder Jacob Kuiper is standing second from left, middle row. Elder J.B. Hulst, who played a prominent role in H.J.'s life, is seated second from right.

the 1912 wedding of Bultema and Dena. An era ended when Hilligje died November 7, 1929, at age seventy-two, in her home at 1009 Bates Street, now going by the Americanized name "Helen." She was predeceased by her husband.

Education

About the time H.J. Kuiper began attending the Williams Street Christian School, the constituency was wrestling with the language issue. In February, 1891, the Spring Street consistory convened a congregational meeting to once again address the nettlesome question. Following deliberation, the decision was reached that for children five through ten years of age, instruction would be in Dutch, thereafter in English, with the proviso that the older students would continue to receive a lesson a week in the Dutch language to maintain their fluency. Provision was made to hire a competent teacher to teach the students English.

At the same meeting, policy was changed to fund the school through subscriptions rather than tuition, and church members who had no children in school were encouraged to participate. Those who chose not to subscribe were informed that they were expected to pay ten

Williams Street Christian School students and teachers in 1895. H.J.
Kuiper is standing directly in front of the doorframe on the right.

cents per week for each of their first two children enrolled and a nickel
a week for each additional child they sent to the school. The meeting
also approved a school board composition consisting of the president
and four members of the consistory and four non-consistory members
elected by the congregation. This marked a step toward Abraham
Kuyper's model, based on his principle of sphere sovereignty, of school
boards being independent of the consistory, elected by members of
an independent Christian school society. Because the Williams Street
school met also in the summer months, enrollment increased then,
when public school children from the church joined the year-round
students.[15]

After completing elementary school, Kuiper enrolled in Grand
Rapids High School. His transcript shows that he matriculated from
Central Grammar School, although it is uncertain when he transferred
there from the Williams Street School.[16] Beginning in September, 1899,
he completed ninth and tenth grades at the high school. While there
he also took two semesters of Greek, a junior-year course, in the second
year. At the time of his enrollment, the high school had between twelve
hundred and thirteen hundred students, including Arthur Vanden Berg,
later a prominent United States senator. Children of such noteworthy
Grand Rapids families as the Wurzburgs, Steketees, Logies, and Stiles
were also in the student body at the time. It was a spiritually menacing
environment for a Christian Reformed youngster, since it featured
dramatic productions, proms, literary magazines like *Helios*, fraternities,

[15]   Material in this paragraph is based on *Centennial*, 39.
[16]   I am grateful to the staff of Central High School for retrieving for me a
copy of Kuiper's transcript and to the archivists of the Grand Rapids Public
Library for access to materials from the school.

athletic competitions, and summers spent at Lake Michigan cottages or trips to Europe by the social elite. Only a sprinkling of Dutch names appears in the student body between 1899 and 1901. If Kuiper did not participate in extracurricular activities—and his name does not appear in the school publications of the day—he certainly marked well the social ambiance and reflected deeply on how religiously perilous such a high school context was.

A case in point was the popular and controversial English teacher, Cornelia Steketee Hulst. She was the daughter of John Steketee, a Grand Rapids mercantile and civic leader and vice-consul of the Dutch government. She was married to Henry Hulst, a son of the Reverend L.J. Hulst who had attended the theological school for six months the year H.J. was born, then dropped out. He next attended Hope College and Princeton University. A graduate of the University of Michigan medical college, Henry had studied hypnotism in Paris, experimented with it as an early form of anesthesia in his Grand Rapids practice, and pioneered in the use of X-ray technology. He had a national reputation and served as president of the American Roentgen Ray Association. He died an agnostic in 1949.[17]

Cornelia became president of the Michigan State Teachers Association, then left teaching and established a reputation as a scholar and author of several books in the fields of Greek mythology and philosophy. Her funeral in 1957 was conducted at the Park Congregational Church.[18] The Henry Hulsts stood in stark contrast with J.B. Hulst, son of the deceased Reverend Frederikus Hulst and L.J.'s nephew, who served with Jacob Kuiper in the Spring Street consistory during H.J.'s high school years. If ever there existed an example of how deep the cleavage of the antithesis could be, the Hulst cousins were it. Covenant fidelity and covenant breaking were entwined in the finest of families. Warnings on the subject undoubtedly sounded from J.H. Vos's pulpit and around the Kuiper family table. Throughout high school, H.J. Kuiper maintained his spiritual defenses.

H.J. Kuiper joined his ethnic and spiritual kinsmen when, in September of 1901, he enrolled in the third year of the theological school's preparatory program.[19] Two years later, he and George Hylkema were examined by the curators and promoted to the fifth year

---

[17]   *Grand Rapids Press*, January 3, 1949, 2 and 25.
[18]   *Grand Rapids Herald*, September 25, 1959, 1-2.
[19]   *Annuary of the Theological School, 1901-1902*, 11.

of the preparatory program—a year devoted exclusively to training those planning to complete the three-year theology or seminary program.[20] Kuiper's high school training allowed him to skip the first two years of the preparatory program and also prepared him well for the fifth and final year.

The theological school had just adopted a modified policy concerning examinations. Until then the curators had examined every student in both the preparatory and the theological programs at the end of the school year. Based on their findings, they and not the faculty had decided whether to promote students to the next year in the two programs. The spring curators' meeting lasted a full two weeks in order to complete the examinations. Now the board delegated examinations of students in the first three years of the preparatory program to committees composed of faculty members and curators. The curators retained exclusive responsibility for examining fourth- and fifth-year students and students in the theology program. They also directed that ministerial students in the first three years who performed dubiously were still to be referred to the curators for examination. Kuiper passed the third and fourth year exams without a problem.

When Kuiper enrolled, all was not well at the school. During his first year, the curators were so concerned about the alarming rates of truancy in the theological program that they recommended to the synod in 1902 that Professor Boer, who had been appointed in 1876 at the time the school was founded and now was well past classroom effectiveness, be retired from teaching and be named librarian and curator. In further corrective action, they also recommended that Professor Hemkes's teaching load be reduced and that two new professors be added. Hemkes, the second appointee, was also past his prime and overworked. Students had been skipping the classes of both men with regularity and consistently attending only the classes of Professor Ten Hoor, a much younger man and a very recent addition to the faculty whose primary responsibility was systematic theology. The synod approved the recommended changes, adding William Heyns and Roelof, better known as Ralph, Janssen to the faculty in 1902. The former taught practical theology and the latter was professor of exegetical theology. Heyns came from a pastorate in Chicago, Janssen from completing a doctorate in philosophy at the University of Halle, in Germany.

[20]   Minutes of the Board of Curators, Calvin College and Seminary, 6/1-11/ 1903, art. 12c. (Hereafter, Minutes, Calvin Board.)

That September the curators met with the entire student body and impressed on them that within their ranks "the spirit of humility and submissiveness leaves something to be desired."[21] They further informed students that concerns and complaints were to be directed to their newly formed committee on supervision. At the same meeting, the curators requested Janssen to teach half his classes in the English language and formed a committee to collect $100,000 in order to start a junior college. Heyns was installed in an appropriate ecclesiastical ceremony; Janssen, who was not ordained and had accepted his appointment with certain stipulations, was introduced with "an appropriate word of installation" (translation mine).[22] Even though H.J. Kuiper was just entering the fourth year of the preparatory program, he undoubtedly was fully aware of these problems, since the combined enrollment in both programs was still less than a hundred students.

The curators reported to the next synod that the addition of Heyns and Janssen had resulted in "a notable improvement" in the teaching of both departments. They not only joined Hemkes and Ten Hoor in the theological program, but also A.J. Rooks, K. Schooland, Jacob G. Van den Bosch, and the young Barend K. Kuiper in the literary or preparatory program.[23] The last four taught exclusively in the literary department and had all been appointed since the mid-1890s. Rooks specialized in Latin and American history; Schooland in Dutch language and history and in Greek; Vanden Bosch in English and mathematics; and Kuiper in German, world history, and natural science. Schooland had been trained in the Netherlands, but the other three held A.B. degrees from the University of Michigan or the University of Chicago.[24] Heyns agreed to teach Dutch history and language and biblical studies in the literary

[21] Minutes, Calvin Board, 9/3-5/1902, art. 13.

[22] *Acta der Synode van de Christelijke Gereformeerde Kerk, 1904* (Grand Rapids: H. Holkeboer, Drukker, 1904), "Bijlage II. Repport van het Curatorium der Theol. School, 1902-1904," 66. (Hereafter, *Acta der Synode*, with the appropriate date indicated in the title. The abbreviated references do not indicate the changes in printers employed over the years.)

[23] B.K. and his brother R.B. Kuiper were sons of the Reverend Klaas Kuiper and were not related to H.J. Kuiper. On B.K.'s contribution to the college, church, and seminary, see Henry Zwaanstra, "Something about B.K." (Grand Rapids: Calvin Seminary, 1977), the pamphlet form of a convocation address.

[24] Henry Ryskamp, *Offering Hearts, Shaping Lives: A History of Calvin College, 1876-1966*, ed. Harry Boonstra (Grand Rapids: Calvin Alumni Association, 2000), 31-32.

department, which helped relieve the pressure occasioned by B.K. Kuiper's leave in 1903 and the years following to pursue his doctorate. The curators also appointed A. Broene to replace him.

The year H.J. Kuiper enrolled, the theological department had twenty-three students, and the preparatory or literary department had fifth-three. Twenty new students were admitted to studies in 1902, twelve in preparation for ministry, but in 1903 the number jumped to forty-four, even rising to fifty-three with late enrollments in September. That year twelve dropped out of the programs, but the unusually heavy enrollment forced the curators to seek the next synod's permission to acquire student housing. The drive for an endowment to create John Calvin Junior College stalled when three denominational leaders in succession declined the invitation to serve as fundraiser. The curators finally named a committee of the Reverend J. Groen; Professor Rooks; S. Postma, school treasurer; and J.B. Hulst,[25] now serving on the synodical committee, to work on the project. The final year H.J. Kuiper spent in the preparatory program there were twenty-one students in the theological program and eighty-eight in the literary program.

Only two students were admitted to the theological program in June, 1904: G.W. Hylkema and H.J. Kuiper. Both passed their final preparatory exams with the curators and both submitted acceptable senior essays in Dutch, as was the custom. Hylkema wrote "Socialism in Its Origin." Kuiper was assigned "Socialism in Its Results." Kuiper's essay began by noting that human conflict existed not just between races and nations, but between classes and stations in societies: rulers and citizens, capitalists and laborers. Socialism arose as an effort to redress the unfair repression of the poor by the wealthy. But its principles must be evaluated in light of a Christian political theory, he argued. When they are, it becomes evident that socialism denies that society is an organism, one distorted by sin. It superficially believes that repression can be corrected by the substitution of one social system for another. Such external analysis ignores the inner, spiritual source of the problem, because socialism does not acknowledge the depth of corruption in the human heart. It attempts to make corrections by absorbing society and the responsibility for its well-being into the state. Such collectivism robs the laborer of freedom to be responsible for his calling, destroys

---

[25] Dr. John B. Hulst informed me that his grandfather had attended the theological school, was widely known as "Elder Hulst," and was licensed to exhort in Christian Reformed congregations.

individual incentive, deprives workers of reaping the fruit of their labor, and eliminates opposition and competition. Its materialism places as much undue emphasis on money as does capitalism and compounds the spiritual problems of society.[26] Socialism was an issue Kuiper would revisit often in later years.

During his first year in the theological program, Kuiper took Janssen's courses in Hebrew language, introduction to exegesis, New Testament history, the book of Amos, and the book of Galatians. Hemkes, now at the end of his long career, taught him sacred geography, archeology, and ancient and medieval church history. With Ten Hoor he had courses in theological encyclopedia, introduction to dogmatics, symbolics, and one of the dogmatic loci. Heyns was his teacher in the history of preaching; text analysis; and sermon outlining, critique, and delivery.[27] It was a meat-and-potatoes theological menu.

To what degree Kuiper was aware of developing problems concerning Janssen's status at the school in Kuiper's final preparatory year or whether he participated in the communication affirming Janssen's 1904 reappointment is unknown. To retrace that issue, it is noteworthy that by the spring of 1903 Janssen had been informed that his teaching was acceptable, but that not being a candidate for ordination might hinder his reappointment. He had been advised to prepare for a theological candidacy examination, and he had even been granted a leave to study overseas for the planned exam. That September he had been instructed to provide a sample of his sermons to the curators, and the board president had been directed to designate a committee to conduct the examination.[28] Janssen chafed under the ecclesiastical pressure. By the next June the curators noted his expressed desire to prepare for the theological examination in a university context rather than by the mechanism they had created.[29] They had also received a petition from "some students" requesting that he be recommended to synod for reappointment and that notice of their support, on behalf of the student corps, be published in *De Wachter*, the denomination's Dutch language periodical.[30] Later in the same meeting

26   See the file of Secretary of the Board of Trustees, Senior Essays, 1904, Calvin Theological Seminary Archives, located in Heritage Hall, Calvin College and Seminary.

27   *Annuary of the Theological School, 1904-1905,* 22-25.

28   Minutes, Calvin Board, 9/2-4/1903, art. 10.

29   Minutes, Calvin Board, 6/1ff./1904, art. 18.

30   Ibid., art. 19.

that heard H.J. Kuiper's examination and accepted his paper, the board considered Janssen's request to be designated a "lecturer" rather than a regular "professor," to which they responded that he was to be regarded as a full member of the faculty. But his reappointment went to synod that month as "lecturer" for two years, which synod approved. When in September the curators named him "rector" or principal for the1904-1905 academic year, he declined the appointment. Initially tabling his decline, they later in their meeting acceded but renewed their reminder that he was to regard himself as a full member of the faculty.[31] It was the outset of H.J. Kuiper's first year in the theological program.

The turmoil during Kuiper's first year in the theological program swirled not only around Janssen, but even more intensely around Ten Hoor. At the fall curators' meeting, the secretary, the Reverend Bernard Einink, informed his colleagues that the board had received a number of student letters complaining about the conduct and attitudes of one of the theological teachers the year before. The board referred the matter to its committee on oversight and to the faculty. By the following spring the student corps sent a communication to the curators noting that a number of students had withdrawn from the student body, one student had "slandered" a professor, and several students had written letters critical of the theological school.[32] Seniors J.J. Hiemenga and P.J. Hoekenga were prominent in the critique. Hoekenga submitted a letter complaining of Ten Hoor's abrasive character and naming eight other students who felt as he did. H.J. Kuiper's name was included on the list. The curators deliberated. The next morning all nine students presented another signed letter asking that each of them be given a transcript of their work successfully completed in order that they might transfer to another seminary. Nine of the sixteen students in the theological program were ready to leave.

The board was facing a crisis. It gave the students a hearing and solicited "testimony" from the remaining students. It learned that students experienced Ten Hoor as caustic and unapproachable, that he strayed in class into issues and people not pertinent to the lecture topic, that he harbored strong antipathy toward Abraham Kuyper and made contemptuous references to him, and that indirectly he was maneuvering against Janssen. The curators hailed the students and Ten Hoor into their meeting. They were all given opportunity to speak. Ten

---

[31]   Minutes, Calvin Board, 9/7-8/1904, arts. 3 and 16.
[32]   Minutes, Calvin Board 9/5ff./1905, art. 9.

Hoor acknowledged truth to the first two complaints and promised to improve. He denied making derogatory remarks about Kuyper as a person and acknowledged his indebtedness to him. As for the fourth complaint, he asserted that it was based on groundless suspicion and misunderstanding. That afternoon the board deferred its consideration of candidacy recommendations, pending its resolution of the unrest. Janssen weighed in with objections to the curators' treatment of Ten Hoor, observing that were he to be so treated by the board, he would resign. The board concluded the session and the week by recording in the minutes that all had sinned and that both Ten Hoor and the students could resolve the tensions by working together in a more Christ-like manner.

The next week they spent another day and a half mopping up. Seniors Hiemenga and Y.P. De Jong were confronted with alleged remarks spoken against Janssen. Pressed, both denied the allegations. Finally, the board left it to their consciences with an admonition then approved them as candidates for ordination. It also dealt with Ten Hoor's pointed statements that theology belonged to the church, which as a matter of principle must maintain ownership and control of theological education. In the turmoil, it refused to take a position but recognized differences between Janssen and Ten Hoor on the matter. As meetings wound down, the board stated that neither Ten Hoor nor the students had dealt with one another properly, accepted Ten Hoor's admission of excesses and his resolutions to do better, rejected conduct unbecoming students toward professors, noted Janssen's statement that his position on the relation of theology and church was still in process, accepted apologies from Hiemenga and Hoekenga for their leadership in the unrest, and received for information a collective statement from students submitting to the board's admonition. As a curator, L.J. Hulst registered his disapproval of the board's neutrality on the issues Ten Hoor had raised. The meetings ended on a high note and with board relief when the nine students let it be known that they had decided not to transfer elsewhere.

That summer Kuiper spent six weeks serving the congregation of believers in Chicago Junction, later Celeryville or Willard, Ohio. A half dozen Dutch families from the Muskegon and Kalamazoo, Michigan, areas had acquired and drained swampland, started muck farms for raising celery and other vegetable crops, and had begun a Christian school and started a congregation in 1896. Though it would be 1910 before they called their first minister, they managed with guest ministers, reading services, and seminarians for fourteen years. In the summer of 1905, Kuiper stayed with the family of Henry Joldersma, one of the village founders and a leading elder in the church. During the course of his stay, Kuiper persuaded the Joldersmas to send their oldest child, a daughter named Dena, who had just graduated from the eighth grade, to Grand Rapids that fall. The parents consented, and in September Dena enrolled in the first year of the preparatory program of the denomination's theological school, planning to become a school teacher. Kuiper had arranged for her to lodge upon her arrival in the home of his parents, Jacob and Hilligje Kuiper.[33]

H.J. Kuiper's first year in the theological program had been turbulent. The second was quieter, but not without incident. Still piqued, L.J. Hulst tried to resign from the board of curators, but his resignation was not accepted. The curatorium registered its disapproval of Ten Hoor's reflection in print on proceedings of the previous June.[34] The following spring second-year students H.J. Kuiper and J.H. Beld were summoned before the board of curators, where the president spoke to them "about the dangers which the curatorium fears threatens these youthful brothers."[35] The minutes do not specify what these "dangers" were. Ten Hoor wrote a letter to the curators, for consideration at the same meeting, objecting to wording with reference to him in the minutes of their previous two sessions. The curators noted that Janssen's second two-year term was expiring. Since he had failed to make progress toward ordination, they did not recommend him for reappointment.[36] That month, the synod by ballot overwhelmingly elected Louis Berkhof

---

[33] Dena Berkhof, "The Story of My Life," mimeographed [n.d.], 20. Chicago Junction does not appear in the Christian Reformed *Yearbook* as a congregation until 1906, the first edition issued after Kuiper's summer assignment. See page 30. Dena Joldersma appears on the list of first-year students, page 59. She later married Herman Heyns, son of Professor Heyns, and after their respective spouses died, Professor Louis Berkhof.

[34] Minutes, Calvin Board, 9/6-7/1905, art. 26.

[35] Minutes, Calvin Board, 5/11-16/1906, art. 5.

[36] In his essay in *Semi-Centennial Volume: Theological School and Calvin College, 1876-1926* (Grand Rapids: The Semi-Centennial Committee, 1926), the Reverend Gabriel De Jong, secretary of the board of curators in 1906, states that the curators were "fully convinced that Dr. Janssen's teaching was not desirable" because it tilted toward higher criticism (37). This judgment is not supported in the curators' minutes and may have been colored by Janssen's second termination in 1922. It probably was an opinion held by some already in 1906.

The 1907 graduates of "the theological school," as Calvin Seminary was then known: Henry J. Kuiper (*left*), John Beld (*seated*), and George W. Hylkema.

as the next professor of exegetical theology from a nomination of three. Ten Hoor was also reappointed by ballot, also by a substantial majority. L.J. Hulst's protest was referred back to the curators with the directive to study the issue and to make recommendations to the next synod. Clearly, reverberations of the previous unrest continued through Kuiper's second year in the theological program.

In Kuiper's senior or last year, Ten Hoor was incapacitated by a serious illness and an extended recuperation; he did not return to the classroom until the September after Kuiper graduated. But that year H.J. benefited from the instruction of Louis Berkhof, Janssen's replacement. By then the preparatory program had been extended to six years, the last two of which were identified as John Calvin Junior College. In January of 1907, the first issue of the *Chimes* appeared, edited by D.H. Muyskens, a second-year student in the theological program. The monthly was identified as being "published by the students of the theological school of the Christian Reformed Church, at Grand Rapids, Michigan." In fact, students in all programs contributed to it, although nothing by H.J. Kuiper appeared during the several months it existed before he graduated.

In June, he and his two classmates successfully sustained their examination by the curators and were declared candidates for ministry.

H.J. Beld accepted a call to Lamont, Michigan; G.W. Hylkema to Volga, South Dakota; and Kuiper accepted the one he received from Luctor, Kansas. H.J. Kuiper was a mere twenty-one-and-a-half years old, and he is probably the youngest person to have achieved candidacy status in the history of the Christian Reformed Church.

Before beginning his ministry, Kuiper married. On July 21, 1907, he married Cornelia Freyling, the daughter of Nicholas Freyling and Clara Alles. The family had lived for a number of years on the north side of Wealthy Street, east of Eastern Avenue, where Nicholas and his partner, Dirk Mendels, ran a successful floral business named Freyling and Mendels. Cornelia had two brothers, Edward and Robert, who continued in the business after Nicholas died in 1905 at age fifty-two. By then the retail outlet had moved downtown to 111 Monroe Avenue, although the greenhouses remained behind the Freyling home.[37] Cornelia had entered the first year of the preparatory program of the theological school in September, 1901—one of the first women to be admitted.[38] The program had first been opened to non-theological students in the fall of 1900. Cornelia had completed the two-year normal or teacher-training curriculum the following year and accepted a teaching position at Westside Christian School in Grand Rapids. How well H.J. and Cornelia knew one another after they matriculated together in 1901, or how their relationship developed in their years together at school or after she commenced teaching is not clear. What is clear is that both young people came from industrious, entrepreneurial immigrant families steeped in the Dutch Reformed faith.

---

[37] Material on the Freyling family is from the *Grand Rapids City Directory* of 1903 and that of 1905.

[38] *Jaarboekje 1902* (Grand Rapids: J.B. Hulst, Boekhandelaar, 1902), 46.

CHAPTER 2

The First Three Pastorates

During his first twelve years in ministry, Kuiper served congregations in Kansas, Michigan, and Illinois. Each was different, and collectively they provided him with a broader perspective on the denomination than his upbringing in Grand Rapids afforded. From his first charge, a rural, homesteading congregation, he moved to a young church at the center of the West Michigan Dutch colony. In his third church, he experienced the tensions of an early English-speaking congregation in one of America's great urban centers. Each contributed to his formation as a denominational leader.

Kuiper as a young minister.

Luctor, Kansas

When Kuiper accepted his call to Luctor, Kansas, in the summer of 1907, the congregation was the sixth largest of the fifty-eight Christian Reformed congregations west of the Mississippi River. With seventy families and 384 members in a flourishing agricultural area, it was a hefty responsibility for a young candidate only mid-way between his twenty-first and twenty-second birthdays. He was selected from a trio of himself, fellow candidate and classmate George W. Hylkema, and the Reverend Tiede Vander Ark, pastor of the First Christian Reformed Church of Pella, Iowa, who had been ordained ten years earlier.

Luctor was a relatively young congregation when Kuiper became its minister. Established in 1885 by hearty immigrant pioneers, it had struggled with adverse weather and financial strains in its early years. Its first minister, the Reverend Evert Bos, had not arrived until 1892 and had moved on to Rotterdam, later named Dispatch, Kansas, in 1896. Three other ministers served the congregation before Kuiper's arrival. By then the church was solidly established, had a Christian school that offered classes in the Dutch language during the summer months, and had just completed construction of a new, never-lived-in parsonage. Reading his letter of acceptance August 5, 1907, a grateful consistory voted to grant Kuiper three weeks of vacation a year so that he could visit his family in Michigan, and it passed a motion to paint the parsonage's barn.

Meeting in Pella, Classis Iowa examined candidate Kuiper at its meeting September 18, heard him deliver part of his classical sermon on 2 John 7, and approved him unanimously for ordination. At the same meeting, two denominational stalwarts were welcomed into classical fellowship: the Reverend Idzard Van Dellen and the Reverend Jacob Noordewier. Van Dellen had served Luctor briefly from 1902 to 1903 and would continue as pastor of the First Christian Reformed Church of Denver until his retirement in 1940. Noordewier, who had begun his ministerial service in 1869 as pastor of the church in Pella, was entering his final charge, in Firth, Nebraska. As a member of the theological school's board of curators in the early 1890s, he had taken time from the pastorate to raise the funds to build the first seminary building. Years later his son would become Kuiper's close friend and staunch supporter on the Neland Avenue consistory and his grandson would marry Kuiper's older daughter. Of the sixteen churches in Classis Iowa, only the First Christian Reformed Church of Pella and

The Luctor Christian Reformed Church and school several years
after Kuiper moved to Holland, Michigan.

Rotterdam had been in denominational existence longer than Luctor.
Young Kuiper had been entrusted with the spiritual care of a significant
congregation.

He began his ministry with the hard work, spiritual sensitivity,
creativity, and discipline that would characterize his subsequent
endeavors. In addition to the preaching, catechism teaching, and
pastoral care expected of him, a month after his ordination H.J. initiated
a second consistory meeting each month to discuss William Heyns's
recent book on church polity. He began a class required for married,
baptized members who had not made profession of faith; it was a
wider practice in the denomination and was a feature of his following
pastorates until the numbers of such couples diminished. He started a
choral society and assumed sponsorship of the young people's society.
Choral societies became a feature of the Christian Reformed landscape
in the early twentieth century, and they provided fellowship and
nurtured joyful, grateful piety. They were precursors of church choirs.
Directing the one in Luctor gave Kuiper an outlet for his musical talent
and interest, an opportunity to know his people better, and the basis for
judging contemporary hymnody with a wary, critical eye.

His most strenuous additional commitment, however, was to Christian day-school education. He fanned the flames, and soon membership in the local Christian school society rose. The next year the school became a year-long rather than merely a summer endeavor, and Kuiper recruited his sister Dena to be its full-time teacher. Kuiper himself taught in addition to meeting his pastoral obligations. By 1909, the consistory relieved him of responsibility for family visiting as long as he continued to teach in the school. Although Dena left after one year, and although the school folded shortly after he left Luctor, Kuiper had inspired a vision for Christian day-school education at a time when the movement was still in its relative infancy in the denomination, and he modeled commitment to it for his congregation.

Under Kuiper's leadership the consistory took spiritual care and discipline seriously. The names of those needing attention appeared in the monthly consistory record with regularity. Elders were expected to make visits and to report in a timely manner. When one member was suspected of belonging to a secret society, he was confronted. Although he denied the rumor, he acknowledged having attended a lodge meeting out of curiosity. He was summoned to meet with the consistory. When allegations persisted, the pastor himself was delegated to investigate, and he reported the next month that the man was in fact a third degree Odd Fellow. The offender was banned from the Lord's Supper, and within six months he had changed his membership to the nearest Reformed church.

Disciplinary work was not done without spiritual concern or emotional investment. In March 1909, the consistory scheduled a special prayer meeting to intercede for those under discipline. That fall young women of the church who were employed by a Long Island, Nebraska, hotel were visited out of concern for their working on the Sabbath. In another instance, a woman involved in a troubled marriage was summoned to discuss the situation with the consistory.

Although only in his first charge, Kuiper soon became involved in denominational issues. He participated in Luctor's overtures to forgive theological student loans, to make the best articles of De Wachter available in book form, and to endorse the Ten Hoor position—still fresh in his mind from the intense debates during his seminary days— that theological education belonged to and must be controlled by the church. The last cause he was able to defend in person as a delegate to the synod of 1910, where he served on the advisory committee dealing with church order. Even closer to his heart was the long overture Luctor had sent to Classis Iowa that spring, which the classis had adopted in full and sent to synod that year. It advocated that synod advise consistories of Dutch-speaking congregations to take steps to improve psalm singing by restoring the original melodies and rhythms used in Geneva, as was recently advocated by Professor Acquoy in the Netherlands. It was Kuiper's overture, and he had crafted thoughtful grounds for it. The synod considered the matter carefully, then referred it to a three-person committee to review, to use in enlightening the church through the denominational papers, and to present recommendations to the following synod.[1] Kuiper was pleased. Good church music stirred his soul, and he had obviously been researching the issue in some depth and experimenting through his choral society with what he advocated. It was his first denominational contribution toward the improvement of congregational singing—the first of many.

The pastor's diligence was respected and appreciated, as is evident from such amenities accorded him as moving his chicken coup closer to the house, refurbishing his sidewalk, repainting rooms in the parsonage and planting 136 shade and fruit trees on his lot. But after a ministry of forty months, H.J. Kuiper left Luctor, Kansas, for Holland, Michigan. The consistory decided to pay promptly the six weeks' salary that was in arrears—a situation not unknown in agricultural communities until the harvest was in and cash flow was restored. Under his leadership the church had gained more than ten families and grown to 409 members. It appreciated his diligent attention to its spiritual vitality and respected his vigilance for Reformed principles and values. Kuiper had established a reputation for hard work and good judgment.

Prospect Park, Holland, Michigan

Prospect Park was Kuiper's briefest pastorate, despite the fact that he had been virtually the unanimous choice of the congregation. He had received thirty votes at the October 10, 1910, congregational meeting, and the two other men being considered with him only one vote each. He notified the church of his acceptance by telegram in early November, and he was installed at 2:30 p.m. on Thanksgiving Day. A reception was held after the service to meet the Kuiper family. Thirty-four months later, in September 1913, he accepted a call to the Second Christian Reformed Church of Englewood in Chicago.

---

[1] *Acta der Synode, 1910,* 68-69.

Prospect Park had been organized three years before Kuiper arrived, one of two Christian Reformed congregations—the fourth and fifth—spawned in 1907 in the growing town. Both new churches lay on the south side, where the expansion was occurring. Skirting but beyond the city limits were the congregations of Harderwyk, Pine Creek, Noordeloos, Niekerk, and Graafschap. Kuiper's congregation had 58 families, 286 members, and 95 children and young people in catechism classes the year he arrived. The Jellema and Peters families were prominent on the rolls, and a young man named William Harry Jellema was active in the young people's society, serving as its president the last year of Kuiper's ministry. Jellema, who had learned Reformed doctrine with precision from Kuiper, would go on to become a distinguished teacher of philosophy at Calvin College.

Since Kuiper had not stayed in Kansas the four years that was customary, Luctor requested that Prospect Park pay Luctor one-fourth of Kuiper's moving expenses to Kansas, to remove some of the sting of a pastor's early departure. Prospect Park's consistory at first declined to pay, but then it yielded. The sum was only fifty dollars. The consistory covered the move from Kansas by soliciting pledges from each family in the church. After he concluded a round of initial family visits, the new minister created a profession of faith class exclusively for married, baptized members. It had been effective in Luctor, and it reflected Kuiper's support of a denominational determination to overcome the *Afscheiding* half-way covenant that had been tolerated for eighty years but was fast falling out of vogue. The consistory approved. It also endorsed a young women's society and Cornelia Kuiper's leadership of it. The consistory delegated the building committee to negotiate with her the necessary improvements in the parsonage and approved her request that the trees around the home be trimmed.

Within four months of Kuiper's arrival, his mettle was tested by William Jansen, a member who had allegedly joined the Socialist Party.[2] Jansen was invited to discuss the matter with the consistory, which he did at length in March 1911. As he had in his senior paper at college, Kuiper pointed out that socialism was incongruent with confessing Christ and was contrary to the Word of God. Jansen declined to terminate his affiliation with the movement, but he did

[2]   A great number of Dutch immigrants in this period were laborers who had socialist sympathies or loyalties. See Pieter R.D. Stokvis, "Socialist Immigrants and the American Dream," in *Dutch-American Experience*, 91-101.

Prospect Park
Christian Reformed
Church as it
appeared during
Kuiper's pastorate,
1910-1913.

agree to "take the matter under consideration." He was then excused from the meeting. The consistory decided to bar him from the Lord's Table. The matter simmered for two months, whereupon Jansen, in an ingenious ploy, agreed to join an acceptable Christian political party as an alternative once one had been formed. The consistory brought the matter to classis for study and advice. It also sent a delegation to Mrs. Jansen to discuss the importance of having her newborn child baptized. Elder A. Peters later reported that William Jansen had promised not to continue his membership in the Socialist Party or to run for office as one of its candidates. The couple was then given opportunity to have their child baptized. Several months elapsed before they complained of unfair treatment by their landlord. The landlord, in turn, noted that Jansen had withheld rent and used inappropriate language with him, and that he had been compelled to turn the matter over to his lawyer for collection and civil action. Through patient counsel, reconciliation was seemingly achieved. But it took another two months and another visit from the elders before the rental obligation was met. In the meantime, the Jansens requested that their membership be transferred. This was approved and a notation of their poor attendance and Socialist leanings was attached to the papers.

The consistory's encounter with socialism led it to approve a motion that the dangers of socialism be addressed in the pastor's sermons. The next January, Classis Holland approved the consistory's request that synod advise the churches on "what stance consistories should take toward members who advocate socialism" (translation mine). That June the synod responded by adding the problem of socialism to the mandate of its study committee on "the labor movement and unions," and it stated that consistories should "take the same approach toward such members as it takes toward all cases of straying from our principles" (translation mine).[3] Jansen undoubtedly found consolation in the fact that three successive synods were of divided opinion on membership in secular unions and that none of the reports on either side tackled the subject of socialism. Kuiper, however, did not ignore it, either as a preacher or later as an editor.

For the most part, however, the church work in Holland was preoccupied with less global issues—a member suspected of larceny, another whose lack of homemaking skills or efforts strained her marriage, and truancy from Kuiper's catechism classes. Both he and Cornelia provided leadership for young people's societies. He again began a choral society and also a first-rate orchestra under his personal direction. He served on the classical interim committee, the finance committee, and the student fund committee.

On a classical level, Kuiper showed his abilities as a thinker and an organizer very early. The area churches had frequently discussed beginning a uniform program of catechism instruction. Just as often, the committee appointed to develop proposals on the matter had returned with no report. At his first classis meeting, Kuiper was named to chair a new committee to revisit the matter. At the next classis, he made an extensive report which included ten points containing "useful suggestions."[4] The report was adopted by the assembly without change. The classis voted to provide each consistory with two written copies of the report, and each was encouraged to implement its suggestions. Kuiper also articulated the strategy for inaugurating a community wide prayer-day service.[5] On theater attendance and "other amusements of a worldly hue," Kuiper assessed the problem for classis and pointed "to the danger for our youth when they seek their diversion in such places."[6] He argued that as ministers they should take their stance in the public

---

[3] *Acta der Synode, 1912,* 38. Neither the brief majority report nor the extensive minority report, in which the Kuyperian Reverend J. Groen argued for temperance and moderation in judging the union movement and suggested this was an area into which the church ought not venture too far, addressed the subject of socialism. The synod reconstituted the committee and directed that a thorough report be presented at the next synod. See *Acta der Synode, 1914,* 13-14, and *Acta der Synode, 1916,* 38-39.

[4] Minutes of Classis Holland, 1/23/1911, art. 3.

[5] Minutes of Classis Holland, 1/3/1912, art. 3.

[6] Ibid., art. 7.

press against such spiritual threats. "A lively discussion" followed his presentation. The prayer-day project was less than entirely successful and was scaled back the following year. When Kuiper later objected to the classis that the local theater had been used for Christian Reformed hymn sings, the classis judiciously refused to go into the matter. He almost certainly endorsed the effort to develop a common Sabbath-day policy by distinguishing work of necessity from that which was not necessary and by listing examples of both kinds in the classical record.[7] His leadership successfully rallied the Classis Holland churches to undertake an English language Sunday school on the north side of the city. A board consisting of one representative from each consistory was created to oversee this cooperative, evangelistic effort. The project was defined and initiated a year before the Reverend William P. Van Wyk published a highly regarded proposal for city evangelism in Grand Rapids entitled, *Stadsevangelisatie, waarom en hoe* (*City Evangelization— Why and How*).[8]

The summer of 1913 found Cornelia Kuiper, who was appreciated for her gracious and supportive involvement in congregational life, convalescing in Grand Rapids from a prolonged illness. The pastor proposed dividing his time each week between Holland and Grand Rapids during her recovery. By September he had received and accepted the call to his third charge.

Second Englewood, Chicago, Illinois

The congregation H.J. Kuiper had agreed to serve had been organized just a decade earlier as the first English-speaking Christian Reformed Church in Chicago and the fourth in the denomination outside Classis Hackensack, a group of English-speaking congregations that had left the Reformed Church in America in the 1820s and joined the Christian Reformed Church in the 1890s. The three earlier, English-speaking churches that were not part of the Hackensack group were La Grave Avenue (1887) and Broadway (1893) in Grand Rapids and Fourteenth Street in Holland (1902).

Second Englewood began with only fourteen families and five single adults. It commenced worship in its own modest building in the summer of 1904. The year Kuiper arrived it had 52 families and 146

---

[7]   Minutes of Classis Holland, 5/26/1913, art. 4.
[8]   William P. Van Wyk, *Stadsevangelisatie, waarom en hoe?* (Grand Rapids: Eerdmans and Sevensma, 1913).

Second Englewood
Christian Reformed Church
in Chicago, built in 1904

baptized and confessing members. That made it the smallest charge he ever held. It was also to be his most troubled and most troublesome. But by the time he left, the congregation respected him and responded appreciatively to his firm positions and clear guidance. It also had become a church with a large heart for evangelism. The congregation under his leadership published its first membership directory in 1915, dedicated a pipe organ in 1917, and acquired electric lights in 1918, the same year it introduced individual cups at the Lord's Supper and opened a fine church library.

The Kuiper family moved to Chicago in mid-October, 1913, and attended welcoming receptions with the consistory members and their spouses and with the congregation on successive evenings. The new pastor soon discovered problems. The young people took a more casual attitude toward catechism instruction and attendance than he had encountered before. He dispatched elders to visit with them and their parents, but the response was not as encouraging as he had hoped and he had to admonish elders to make these calls with greater faithfulness and enthusiasm.

Sabbath observance in the thriving metropolitan area was not what it should have been, in his estimation. A baker in the congregation mixed his dough on Sunday evening so as to have fresh bread on the shelves first thing Monday morning. The consistory discussed the situation, made a statement disapproving of Sunday labor, but maintained the brother as a full communicant member and left his practice to his own conscience. More problematic were the members who had recently acquired automobiles and were engaging in Sunday joy rides, either between or during the services. They were admonished—both from the pulpit and in focused visits. So were any number of families who were "oncers," attending services only once instead of twice a Sunday.

A host of other problems greeted the new pastor. One member was unaware that he had been placed under silent censure, the first step of ecclesiastical discipline, for his views on prayer and scripture. The nearest police precinct was not only asked to provide an officer to guard parked cars during services, since several had been vandalized, but one was requested to keep order among unruly young people in the rear of the church during worship. The congregation seemed inattentive and unresponsive to meeting the church's financial and ministry obligations. Special steps were taken to correct the problem. Among the leadership there seemed to be an undercurrent of defiance. The consistory reined in the pastor for making arrangements for substitute preachers when needed, and directed the clerk to handle the responsibility. One elder, irked that meetings were running beyond the agreed-upon hour for adjournment, finally asked one evening to be excused. Kuiper refused, but the brother left anyway, noting as he walked out the door that the meeting was already more than an hour longer than scheduled. Several members reacted negatively to the consistory's practice of preparing nominations for elder and deacon and advocated the past practice of accepting nominations from the floor at congregational meetings. Kuiper resisted such intrusions of American democracy into the arena of Reformed church polity, and the congregation responded to his firm leadership by giving him an 8 percent pay raise in appreciation for his work after a year and by eliminating the church deficit.

After a year in Englewood, Kuiper had enough cause for concern that he took a calculated and bold step. He presented a three-page, single-spaced "State of the Church" white paper to a combined meeting of retiring and newly elected office bearers. Two-year terms were too short to give adequate spiritual leadership in the church, he began. By his count thirty members were delinquent in doctrine or life, and over half the youth did not attend catechism or worship regularly and were critical of the church. He related how troubled he was over the seeming lack of spirituality in the homes and the local Christian school. The budget system was not working and needed reinforcing. Facilities for teaching catechism were poor and appeared to have low priority. The office of deacon needed review and development. A benevolence ministry in the neighborhood was badly needed. Little religious literature existed in members' homes and a church library should be opened. New office bearers needed to become thoroughly familiar with the church order and their responsibilities.[9]

Reaction to the pastor's assessment is not recorded. His litany was as sobering as it was unprecedented. It demonstrated emphatically how deeply concerned he was for the spiritual welfare and growth of the congregation. The consistory had to respect him for that. It also indicates that, for the first time, Kuiper had to contend with an Americanizing congregation in a major American urban setting. The members of Second Englewood lived in a world less sheltered and less outwardly devout than Luctor or Prospect Park. It was a setting in which survival, let alone success, demanded that one be more engaged and more assertive than in the Dutch-speaking, agrarian colonies of the great plains or the Dutch villages of western Michigan. Moreover, Second Englewood witnessed a steady influx of members, particularly from the Dutch-speaking First Christian Reformed Church of Englewood. These people were likely more culturally engaged with American society than the members of Kuiper's previous two charges. In any case, the next five years show a deepening rapport and mutual understanding between pastor and consistory.

Problems did not disappear, however. If a steady stream of people joined, a steady stream of people also left. Many who could not tolerate Kuiper's rigorous spiritual conformity, devotional discipline, doctrinal precision, and expectations for accountability left for the Second Reformed Church in Englewood, for several Presbyterian congregations, and for the Third Christian Reformed Church of Roseland—the last probably for geographic reasons as much as for disaffection with the pastor. One woman reported that since her marriage, she no longer felt at home in the congregation, was not stirred by the preaching, and just disliked the pastor. The director of the women's glee club chafed under the requirement to have all music preapproved. He contrived a Christmas program which, by official assessment after the event, failed to open with prayer, presented the women costumed for an opera house rather than a church, and neglected to request preapproval of an especially offensive number. Called before the consistory, he dissembled when asked whether, as reported, he had said that it was his desire "to

---

[9]   Minutes of the Consistory of the Second Christian Reformed Church of Englewood, 1/15/1915, art. 21. The assessment is incorporated in its entirety into the consistory record.

put one over on the consistory."[10] The consistory required a public apology, which he refused to make. He stopped attending church.

More seriously and more sadly, the consistory had to deal with a woman who abetted, although did not approve, another member's abortion—a covert procedure whose complications cost her her life. A public statement was prepared, and the enabler's husband strenuously objected to the pastor's handling of the delicate situation. Another member was admonished for uncivil discourse at a congregational meeting. A teenage catechumen from the First Christian Reformed Church of Englewood, who asked the consistory to be catechized in English at Second Church, was accepted skeptically and only after promising to attend faithfully. He did not and was visited repeatedly about his absenteeism. Another contended that he was attending catechism at the Third Christian Reformed Church of Roseland, which was investigated and proven false. "Tending the flock" was a solemn obligation diligently met but often resented in a Kuiper church, because of his heavy-handedness.

But, how deeply the majority of the church came to understand, respect, and value its pastor is indicated by the 23 percent raise it voted for him at the September 8, 1918, congregational meeting—retroactive to January 1! Kuiper was firm and direct, but also fair and respectful. He set high standards and expectations. He had no patience for casual Christianity. But what he expected of church members, he lived in his own life—for the glory of God and the honor of the Lord he served. When in May, 1919, he informed the consistory that he had received a call to Broadway Christian Reformed Church in Grand Rapids, the members "unanimously" congratulated him and expressed "the wish that he may stay with us."[11] The congregation had grown by 50 percent during his ministry and was on a much more solid footing spiritually than when he had come.

As intense as his ministry to the congregation was, Kuiper also accepted wider assignments. On the classical level he served on the student fund, Sunday school, and interim committees. He was a deputy for local Jewish evangelism. His effectiveness with young people is reflected in his being elected president of the Chicago-area young people's league. In 1916, he was delegated to the denominational synod, where he was placed on the committee on appointments and

[10]   Minutes, Englewood, 12/19/1916, art. 6.
[11]   Minutes, Englewood, 5/28/1919, art. 19.

was chosen as a reporter for the advisory committee on protests and appeals. The following synod named him to the study committee on worship, whose interests would occupy his time substantially and benefit from his insights and diligence for the next two decades.

Three prominent features of H.J. Kuiper's life developed more fully during his years in Chicago. The first is evangelism. The second is his involvement with the *Banner,* the denomination's weekly magazine. The third is his contributions to Christian Reformed worship. Each warrants some attention.

Five Chicago Christian Reformed congregations—the three Roseland churches did not participate—had approved a jointly sponsored city mission the spring before Kuiper had accepted the call to Second Englewood. His predecessor, John R. Brink, had been a prime force behind the project but had moved on to become the home missionary for the Grand Rapids area. The five churches called the Reverend Peter J. Hoekenga of Lynden, Washington, for this work about the same time Second Englewood called Kuiper. When he arrived, Hoekenga and his family joined Second Englewood, where he attended consistory meetings regularly.

Kuiper took a special interest in Hoekenga's work and was his staunch supporter and ally. The two seminary dissidents were now yoke-fellows in evangelism. The next February, Kuiper was designated to investigate with Hoekenga whether work on State Street really fell within the purview of the Helping Hand Mission, as the joint project had been named.[12] The Englewood consistory appointed several members to bring the message at the mission from time to time. The congregation welcomed John Vande Water as Hoekenga's assistant in 1915. Kuiper encouraged Vande Water, and the two began a close relationship that would endure into the 1940s, first in Chicago and then in Grand Rapids.

By 1919, the Chicago City Mission had work at four sites, and Kuiper was its great encourager and strategist. He welcomed "Miss Josie [almost certainly, Johanna] Veenstra" on a Sunday evening in 1919 to speak to the congregation about her work.[13] She had been involved in city missions in Grand Rapids and that fall would depart for Africa, where she would eventually become the Christian Reformed Church's patron saint in missions. Kuiper's passion to evangelize the lost was a hallmark of his ministry and it mobilized Second Englewood.

[12]   Minutes, Englewood, 2/3/1914, art. 10.
[13]   Minutes, Englewood, 4/28/1919, art. 13.

Kuiper's interest in the *Banner* emerges in an overture he crafted asking that synod renew negotiations to purchase the paper, to that point an independent publication, or to begin its own "official organ" in the English language. He argued that it would place English-language churches on an equal footing with Dutch-speaking congregations, which had *De Wachter* as their source of inspiration and information on denominational matters. Further, the paper as it had existed for a decade under the editorship of Henry Beets, represented, Kuiper contended, the Christian Reformed position and should be owned and controlled by the church, not by individuals. The classis approved the overture in January, 1914, and the synod adopted it that June, purchasing the paper for the asking price of five thousand dollars.[14]

For the next several years, Kuiper read and critiqued the paper with increasing concern. Finally, he drafted an extensive letter and laid it before his consistory. In the draft, Kuiper stated that the *Banner* needed a more pronounced Calvinistic emphasis than it had, and that it deserved an editor who could and would supply this. The consistory reflected on the matter for six weeks and decided to send a revised version to the publication committee of the synod. In the revised draft, the consistory argued that the entire denomination needed to be instructed and mobilized in a unified approach to Americanization. Not all departments of the paper propagated Calvinistic principles, the consistory said, and things showed no prospect of changing under the current editor, Henry Beets.[15] The consistory had considered who could best serve in this capacity and recommended Professor B.K. Kuiper, strong advocate of Kuyperianism, or the Reverend Gerrit Hoeksema as replacements. Little did Kuiper know that a decade later the denomination would turn to Kuiper himself as Beets's successor!

If Kuiper's clash with the leadership of the women's choral society reflected his determination to assure respectful, Reformed worship in God's house, he had earlier suggested changes in the liturgy that demonstrated a willingness to consider innovation that fostered congregational involvement and was more consistent with proposed changes in the Netherlands and with American Presbyterian services. In March, 1914, he suggested that the congregation recite the Apostles' Creed in unison. The consistory reflected on the idea for a month, then

---

[14] *Acta der Synode, 1914*, 22.
[15] Minutes, Englewood, 2/27/1918, art. 13. It has not been confirmed that the letter was sent, but it is assumed that it was.

approved it.[16] Several years later it asked the classis whether another American liturgical practice, the use of individual communion cups at the Lord's Supper, was permissible. Classis appointed a committee to look into the matter, discussed its report at length at a following meeting, tabled it overnight, and the next day referred it to the synod and advised Second Englewood to use "wisdom" in making the change congregationally, "since circumstances demand it."[17]

No liturgical initiative during his Chicago days was to have as significant an impact on Kuiper's life as the overture by Classis Illinois in 1916, submitted by the consistory of the Third Roseland Christian Reformed Church that January,[18] that the synod direct the American-speaking congregations of the denomination to develop and follow a uniform order of worship that would feature greater congregational participation in worship. The synod judged that the idea held sufficient merit for both Dutch-speaking and English-speaking congregations that a committee should review it carefully and present its findings and recommendations to the next synod.[19] The committee presented a perceptive review and critique of Christian Reformed worship in the light of Reformed principles. It affirmed the need for uniformity, greater coherence, and congregational participation. It also proposed that a larger committee be appointed and mandated to develop such a uniform order of worship and to articulate the principles that supported it. The synod agreed. H.J. Kuiper was named to the committee and became its secretary. For the next eighteen years he would be at the center of denominational developments in liturgy and hymnody.

By the end of his third pastorate, H.J. Kuiper was a seasoned, competent pastor who had demonstrated vision and initiative on several fronts. His assessment of the church's needs, as well as the dangers it faced in an era of emerging Americanization, was keen and realistic. He had a clear sense of the direction that a confessional Reformed church should take in that context. That sense was articulated in a

---

[16] Minutes, Englewood, 4/14/1914, art. 6.
[17] Minutes of Classis Illinois, 9/25-27/1917, arts. 19, 33, and 39.
[18] Minutes of Classis Illinois, 1/25-26/1916, art. 52.
[19] *Acta der Synode, 1916*, 30. For a complete review of Christian Reformed liturgical developments from 1916 to 1932, including English translations of pertinent materials in Dutch, see Carl G. Kromminga, "A History of the Efforts toward a Uniform Order of Worship in the Christian Reformed Church, 1916-1932" (Grand Rapids: mimeographed by Calvin Theological Seminary, 1972).

Former pastors of the Second Englewood Christian Reformed Church in 1953, at the fiftieth anniversary of the congregation: (*left to right*) J.R. Brink, H.J. Kuiper, E.J. Tanis, William Masselink, and Oliver Breen.

steady stream of proposals and overtures, a number of which yielded new programs and organizations. (The story of his pivotal role in the founding of Chicago Christian High School is told in chapter 5.) By 1919, Kuiper had become a recognized and respected denominational leader who would come into the full bloom of his influence during his ministry at the Broadway Christian Reformed Church in Grand Rapids, Michigan.

CHAPTER 3

Broadway: The Making of an Editor

When Herman Hoeksema, the overwhelming choice over H.J. Kuiper and H. Henry Meeter, declined the call to the Broadway Christian Reformed Church in Grand Rapids, Michigan, in the spring of 1919, the consistory put Kuiper on the next trio of names proposed to the congregation. This time it was he who received a substantial majority. He visited with the consistory, negotiated numerous improvements to the parsonage, and accepted the call. By July the Kuiper family's membership papers had been received and they had moved into temporary housing until work on the parsonage could be completed.

The Dutiful Pastor

Broadway represented a hefty increase in Kuiper's pastoral responsibilities. The year he arrived, it reported 192 families and 903 members. The congregation was six times larger than his previous charge had been when he arrived. Some of the families were very large. The Thomasma family had fifteen children; a dozen others had between seven and twelve offspring. The number of children in catechism classes was overwhelming. An added challenge was assimilating seventy servicemen back into congregational life after World War I. Broadway reported a larger number of veterans than any other congregation in the denomination.[1] One member had been killed in the Great War and

---

[1] *Jaarboekje, 1920*, 191-99. Several larger congregations, like Grandville Avenue and Alpine Avenue in Grand Rapids, did not submit reports and

four had been wounded. That such a high percentage of Broadway's members had worn a U.S. uniform sometime during the conflict only accelerated Americanization in a congregation already in the vanguard of this process in the Christian Reformed Church. It also raised Kuiper's sensitivity to the spiritual dangers that Americanization presented.

Two months after the catechism season began, Kuiper gave the consistory a complete report on truancy. He also began his mandatory class for married members who had not yet professed their faith; exceptions were allowed only for those who had scruples against full membership. He was more usually late than on time for the biweekly consistory meetings, since the starting time overlapped with catechism teaching. He not only paid close attention to attendance, he again assigned elders to visit the homes of children and young people who were irregular in attendance or unprepared. At one meeting he unfolded and read a list of fifty names of married and unmarried members who should have been in catechism classes but were not. Throughout his ministry at Broadway, the effectiveness of the catechism program was reviewed almost monthly.

Kuiper was not only dutiful and faithful in his pastoral care of the church, he was resourceful in developing the eldership. At one point he identified eight practices of spiritual life that elders should review in their family visits, commonly scheduled the week before the quarterly celebration of the Lord's Supper. These were attendance at evening as well as morning worship, support of the catechism program, loyalty to the Christian school, tithing, personal and family devotional life, participation in church programs, presence at the Lord's Table, and intercession for the church and its members.[2] The list is a reliable, comprehensive indicator of prevailing denominational mores and expectations.

Similarly, neglect of the means of grace was a matter of great concern. Visits, warnings of probation and discipline, and eventually steps toward censure and excommunication followed where the response so dictated. This was the most frequent offense for which the Broadway consistory sought the required permission of the classis to proceed with formal discipline. But cases of violating the seventh, eighth, and ninth commandments surfaced from time to time. Alcohol

---

may have had more men in the armed forces. Several larger congregations reported fewer members in the armed forces than Broadway.

2   Minutes of the Consistory of the Broadway Christian Reformed Church, 8/8/1927, art. 13.

A church picnic at Broadway in the 1920s.

abuse, including public intoxication; embezzlement; and divorce were also faced during Kuiper's ministry at Broadway. A member who owned a restaurant that was open on Sundays for regular customers was judged to be engaged in "a work of necessity," but was urged to sell the establishment for his own spiritual good. A single woman who occasionally attended movies was placed on "the watch list." The clerk carefully recorded membership transfers in and out of Broadway. They were about even, and the size of the congregation at the end of Kuiper's ministry there was slightly larger than when he had arrived.

Kuiper recognized that his work was under the supervision of the consistory, particularly the elders. He respected their office and deferred to their judgment. The respect was mutual. When he asked their permission to teach a half day a week at Calvin College, they approved.[3] From time to time he requested and was given permission to preach at other churches. On other occasions the consistory withheld permission. The body thought enough of his sermons that it accepted the offer of a member to mimeograph them at no charge to the church,[4] and another time it directed that a series of sermons be printed for the congregation.

When Kuiper began to receive calls to other churches with frequency, the consistory recorded its request that he remain at

[3]   Minutes, Broadway, 2/20/1920, art. 28.
[4]   Minutes, Broadway, 1/29/1923, art. 31.

Broadway. In the case of an especially tempting call to the Fuller Avenue Christian Reformed Church, also in Grand Rapids, it called a special consistory meeting to make its sentiments known. The consistory recorded its desire and attached the grounds that (1) much work along "spiritual lines" remains to be done; (2) Kuiper's ministry at Broadway is incomplete; and (3) the consistory supports him, "especially on the doctrinal end of the work."[5] The third ground was both a statement of the church leaders' convictions and a direct reminder that in Kuiper's strong, articulate positions on Reformed doctrine he had their unwavering support. He declined the call.

On another occasion the consistory refused to grant him two weeks to promote the Federation of Young Men's Societies on the East Coast but relented a month later when young professor W. Harry Jellema, a leader in the organization, made the case before them in person. The consistory members' affection as well as respect for their pastor is evident from the surprise party they held for him at his Gun Lake cottage in August 1927, as well as from the generous salaries they successfully proposed annually to the congregation. After he was excused early from the March 1929, meeting to visit with the consistory of Neland Avenue Christian Reformed Church about the call that church had extended him, the consistory voted unanimously to ask him to stay at Broadway. Its support of him had been consistently strong and its respect for him had only increased through the years.

Throughout his ministry at Broadway, the spiritual health and development of his congregation had been of paramount importance to Kuiper. But in addition to the preaching, catechetical instruction, spiritual supervision, and pastoral care expected of ministers, Kuiper became heavily engaged in the wider denominational issues of worship, hymnody, evangelism, opposition to worldly influences, doctrinal controversy, and synodical policy-making. This engagement was so extensive and his contributions were so substantial that by the end of his Broadway pastorate the denomination entrusted him with one of the most sensitive and influential positions in the church.

Uniform Worship

As already noted, Kuiper had been appointed by the synod of 1918 to a study committee on a uniform order of worship. It was

---

[5]   Minutes, Broadway, 9/21/1925, art. 3.

his first synodical study committee assignment and one of his most important. It would lead to subsequent committee appointments in the areas of liturgy and hymnody. Collectively, these assignments would occupy him for eighteen years and make him the most significant leader of his era in shaping the Christian Reformed Church's worship and music. The original committee of three appointed in 1916 had gone on record as desiring a uniform order of worship that would foster greater denominational unity. It had provided an analysis of the state of Christian Reformed worship and articulated basic principles of Reformed worship. It also had recommended that an expanded committee develop specific proposals for the following synod. The synod of 1918 approved these proposals and added Kuiper and three other new members to the original committee.

Kuiper became the expanded committee's secretary. The committee produced a thorough, theologically thoughtful, coherent order of worship.[6] It proposed a number of modifications that brought liturgical cohesion into corporate worship: reciting the Apostles' Creed and the Lord's Prayer in unison; introducing a statement of absolution; and presenting the basic morning service and four variations for evening worship and special occasions. The committee insisted on the principle that uniformity in worship was, along with common confessions and a common church order, one of three nonnegotiable pillars of denominational unity. It envisioned that all congregations would be bound to follow the common order of worship. In considering the committee's proposals, the synod of 1920 judged that the churches and classes should have ample time to review and discuss the proposals and that the committee should write explanatory articles in the church papers before action was taken by the following synod.

The committee's proposals elicited an unanticipated and wide-ranging list of objections from nine of the thirteen classes in the denomination in 1922. Understandably, that synod deferred any action, continued the committee, urged it to explain often and plainly its proposals in the church papers, and asked it to reflect on the content of the classical objections and suggestions. The committee was demoralized. In 1924 Kuiper's own classis, Grand Rapids West, overtured the synod to discontinue the committee. But that synod renewed the committee's mandate, noting the liturgical arbitrariness and absence of unity in Christian Reformed worship. The committee

---

[6]   *Acta der Synode, 1920*, 185-204.

provided an interim report in 1926 but also asked that the synod go on record as affirming synod's right and obligation to articulate the principles and order of worship for the denomination. The synod said it wanted "a uniform but flexible" order of worship for all the churches. On the strength of that commitment, the committee provided an extensive report for the synod of 1928. It was a refinement of what it had presented in 1920 and defended again in 1922, but this time the committee prudently designated a number of elements in the service as "optional" and provided choices for implementing others. Extensive, point-by-point discussion in committee and on the floor of synod went substantially the study committee's way, although some details, particularly concerning the evening and special services, were referred back to the study committee for further consideration. One point of controversy, the absolution—a declaration of God's forgiveness after the congregation's confession of sin—was retained. But choirs remained a congregational option, as decided by the synod of 1926 and despite the study committee's significant reservations about them.

H.J. Kuiper must have been pleased with the outcome at the synod of 1928 concerning the order of worship. As committee secretary he had invested ten years of research, of drafting proposals and reports, and of explaining committee positions in public and at synods. That matters turned out as they did was due in large part to his perseverance and enhanced denominational stature. He had been elected vice president at this his fifth synod. It was his first attendance, but not his last, as an elected officer. That he had also chaired the committee that proposed the composition of the advisory committees for the synod of 1928 probably had little determining influence on the final decisions. He was unhappy, however, with the synod's action concerning choirs. The synod upheld the 1926 decision that "in principle" no biblical objection to choirs existed. Kuiper and nineteen others—almost a fourth of the ninety delegates—registered their negative votes, since making choirs optional, at each congregation's discretion, conflicted with the ideal of a uniform order of worship as already approved by the synod.[7] For Kuiper, choirs also displaced the important involvement of the congregation in praising God. But, undoubtedly because of his recognized work on the about-to-be-released hymnal, *The New Christian Hymnal,* the synod named him to a new committee appointed to articulate the case for using hymns in worship and to propose a

---

[7]   *Acta der Synode,* 1928, 59.

The New
Christian Hymnal

Edited by
REV. H. J. KUIPER

Title page of *The New Christian Hymnal.*

WM. B. EERDMANS PUBLISHING COMPANY
Grand Rapids   Michigan

collection of acceptable hymns, whose texts were to be circulated to the churches six months prior to the following synod.[8]

Kuiper's work on the order of worship, hymns, and choirs made an impact on worship at Broadway, especially toward the end of his ministry there. He did not force liturgical change on the church. As late as 1926, he objected when the consistory assented to the request that a children's choir sing for the offertory at the Thanksgiving Day service; he did so despite the latest synodical ruling. In early 1928, the consistory informed the classis that it favored adding several "doctrinally sound hymns" to the psalter. But only after the synod had approved the new order of worship was this implemented at Broadway. Then the congregation was given two weeks advance notice and the pastor was asked to preach a sermon on the sensitive issue.[9] Changes were introduced in the evening service, and saying the Lord's Prayer in unison was begun. Even carefully introduced, temperate changes

[8]   Ibid., 48 and 155.
[9]   Minutes, Broadway, 8/27/1928, art. 11.

aroused some, including a member who protested in writing the use of the absolution and appeared before the consistory to argue his case.

The congregation and consistory were well aware of their pastor's work on *The New Christian Hymnal*, a project long espoused by Kuiper as an alternative to the Arminian hymnody that flooded the religious market. The task of completing the book for publication had fallen substantially on his shoulders, and when it was about to appear, the Broadway consistory overtured the synod of 1928 to examine it with a view to its use in Sunday school, societies, and Christian schools.[10] Although the synod declined because the project was private and nonecclesiastical, while commending it as a praiseworthy endeavor, delegate Kuiper[11] did not hesitate in selecting sample numbers from it when it was his turn to lead synodical devotions. Once it was published, the book became *de facto* a Christian Reformed institution.

Both the approval of a uniform order of worship by the synod of 1928 and the publication of *The New Christian Hymnal* were crowning achievements at the end of Kuiper's ministry at Broadway. The former was to be short-lived, the latter enduring.

Evangelism and Missions

Broadway was a generous, mission-minded congregation. That pleased Kuiper greatly and suited him well. The consistory regularly voted special gifts to heathen[12] missions, home missions, the Chicago Helping Hand Mission, the Chicago Jewish Mission, the Paterson Hebrew Mission, the Chicago Tract Society, Rehoboth Hospital in New Mexico, the Crown Point Christian School among the Navajos, and other evangelistic endeavors. A young congregant, Wilhemina Kalsbeek, was encouraged to receive special training in missions, and the congregation supported her financially in her studies at the Kennedy School of Missions in Hartford, Connecticut. Later, as a missionary to China, she was sponsored by the congregation.

So was the Reverend Harry Dykstra, a missionary to China whose lively and unconventional preaching when on home service delighted many members because of its marked contrast to Kuiper's heavily doctrinal, formal, serious pulpit style. Kuiper led the efforts of the

[10]   Minutes, Broadway, 5/28/1928, art. 12.
[11]   *Acta der Synode, 1928*, 63-65.
[12]   While offensive by today's standards, the term was common parlance in religious writing of that era.

churches on Grand Rapids' west side to have Dykstra's salary increased by the foreign mission board. He even led his classis in an unsuccessful attempt to have the synod rule that the calling churches of missionaries rather than the mission board should set and pay their salaries; for Kuiper it was an initiative against "boardism."

Early in 1921, John Vande Water was invited to show slides at Broadway, which took a collection for his evangelistic and city mission work in Chicago. By 1925 Broadway had submitted a proposal for united city mission work with three other west-side churches. A joint board was formed. Vande Water was consulted for advice on a location, and the next year he was hired away from Chicago as the evangelist of the West Fulton Street Mission. His family joined Broadway, and the tandem of pastor and evangelist forged in Chicago resumed in Grand Rapids.

The Janssen Controversy

During Kuiper's pastorate at Broadway, the denomination addressed a number of substantial doctrinal issues. Nothing exists in the official record of either Englewood or Broadway to suggest that Kuiper initiated or participated in any action concerning the premillennial and mildly dispensational thinking published by his brother-in-law, Harry Bultema, in his controversial book *Maranatha*, in 1917. The synod of 1918 had reviewed and rejected Bultema's views, and it dispatched three deputies to work with his consistory in handling the errant brother. Eventually Classis Zeeland deposed Bultema. About the time Kuiper began his ministry in Grand Rapids, the popular Bultema and the majority of his consistory and members at the First Christian Reformed Church of Muskegon had left the denomination and formed the Berean Church. If he avoided that skirmish, Kuiper was heavily engaged in directing the outcome of several other major issues faced by the denomination in the 1920s.[13]

Already in the summer of 1920, the Broadway consistory protested to Classis Grand Rapids West the synod's refusal to reject the allegedly problematic views of seminary professor Ralph Janssen, as his other four faculty colleagues had asked. Janssen, who had not been reappointed in 1906, had been appointed—still unordained—to the seminary faculty for a second time in 1914. He soon became the object

---

[13] For their reviews of these controversies see Kromminga, *The Christian Reformed Church*, 75-79, 82-86, 120-21; and Bratt, *Dutch Calvinism*, 105-18.

of many of the same concerns that had attended his earlier tenure. These concerns revolved around scripture as divine revelation, miracles, and the relationship of biblical material to earlier Near Eastern literature. Janssen allegedly suggested that biblical writers depended on outside sources; he posited natural explanations for accounts of Old Testament miracles; and he stressed the human more than the divine side of scripture. When Janssen's colleagues' concerns, based on student reports and uneasiness with emphases in his teaching, had been rebuffed by the board of curators, they had appealed to the synod. The synod of 1920 had reviewed the matter, issued a caution to Janssen, and admonished the four to be more collegial and open with Janssen.

H.J. Kuiper was not satisfied. He had studied with Louis Berkhof, William Heyns, and Foppe Ten Hoor as well as with Janssen during Janssen's first term of service at Calvin Seminary. He knew firsthand the style and content of every professor's teaching except that of Samuel Volbeda, who had joined the faculty in practical theology after Kuiper had graduated. If the four were concerned about Janssen, that resonated with Kuiper. The four were disturbed that the liberalism raging in mainline Protestant schools might be infecting Calvin Seminary. So was Kuiper. He immediately took the board's and synod's dismissal of the matter to his consistory in the form of an ecclesiastical protest.

At the late summer meeting of the classis in 1920, Kuiper produced Broadway's carefully crafted protest against the synod's inaction. Much later the four professors, along with four ministers, including Kuiper,[14] published their exposé in pamphlet form, prompting exchanges in the church papers and a flurry of subsequent pamphlets. The classis dutifully appointed a committee that for the next two years announced at every subsequent classis meeting that it had no report. Finally, in May 1922, a month before the next synod was to assemble, Broadway's by now exasperated delegates "insist[ed] on action."[15] The classis decided to forward the original protest to synod without taking a position, but urged that body to give its content "careful consideration."

Classis Grand Rapids West hesitated to take a position on the Janssen case for several reasons. The issues were complex and were evaluated on the basis of notes and the testimony of students, whose

---

[14]   The pamphlet "Waar het in de Zaak Janssen Omgaat," was signed by Henry Danhof, Y.P. De Jong, and Herman Hoeksema as well as by H.J. and the four professors.

[15]   Minutes of Classis Grand Rapids West, 5/16/1922, art. 45.

opinions on the matter were sharply divided. Because neither the board of curators nor the synod of 1920 had found any substantive basis for action against the professor, the classical committee hesitated. William Stuart, one of the most respected pastors in the denomination, joined the board of curators in 1921 from Classis Grand Rapids West; he was much closer to the issue than were most of the other pastors and elders of the classis. Three of its ranking ministers—Kuiper, Y.P. De Jong, and Henry Danhof—had examined the student materials, signed the early pamphlet in opposition to Janssen, helped start a new journal that began in the context of the controversy, and in the spring of 1921 been appointed to an expanded investigating committee that the curators had named in response to pressure from the churches. To complicate the situation further, opinions among the ministers of the classis were deeply held and sharply divided. Kuiper represented those who had lost patience with and confidence in Janssen. Bright young Quirinus Breen, who had just completed his seminary studies and had accepted a call to the Twelfth Street Christian Reformed Church in May 1920, as the crisis was coming to a head, articulated the opposing view.

Prudently, the classis deferred to its representatives on the board of curators and to the expanded investigating committee; it seemed content to wait patiently for the committee's findings, the board's action, and the synod's resolution of the matter. In the months after Broadway submitted its protest, therefore, it became increasingly obvious, given the volume and intensity of publications and speeches on the matter, that for the classis to consider its substance would have been to take on a denomination-wide issue that was already being handled. It would also have seriously divided its own delegates and churches. So the classical committee stalled.

While the classis waited, however, Kuiper pressed his position. The Broadway protest crafted in the summer of 1920 had taken exception to two points. It protested the synod's conclusion that "it is not apparent to the synod that Dr. Janssen teaches anything that is inconsistent with the Reformed doctrine of the verbal inspiration of Holy Scripture and its absolute authority for faith and life"[16] (translation mine). It also protested the conclusion that "it appears to the synod, however, that in his exposition of Holy Scripture Dr. Janssen sometimes lays too heavy an emphasis on the human component and on natural instrumentality,

---

[16]   *Acta der Synode, 1920*, 96.

so that in the opinion of some students this leads to an under-emphasis on the special, divine component of scripture"[17] (translation mine).

The Broadway protest was based on a careful reading of the concerns brought by the four professors, Janssen's reply, and typed "lecture outlines" from Janssen. It argued that the outlines contained expressions that contradict verbal inspiration, that they were inconsistent with the doctrine of biblical infallibility, subverted biblical inspiration and infallibility, and ignored and weakened rather than strengthened the conviction that Israel's religion has a supernatural origin and content. The protest documents and develops these conclusions from material in the outlines. It concludes, "The question confronting the synod was what Dr. Janssen taught in his classes rather than what he personally believed or in his defense claimed to believe."[18] By not facing the real issue, the synod in effect made it possible for Janssen to continue teaching as he had been doing and to represent his views as sanctioned by the synod. The effect allegedly was that "synod has unwittingly sanctioned certain tenets of an unbelieving higher criticism."[19]

Through the Broadway protest, H.J. Kuiper got the wider church's attention. In the ensuing months he spoke out and wrote on the problem. So did the four professors, their ministerial allies, and many others.[20] The church became riled. By 1921 two-thirds of the classes demanded an investigation. Increasingly defensive, the curators appointed the expanded committee to investigate Janssen's views and gave him a paid leave for the 1921-1922 academic year, until the

---

[17]   Ibid.

[18]   *Acta der Synode, 1922*, 96. The entire protest is incorporated into the *Acta der Synode, 1922*, pages 89-97. A thoughtful review and assessment of all the materials in the Janssen controversy is David E. Holwerda, "Hermeneutical Issues Then and Now: The Janssen Case Revisited," *Calvin Theological Journal*, 24/1 (April, 1989), 7-34.

[19]   *Acta der Synode, 1922*, 96.

[20]   Herman Hoeksema and Henry Danhof gathered and studied student materials early in the controversy. They were two of the four ministers who signed the brochure noted in footnote 13. Hoeksema also assessed the issues in his column, "Our Doctrine" in the *Banner*. He and Danhof joined H.J. Kuiper, Y.P. De Jong, D. Zwier, and professors Berkhof and Volbeda in launching the *Witness* in the context of this controversy. Kuiper was assigned to the board's committee formed in 1921 to examine Janssen's views, as were Hoeksema and Danhof. For Hoeksema's account, see Herman Hoeksema, *The Protestant Reformed Churches in America*, 2nd ed. (Grand Rapids: 1947), 17-20.

matter was resolved. That the committee included such noncurators and Janssen critics as Kuiper and Herman Hoeksema upset Janssen and his supporters. It also caused Janssen to refuse to meet with the committee or to supply it with his lecture notes when requested. When the curators' committee submitted its report, the board voted by the narrowest of margins to recommend that the synod terminate Janssen. If the committee of Classis Grand Rapids West had remained inactive, superceded by the curators' own committee, the classis was not similarly disinterested. It delegated H.J. Kuiper to the synod of 1922. Furthermore, at its May 1922, meeting, the classis did not concur with an overture from the Twelfth Street church to disapprove of the curators' decision to pass judgment on Janssen's views that spring without first hearing him or inviting him to defend himself.[21] Kuiper's position had gained the upper hand in his classis.

At the synod of 1922, Kuiper served on the advisory committee that dealt with the Janssen case. The synod sustained the two major points of Broadway's protest and rescinded the actions of 1920.[22] It also named Kuiper and Henry Beets to translate key Janssen materials into English for wider circulation in the church. Finally, with keen sorrow it voted to terminate Janssen. No negative votes by any delegates were recorded. The sessions had been "tense with excitement, but there was no widespread and emphatic dissent" from the decisions.[23] Kuiper

---

[21] Minutes of Classis Grand Rapids West, 5/16/1922, art. 46.

[22] *Acta der Synode, 1922*, 124-25.

[23] D.H. Kromminga, *The Christian Reformed Tradition* (Grand Rapids: Eerdmans, 1943), 145. Kromminga's assessment is significant. He served with Kuiper as a noncurator on the board's committee of seven to investigate Janssen's views, signed the more temperately critical minority report to the board, then served as the official advisor to the synod's advisory committee on Janssen matters in 1922, and two years later chaired the synod's advisory committee dealing with appeals on behalf of Janssen, again with Kuiper, its reporter. Kromminga's observation above is notably more temperate than the accounts of either Harry Boer, "Ralph Janssen: The 1922 Loaded Court," the *Reformed Journal* 23 (January 1973), 22-28, or of James Bratt, *Dutch Calvinism*, 264 n. 15. If some of those involved served, as Bratt observes, as "prosecutor, judge, and jury," they were legitimately appointed to these roles by the church's mechanisms. The curators were more closely divided on the disposition of the Janssen matter than were either the curators' investigating committee or the synods of 1922 and 1924 or their advisory committees. A balanced assessment must begin with a close reading of the relevant section of the curators' report to synod, *Acta der Synode, 1922*, 175-79, and the synodically approved English translation

had been involved in more aspects of the public proceedings against Janssen, start to finish, than any other person in the church. His critique of 1920 had prevailed at the synod. The synod of 1922 also elected him to replace Hoeksema as author of the column, "Our Doctrine," in the *Banner,* an appointment which he felt compelled to decline.[24]

That September Quirinus Breen informed classis that he reserved the right to protest synod's action against Janssen. In January 1924, sixteen months later, he and three elders and five deacons filed a protest. The classis asked Breen to provide copies for every consistory and deferred consideration until the following meeting. In May, Kuiper had an overture waiting for them. In an astute move, it recommended that the Breen protest be forwarded to the synod with a notation. The classis approved. The notation stated that on the formal or procedural side of the protest the classis took no position, since it had inadequate time to consider the matter. On the substantive or material side, it asked the synod "to demand of the protestant to justify his doctrinal position as expressed in this part of the protest and the charges which it contains to the satisfaction of synod or retract them."[25] The protest alleged that those who had opposed Janssen at the synod of 1922 held un-Reformed views of inspiration, the unity of scripture, and miracles; a Lutheran view of Abraham and the afterlife; and that it rejected common grace. By approving the overture from Broadway, the classis put Breen on the defensive. Significantly, at its previous meeting it had also delegated Kuiper to the following synod.

For Kuiper, sympathy for Janssen was a very serious matter. He judged that it disqualified one from key positions. That April he convinced the Broadway consistory to submit a protest to the forthcoming synod opposing the *curatorium's* inclusion of Clarence Bouma's name on the list of nominees for the seminary's systematic theology opening created by the imminent retirement of Foppe Ten Hoor. The reasons were (1) that Bouma had been supportive of Janssen and (2) that the names of Louis Berkhof and Samuel Volbeda, suggested by many churches, including Broadway, had been ignored.[26]

---

of its full proceedings on the matter, *Acta der Synode, 1922,* 256-78. This counsel in no way condones the inappropriate rhetoric and accusations present in much of the discussion and writing on all sides.

[24] *Acta der Synode, 1922,* 77. When Kuiper declined, the position was offered to the Reverend Herman Kuiper of Rock Valley, Iowa, who accepted.

[25] Minutes of Classis Grand Rapids West, 5/13/1924, art. 40.

[26] Minutes, Broadway, 6/9/1924, art. 12.

When the synod of 1924 convened, it placed H.J. Kuiper on the advisory committee to deal with the sixteen protests against the previous synod's disposition of the Janssen case. That fourteen were from individuals or groups of individuals, only two from consistories, and none from a classis indicates that by then Janssen enjoyed only weak support in the denomination. Clearly he had fallen out of favor with the Christian Reformed majority. Kuiper was designated as reporter of the advisory committee that dealt with these materials; it was chaired by Kromminga, then serving as minister of the congregation in Peoria, Iowa.

Kuiper worked industriously and in scrupulous detail on the submitted materials. For eighty pages, in point after point, the advisory committee's analysis examined and answered the issues raised in each of the protests. Their rebuttal is overwhelming in precision and detail. Every member of the advisory committee agreed with the analysis exonerating the synod of 1922.

Synod approved all their recommendations concerning the procedural and material protests. Then it considered the notation attached by Classis Grand Rapids West to the Breen protest. The advisory committee recommended that because of the "seriousness" of disagreeing with the material or substantive positions of 1922, as now upheld by the synod of 1924, Breen should be given ample time to reflect on what he had alleged. It judged that what now looked like it had become "the Breen case" should be referred to Classis Grand Rapids West, with the suggestion that it solicit the assistance of Classis Grand Rapids East "if necessary," for final disposition. If synod concurred, the fate of Quirinus Breen would be sealed by Classis Grand Rapids West, on Kuiper's home turf.

But at this point the synod added a caution: "In the mind of synod, it would be less responsible procedurally to direct complaints toward a person than toward the protest submitted to synod by that person"[27] (translation mine). It is a telling caution. The synod had seen Kuiper at work, and its delegates were thoughtfully aware of what Kuiper was capable of inflicting. With that, the synod referred final disposition of the matter to Classis Grand Rapids West, advising it to be guided by the light shed in the advisory committee's report. The synod thanked the committee, particularly the chairman, D.H. Kromminga, and the reporter, H.J. Kuiper, for their "comprehensive and important" work on behalf of the synod.

[27] *Acta der Synode, 1924,* 242.

H.J. Kuiper's involvement in the Janssen controversy reveals that he was a consummate ecclesiastical tactician. Breen had had enough. He resigned from the ministry even before the September classis met and went on to a noteworthy career as a university professor.[28] Kuiper had more do to with the resolution of the Janssen matter than anyone else in the church. Those who were alert took note.

Common Grace

A major theme in the Janssen controversy was the doctrine of common grace.

Janssen and his defenders argued that the dependence of Israel's religion on earlier literature and ideas in other religions could be explained by the Kuyperian doctrine of common grace. As a manifestation of his goodness or grace to all people generally, whether or not they were Christian believers, God had been active in other religious traditions than Israel's, they contended. By virtue of this divine goodness, all people had at least the capacity and potential for discerning glimpses of religious truth and contributing significantly to the welfare and progress of humanity. In the minds of people like H.J. Kuiper and Herman Hoeksema, this line of reasoning made relative the uniqueness of Israel's religion and of God's special, biblical revelation. Before 1922, Herman Hoeksema had used his column, "Our Doctrine," in the *Banner* to probe, test, and ultimately question the doctrine of common grace. He pursued the matter relentlessly, and his theological and exegetical investigations led him to deny common grace altogether, and to preach and teach that position in his congregation. Reaction soon followed.

From across the Grand River, H.J. Kuiper watched the developing turmoil in Eastern Avenue Church over pastor Hoeksema and the consistory's handling of congregational dissent on the matter and between Classis Grand Rapids East and Hoeksema and his consistory

---

[28]   Quirinus Breen completed a Ph. D. at the University of Chicago in 1931, submitting a thesis, "John Calvin: A Study in French Humanism." It was revised and published under that title in 1968, with a foreword by John T. McNeill. Breen taught in the History Department of the University of Oregon after leaving the ministry. He specialized in Renaissance studies, Calvinism, Dutch colonialism, and Protestantism generally, publishing a number of articles and several books. His papers are contained in "Collection 23," Archives, CRC, and contain a paper entitled, "My Reflections on Ralph Janssen."

for disciplining the dissenters. The Reverend Henry Danhof, pastor of the First Christian Reformed Church of Kalamazoo, which then belonged to Classis Grand Rapids West, was on the board of curators, had served with Kuiper and Hoeksema on the committee investigating Janssen's views, and like both of them had been a delegate to the synod of 1922. Danhof supported publicly points Hoeksema was making and joined him in print challenging the doctrine of common grace. This elicited from the Reverend Jan Karel Van Baalen, pastor of the Munster, Indiana, Christian Reformed Church, a detailed protest against Danhof and his consistory at the May 1924 meeting of the classis. He lodged a similar protest against Hoeksema and Eastern Avenue with Classis Grand Rapids East. However, Classis Grand Rapids West took no immediate action, since Danhof and Van Baalen believed that discussions they were having would yield a resolution. It did approve the calling of a special classis meeting before the synod met that year, should talks between the two fail and Van Baalen desire such a session.[29] The talks did fail. Van Baalen asked for the meeting. It was held, in spite of procedural protests, June 10. Kuiper was named to the advisory committee that recommended that the classis refer the matter to synod, which classis decided to do. When the synod convened in Kalamazoo eight days later, it had almost two dozen protests and communications before it on common grace, a third of them generated by Classis Grand Rapids West's special session.[30]

Preoccupied with protests on the Janssen matter, Kuiper was not centrally involved in resolving the controversy about common grace. He had to have had a significant measure of sympathy with the concerns of Hoeksema and Danhof, since they had been allies through two years of work on the Janssen issue. Synod convened on a Wednesday morning, met for three days, broke for the weekend, spent the entire following week on other matters, and recessed on Friday for the second weekend. Finally, on the Tuesday of the third week, July 1, it began consideration of the common grace controversy.

The next three days were entirely devoted to the problem. Hoeksema, Danhof, and Van Baalen all made lengthy presentations. After the Thursday evening session, the synod recessed for the third weekend. It concluded the matter on the next Monday, devoting the entire day to it. The synod wanted desperately to find a position on common grace acceptable to everyone. Its three-point settlement

[29]   Minutes of Classis Grand Rapids West, 5/13/1924, art. 40.
[30]   *Acta der Synode, 1924*, 114-15.

recognized that God has an attitude of favor or mercy toward the unregenerate, that by his Spirit he restrains sin in unbelievers without changing their hearts, and that he accomplishes good and noteworthy civic benefits through them that bless others and yield a sustainable social order. The synod stated that the intent of both Hoeksema and Danhof was laudable and Reformed; they wanted to prevent any theological basis for the church's conformity to the world. The synod cited Abraham Kuyper and Herman Bavinck at length on the danger inherent in a misuse of the doctrine of common grace. But, it continued, Hoeksema and Danhof have distorted Reformed doctrine by overreacting and rejecting common grace in the way that scripture and the confessions suggest or imply. The synod also acknowledged that a common understanding or mind, which it labeled a "*communis opinio,*" did not exist in the Christian Reformed Church on this subject. But it expressed the belief that through widespread, civil, perceptive discussion of the matter one would emerge in time.

The next day the synod concluded its business, handling almost as many protests on the Janssen case in the span of one afternoon and evening as it had on the matter of common grace in three days of consideration.[31] In addition, it received a number of protests from delegates against saying more than could be substantiated and more than was good for the church to say on common grace. Among these responses on common grace was a six-page statement by delegate Danhof noting that the synod's extended discussion had dealt predominantly only with the first of its three points, that his statements and those of Hoeksema had been misunderstood and misapplied, and that the scriptural and confessional support for its three statements had not been demonstrated.[32] He concluded that he was conscience-bound to oppose the position the synod had taken and to work to overturn it. It was a forthright, honorable declaration. If H.J. Kuiper had similar misgivings, he did not enter them into the synodical record. By the next January, it was clear that his sympathies were not with Hoeksema and Danhof.

[31]   Edward Heerma's conclusion that the common grace issue "apparently did not take as much of the synod's time" as did protests on behalf of Janssen is based only on the sheer volume of Kuiper's and the advisory committee's extensive analysis. In point of fact, it spent only about a half day on the protests, but at least several days on common grace. See Heerema's insightful study *R.B.—A Prophet in the Land* (Jordan Station, Ontario: Paideia, 1986), 69.

[32]   *Acta der Synode, 1924,* 194-99.

In December 1924, Hoeksema's unyielding position on the points of doctrinal discussion and especially his defiance of Classis Grand Rapids East's directive to lift disciplinary measures against his members critical of his position precipitated his suspension from office and that of virtually all his consistory members from theirs. The classis had met sporadically in special sessions from November 19 through December 12 in its unsuccessful effort to resolve the points of conflict.[33] The controversy had been acrimonious, the press coverage detailed and relentless. Civil action ensued over control of the Eastern Avenue church property. Finding in favor of the minority opposed to Hoeksema, the court precipitated bitter and sustained resentments among Hoeksema's followers over their sense of doctrinal compromise and of the legal injustice imposed on them.

The turmoil in Classis Grand Rapids East was not lost on the churches and leaders across the river. The concerns voiced in the protests at synod a half year earlier surfaced for Classis Grand Rapids West in connection with the candidacy of B.J. Danhof, a nephew of Henry. B.J. Danhof had accepted a call and was scheduled for a classical examination January 13, 1925. The week before, the Broadway consistory approved a series of interrelated overtures. It asked that B.J. Danhof's candidacy examination be suspended until he affirmed the synod's three points on common grace. It asked that classis meet in executive session when the fall-out on common grace was considered and that one person be designated to deal with the media about any action classis might take. In a fourth overture, it asked that classis confront two of its pastors about having conducted services at Eastern Avenue after that church had broken with the 1924 synodical position on the issue. And finally, it asked the classis to require the consistories of Hope Church in River Bend and of the First Christian Reformed Church of Kalamazoo to compel their pastors, the Reverend G.M. Ophoff and the Reverend Henry Danhof, to indicate their support of the synod's statements on common grace. Clearly Kuiper intended by these overtures to foster a united position and to keep any further dissension out of the secular press. The theological discourse had not been civil, as the synod had hoped. Progress toward achieving a common mind had not only foundered, but words were sharper and the church was more divided than was the case the previous summer. The classis approved Broadway's proposals.

---

[33]   See Hoeksema, 128-221 for the most detailed account of these events. Also see Henry Beets, *The Christian Reformed Church* (Grand Rapids: Baker Book House, 1946), 108-109.

B.J. Danhof protested the classis's decision to make his assent to the three points a precondition for proceeding with his examination. He had support from Uncle Henry and Ophoff and their consistories, as well as from individuals in other churches in the classis. Procedural debates dragged into the third day. Then the classis gave the consistories of the Hope and Kalamazoo churches until Wednesday of the next week to return with commitments from their pastors that they would neither preach against nor oppose in other ways the three points of 1924.

When the classis reconvened, delegates from First Kalamazoo reported that their consistory had in fact put the demand before its pastor, but also that the consistory objected strenuously to the legitimacy of making these points a litmus test of Reformed orthodoxy when synod had acknowledged the absence of a common mind and had called for further reflection and discussion. The consistory had also noted that proper Reformed procedure required that charges and grounds should be brought against its pastor in writing and that he should be given the opportunity and adequate time to respond to them. Hope Church in River Bend and Ophoff had not complied. The next day Classis Grand Rapids West deposed Ophoff and the Hope consistory on grounds of insubordination and schism. Two days later, on Saturday afternoon, the same action was taken against Danhof and every member of the First Kalamazoo consistory, save for one elder who sided with the classis. Classis Grand Rapids East met a week later and deposed the already suspended leaders of the Eastern Avenue church.

By the time the matter was concluded, the classis had been in session for seven of the previous eleven days, the Broadway procedural overtures had substantially been followed, two pastors and two consistories had been deposed, and B.J. Danhof had not been examined for ordination. H.J. Kuiper's hand on the tiller had guided the outcome. In three balanced sermons, subsequently published at his consistory's request, he helped his people understand the doctrinal aspects of the subject.[34] A year later a penitent B.J. Danhof requested reinstatement as

---

[34] H.J. Kuiper, "The Three Points of Common Grace" (Grand Rapids: Eerdmans, 1925). Kuiper's foreword is dated February 24, 1925, suggesting that the sermons were delivered in the heat of the fray. That Hoeksema came to regard H.J. Kuiper as a central player in the common grace controversy is evident from an undated pamphlet he subsequently wrote claiming to illustrate that the Christian Reformed principals in the outcome were not followers of Calvin in the matter: "Calvin, Berkhof and H.J. Kuiper—A Comparison" (Grand Rapids, n.d.).

a candidate. Because he had meanwhile been ordained as the Protestant Reformed pastor in Hull, Iowa, he was given a doctrinal examination, known as a *colloquium doctum*, passed it, and was installed properly as pastor of the Christian Reformed Church in Grand Haven.

Crusade against Worldliness

If Kuiper was enthusiastically committed to evangelism, he was equally vigilant regarding worldliness, of which secret societies were in his estimation a noxious example. In September, 1921, he convinced his consistory to investigate the Grand Rapids Boat and Canoe Club and the American Legion to determine whether they should be classified as secret societies. The next classis meeting responded to a Broadway overture by appointing a committee to investigate these two organizations.[35] Early in 1922 he led the review of the Westside Y.M.C.A. by the four west side Christian Reformed pastors, who recommended to their consistories that the organization not receive financial support from their churches, as requested. H.J. reported that he had admonished a young man of the church for patronizing the Shrine Circus. Both his capacity for thorough work and his vigilance against worldliness earned him a position, along with seminary professors Ten Hoor and Volbeda, on the committee mandated by the synod of 1924 to study once again the problem of divorce.

Concerned with trends in American society and culture, Broadway overtured the classis in 1926 to ask synod to take a strong stand against worldliness, especially the evils of "card-playing, theater-attendance (including movies) and dancing." These practices are much too prevalent and will only proliferate, the elders judged.[36] The classis agreed and approved the overture. It appears in the synod's printed agenda.[37]

The initiative was reinforced by a later overture from Classis Illinois, initiated by Kuiper's former consistory at the Second Christian Reformed Church of Englewood, submitted after the printed agenda appeared but read on the floor of synod and printed in the synodical acts.[38] The latter warned of the dangers inherent in the same practices but raised the further question of whether and to what extent

[35]   Minutes of Classis Grand Rapids West, 1/19/1922, art. 32.
[36]   Minutes, Broadway, 1/6/1926, art. 10.
[37]   *Agendum der Synode van de Christelijke Gereformeerde Kerk, 1926* (Grand Rapids: n.p., 1926), xxxv-xxxvi. (Hereafter, *Agendum*).
[38]   *Acta der Synode, 1926*, 57-58.

ecclesiastical discipline was warranted for members who exhibited "worldliness."

Second Englewood's pastor, the Reverend E.J. Tuuk, had published an expose of worldiness a year earlier.[39] No evidence exists in the record of collaboration between Kuiper and either the Englewood consistory or Tuuk in preparing and submitting the two overtures, although it may have existed. Classis Pacific weighed in with an overture in support of the Grand Rapids West overture. The synod responded to these expressions of concern by taking a clear, preliminary position against worldliness and by naming H.J. Kuiper and E.J. Tuuk to a synodical committee to formulate and propose a definitive, denominational statement on worldly amusements.[40] The synod's preliminary statement was duly noted at Broadway's first consistory meeting after synod that year, clipped, and pasted in its entirety in the consistory minute book for future reference.[41]

The synodical committee was a high-profile group that included such leaders as Henry Hekman, the Reverend R.B. Kuiper, and Professor Henry Schultze, as well as H.J. and Tuuk. Hekman was a prominent Grand Rapids businessman who would soon serve with H.J. on Neland Avenue's consistory and whose son would marry Kuiper's younger daughter. R.B. Kuiper was the new pastor of La Grave Avenue Christian Reformed Church, who would shortly and successively be named president of Calvin College, president of Westminster Theological Seminary, and eventually also president of Calvin Theological Seminary. Schultze had been appointed by the synod that year as the seminary's professor of New Testament and in time would also become president of Calvin College. Tuuk was respected as the author of widely used catechism booklets. Kuiper was named secretary of synod's committee, and as such he became the primary author of the report on worldly amusements.[42] Its conclusions and recommendations were adopted by the synod of 1928. The synod directed that they be reproduced in the

---

[39]   Edward J. Tuuk, *As to Being Worldly*, 2nd ed. (Grand Rapids: Eerdmans, 1925).

[40]   *Acta der Synode, 1926*, 179 and 181-82.

[41]   Minutes, Broadway, 7/12/1926, art. 24.

[42]   Kuiper's position as reporter on the committee, while not stated in the agenda or acts of synod, is supported by his name appearing second on the committee list (the customary spot for the reporter) and by the notes and members' names appearing in his handwriting in the draft report submitted to the synod. *Acta der Synode, 1926*, 179. The draft report is on file in Archives, CRC.

R.B. Kuiper in 1931, about the time of his work on worldly amusements and when he was briefly president of Calvin College.

two church papers and in booklet form. Both venues assured that they were distributed and discussed widely throughout the denomination.

Kuiper's assignment to the committee on worldly amusements and his work on it did as much as any other association in his career both to express his convictions and to define his image in the church. As he was finalizing the report, Broadway elders were dispatched to view and assess the films that the Berkey and Gay furniture factory, where a number of their fellow church members were employed, showed employees on Saturday afternoons. The elders' report was not encouraging, and the consistory warned parents and factory officials that these movies were inappropriate and "profane."[43] Kuiper's synodical assignment was more timely than he had imagined when appointed two years earlier.

The fifty-three page report is divided into two sections.[44] The first, theological, section develops four cardinal principles of a Reformed or Calvinistic worldview. The honor we owe God requires believers,

[43]   Minutes, Broadway, 4/2/1928, arts. 9-11.
[44]   *Agendum, 1928,* I, 4-56.

remembering their covenantal status, not to participate in amusements and recreational activities that conflict with God's will or that promote Satan's kingdom at the expense of God's kingdom. The legitimate place good leisure-time activities have in life is for the well-being of body and mind, but they should never be primary or dominant nor should they subvert spiritual and moral health. Christians must always remember that they are called to be separate from the world. Their Christian liberty is a release from sin's bondage, from the yoke of the law, and from a restrictive conscience on indifferent matters. Further, it is a freedom to exercise Christian love and self-denial in recreational and diversionary activities.

The second, practical or ethical, section of the report deplores the prevalence among Christian Reformed members of such practices as theater attendance, social dancing, and card playing. It urges consistories to work and pray fervently for spiritual awakening and renewal in the church, to warn repeatedly against worldliness, and in its spiritual care of the congregation and its nomination of office bearers to be guided by a strenuous opposition to worldliness. That the thought and spirit of the report would later be eclipsed by the three identified prohibitions was not the intent of either the committee or the synod of 1928. The fervent desire was to give tangible form to what it meant for a denomination emerging from its isolation to be both Reformed and North American. That remained H.J. Kuiper's agenda to the end of his ministry. The report had wide support, including by Tuuk and R.B. Kuiper, who just a few years earlier were espousing cultural engagement in their magazine *Religion and Culture*.[45] As prime movers against encroaching worldliness in the CRC and as the chief architects of the newly constructed case against it, these leaders meant to see the position enforced denominationally.

An especially poignant dimension of this resolve is what might be called "the Kuiper entanglement." In addition to being primary author of the 1928 report, H.J. Kuiper had been embroiled in the subject as a member of the Calvin board of curators since his election to it in 1924. The board was deeply concerned with a perceived increase in worldliness among students. It had designated a committee to confer with the faculties of the college and the seminary about the problem, and it had held up the admission of several students to the seminary

[45]   On *Religion and Culture* and the *Witness*, an alternative magazine, see chapter 6, pp. 111-14.

as a result. In 1926, Kuiper was elected as the board's president, and three months after the synod had appointed its committee on worldly amusements, the Calvin board convened a special meeting to deal with strenuous protests against B.K. Kuiper's new appointment as professor of church history at the seminary because of his alleged patronage of movie theaters. He had been living under a cloud since resigning from the college faculty eight years before, then from the editorship of *De Wachter* in 1922, and also for writing a pamphlet in support of Janssen. The board had refused several requests he had made to be approved for ordination. And now, as its new chairman, H.J. Kuiper had to guide the board in dealing with a public relations problem of substantial proportions, much of it generated within his own classis.

The board put four pointed questions to B.K, gave him the night to reflect on his answers, recalled him the next day to elaborate on them in person, then designated a subcommittee to refine and approve his written formulations for publication in the two church papers. The unrest seemed to have been quelled. Unfortunately, B.K. Kuiper proved to be something of a backslider. He returned to his theatrical haunts and consequently was not recommended by the board, H.J. presiding, for reappointment in 1928. At the synod that year the report on worldly amusements, substantially written by H.J. Kuiper, was presented and defended by R.B. Kuiper, reporter for the advisory committee and B.K.'s brother. R.B. had also served on the study committee with H.J. The report of H.J. and R.B. was approved; B.K. was not. Spiritual ties on this matter were stronger than bonds of the womb.[46] So embroiled in the issue was R.B. that after the synod he preached a series of eight sermons on the Christian's relationship to the world and dedicated their published form to his La Grave Avenue congregation the next year.[47]

Synodical Policy

In addition to all his other preoccupations during his Broadway ministry, H.J. Kuiper through his consistory was a fount of ideas for improving a number of denominational policies and procedures. Some have already been noted. Others deserve mention. Collectively they

---

[46]   Much in this paragraph is based on the more extensive treatment by Henry Zwaanstra, "Something about B.K.," (Grand Rapids: Calvin Theological Seminary, 1977), 7-16.

[47]   R.B. Kuiper, *'Not of the World': Discourses on the Christian's Relation to the World* (Grand Rapids: Eerdmans, 1929).

reflect a prodigious worker with a keen interest and generally perceptive judgment on almost all matters denominational.

In the context of the Janssen problem, Broadway proposed that, all things being equal, people appointed to the seminary be ordained men with pastoral experience and that the churches be given the opportunity to react to nominees. The proposal can best be understood against the church's experience with Janssen. The classis endorsed the former idea, but not the latter. The synod approved both, since both had also come via an overture from Classis Hudson.[48]

Kuiper was vitally interested in the denomination's ecumenical contacts and offered proposals on the subject. The synod of 1924 approved an overture from Classis Grand Rapids West, submitted originally by Broadway, that the synod select and send, at its expense, a delegate to the 1926 synod of the Gereformeerde Kerken in the Netherlands because of the significant issues before that body and because of that church's close ties with the Christian Reformed Church.[49] The European church was in the throes of dealing with the sensitive issue of interpreting the early chapters of Genesis regarding human origins. Another sensitive ecumenical issue receiving mixed reviews was continuing membership in the Federal Council of Churches, which the Christian Reformed Church had joined during the First World War. The synod of 1924 received a positive report from its three representatives to this body, two of whom—the Reverends Dolfin and Timmerman—served on its executive committee and one of whom—Henry Beets—was a vice president. In their report, the delegates mounted arguments why the denomination should continue its affiliation.[50] But the synod had also received overtures from four classes to sever relations with the council, one of which was from Grand Rapids West as submitted by Broadway. The advisory committee recommended maintaining membership. After a lengthy discussion, the synod adopted the position of Classis Grand Rapids West, with slight modifications of its several grounds. The synod concluded that (1) the conviction exists in the churches that alliances between liberal and orthodox bodies are contrary to scripture; (2) liberalism is entrenched in the council, as its emphasis on the social gospel and social programs indicates; and (3) the council

---

48 *Acta der Synode, 1922,* 12-13.
49 *Acta der Synode, 1924,* 40.
50 *Acta der Synode, 1924,* "Bijlage XII," 322-28.

Henry Beets (*left*), secretary of foreign missions and editor of the *Banner*, and the Reverend John Dolfin (*right*), Christian Reformed pastor in Muskegon who was both a *Banner* columnist and treasurer of the mission board, pictured in 1924 while on a visit to Christian Reformed missions among the Navajos.

is committed to programs that are outside the sphere of responsibility and competence of the institutional church.[51]

Kuiper's longstanding desire for a uniform church education program for the churches and his unhappiness with the International Lesson System, which was used in many churches of the denomination, led to a Broadway proposal that the denomination, under the direction and control of the synod, develop its own materials.[52] The matter had been before the synod several times since 1920. This proposal carried a step further the decision of the previous synod, that a standing committee on education be appointed to advise the churches on ways to enhance the instruction of their youth.

[51] Ibid., 111-12.
[52] Minutes of Classis Grand Rapids West, 4/10/1928, art. 16.

Kuiper's overture contained a thoughtfully crafted background section and five grounds. Kuiper believed the material was too oriented toward a social gospel and not sufficiently Reformed in doctrinal emphasis. The advisory committee recommended that the overture not be adopted, as the entire enterprise seemed far too ambitious and expensive and because the International Lesson System was being used in some two hundred Christian Reformed churches at the time. The synod, however, followed neither course. It referred the issue of producing its own Sunday school material to the standing committee on education for study and with a request that it submit its recommendations to the following synod. The standing committee reported in 1932 that it saw too many obstacles to moving in that direction. The issue, however, resurfaced two years later, when Kuiper's position prevailed.[53]

Conclusion

As the end of the decade approached, H.J. Kuiper had earned the respect and trust of his own, large congregation. He was an organized, faithful, and effective pastor in all aspects of his ministry at Broadway. But the decade had also seen him emerge as a leader in a variety of denominationally significant endeavors. He served for the entire period on the denomination's strategic and controversial committee on worship. He was the secretary on its worldly amusements committee. He had been a delegate to synod in 1922, 1924, and 1928—three determinative assemblies for the Christian Reformed Church. As reporter on the advisory committee handling protests in the Janssen case, he formulated the analysis and resolution that reunified the

[53]   His first year as editor, Kuiper analyzed the International Sunday School lessons for the fall quarter, since they were being used by his own Sunday school teachers at Neland Avenue, and he reviewed the forthcoming lessons with them weekly. The lessons present "the social gospel," ignore the main themes and organic unity of scripture, and consistently distort the biblical passages adduced, he pronounced in his editorials that December. These lessons are "a standing menace to the purity and welfare of our church and of every church which uses them," he alleged. "If we ever drift into modernism no one will be able to say without blushing that the International Lesson Committee had no share in our defection," he stated. *Banner,* 64/1713 (12/20/1929), 956-57. For helpful background on the International Sunday School Committee and its materials, see Marvin J. Taylor, ed., *Religious Education: A Comprehensive Survey* (New York and Nashville: Abingdon Press, 1960), particularly chaps. 30-32, pp. 326-58.

denomination in 1924. In 1928 he was synod's vice president. Less visible synodical assignments were his service on the tract committee, on the 1924 committee named to study divorce, and as a synodical deputy. The Young Men's Federation elected him president and used him in its promotional work. The Calvin curators placed him on the committee to investigate the views of Ralph Janssen, and in 1924 he was elected to the Calvin board, which he served successively as vice president, president, and secretary. On a classical level he was the father of numerous overtures, was briefly stated clerk, and spearheaded local evangelism. By 1928 he had become a denominational leader who had had a determinative influence on many of the most important decisions and policies of the church.

That synod that year entrusted him with the responsibility that would define the rest of his professional life, therefore, is understandable. Still smarting from the Janssen experience, the Calvin board of curators in 1928 recommended that B.K. Kuiper not be reappointed to the seminary faculty. He had held the position of professor of church history for only two years, but he had reneged on his promise made at the time of his appointment to cease and desist from theater attendance. The Oakdale Park consistory, via Classis Grand Rapids East, had asked the curators to investigate reports that B.K. had been seen attending the theater on more than one occasion. When they verified the reports, they made their recommendation to synod. H.J. Kuiper not only wrote the report and recommendation for the synod in his capacity as secretary of the board of curators, he was on the synod's advisory committee that processed the recommendation and concurred with it. And H.J. Kuiper served on synod's committee of appointments that assigned himself to this advisory committee! As he had been in the Janssen situation, he was positioned to guide the matter to its proposed outcome.

But the decision not to reappoint B.K. Kuiper presented a set of circumstances that would lead to an unanticipated but life-changing opportunity for H.J. Kuiper. Early in its sessions the synod of 1928 had appointed the Reverend D.H. Kromminga, pastor of Neland Avenue Christian Reformed Church, as the new editor of the *Banner* to replace Henry Beets. Kromminga had accepted. When B.K. was not reappointed later in synod's sessions, it again turned to Kromminga, this time as its first choice as professor of church history. He accepted. Judging it impossible to serve in both capacities, he informed the synod that he would relinquish the editorship. In one of its last matters of business, the synod of 1928 elected H.J. Kuiper, its vice president, to be the next editor of the *Banner* in Kromminga's place.

It was Friday afternoon. The synod adjourned that evening. Kuiper was conflicted. He did not immediately accept. He did not seek or want the position, he admitted in his opening editorial January 1, 1929. He had withdrawn from the first nomination for it at the synod of 1928. After the synod turned to him in place of Kromminga, H.J. took "several months" to accept. The reason was, he stated, "a strong, almost painfully strong, sense of our incompetence and insufficiency, especially in view of the limited time at our disposal for the big task involved in this editorship."[54] But in the end he accepted.

Henry J. Kuiper, pastor of the Broadway Christian Reformed Church, began his tenure as editor of the *Banner* January 1, 1929. He held the position until his retirement at the end of the summer, 1956.

---

[54] *Banner,* 64/1664 (1/4/1929), 4.

CHAPTER 4

Neland Avenue: Wearing Two Hats

D.H. Kromminga's acceptance of the church history position at Calvin Seminary yielded a second change in Kuiper's life. Kromminga relinquished his pulpit as pastor of the Neland Avenue Christian Reformed Church in the summer of 1928. By March of the next year, that congregation extended a call to be their pastor to H.J. Kuiper. On March 18, 1929, Kuiper left the Broadway consistory meeting early to visit with the Neland consistory about the call. After he left, the Broadway consistory unanimously passed a request that he stay with them. But by the first of April he had decided to move across town, and by the first of May he had begun his last pastorate. At his first Neland consistory meeting, Kuiper announced his intention to visit all the church families socially. Membership papers of his family were received, including the confessing membership of his older daughter, Helen, and the baptized membership of his younger daughter, Clara. A mid-week Bible study for all age groups was approved for the summer months, as Kuiper had recently proposed in a *Banner* editorial. Before his arrival, the consistory had approved motions to redecorate the parsonage, build a two-stall garage, and welcome the Kuipers at a reception. It was an auspicious beginning.

As Neland's pastor, Kuiper followed many of the patterns he had established in his previous pastorates. He provided regular and detailed reports on catechism attendance. He led several societies. He was dutiful in family visiting and pastoral calling. That he volunteered several salary reductions during the Great Depression while maintaining a positive

The Neland Avenue church and parsonage in the Kuiper era.

outlook modeled a mature spirituality admired and appreciated by the congregation. The church recognized the Kuipers with a special event on their thirtieth wedding anniversary, and the consistory surprised its pastor with a fiftieth birthday party at the family's Gun Lake cottage. The young people looked forward to the parties the pastor threw at the conclusion of the catechism year. Cornelia Kuiper was known for her winsome hospitality. Kuiper's preaching continued to stress the purity of biblical truth, to encourage diligent spiritual discipline, to warn against all forms of worldliness and compromise, and to proclaim a Calvinistic world view. Both of the church's previous pastors were members: H. Henry Meeter as chairman of the Calvin College Bible department and D.H. Kromminga as the seminary's professor of church history. Kuiper's attention to Calvinism pleased Meeter, who noted that the congregation's proclivity for *Afscheiding* experientialism did not always find that emphasis palatable. Kromminga's tendency toward a mystical Reformed spirituality was not incompatible with Kuiper's homiletical emphases. The fact that the entire seminary faculty save one, and many college professors, were members put Neland Avenue at the center of denominational life, although the academic leaders did not control the church.

Kuiper served in classical and denominational capacities while at Neland Avenue. He continued on the synod's worship committee and its new committee to introduce hymns. He soon dropped his role as associate editor of the *Young Calvinist* and his position on the Calvin board, which he most recently had served as secretary. In the early years he for a time held a seat on the classical interim committee.

H. Henry Meeter, Neland pastor from 1917 to 1926, subsequently professor of Bible at Calvin College.

Later he was named to various classical committees. Four times he was delegated to synod: 1930, 1932, 1936, and 1937. In 1932 he was elected vice president and in 1936 and 1937 he was president. In 1932 the synod appointed him to a committee to formulate principles of evangelism and to its new emergency committee, which was mandated to propose creative ways to match the oversupply of ministers with needy churches and to subsidize their ministries. In 1934 he became acting chair of the committee to produce the first edition of *The Psalter Hymnal*. His load was heavy; but he bore it with dignity, grace, and competence.

Under his leadership, Neland Avenue also engaged the issues of the day.

Worldliness

Worldliness continued to be a major preoccupation of H.J. Kuiper during his Neland Avenue pastorate. He was constantly vigilant regarding catechism attendance and issued specific reports to his consistory on who skipped and how often. Committees assigned to work with problem families and members dutifully made monthly reports. Community activities and denominational ministries were scrutinized for signs of spiritual deviance. In 1932 the consistory sent

D.H. Kromminga, Neland pastor from 1926 to 1928, subsequently professor of church history at Calvin Seminary.

a letter to the Michigan Christian Teachers Association protesting an objectionable title to a play the organization was advertising, and it noted incidentally that the consistory was in principle not supportive of dramatic presentations. Young people appearing to make profession of faith were quizzed on worldly amusements, and a few were not approved because they did not measure up to denominational expectations. One young woman, resolute in her determination to attend movies she judged worthwhile despite a personal visit from Kuiper to dissuade her, was told she could be admitted to the Lord's Table if she changed her mind on evolution and her practice on theater attendance. When an alert elder discovered that two young men attended dances, he so reported and a committee was dispatched to confront them about the problem.

One of the saddest cases during Kuiper's long pastoral career involved a young woman who had made profession of faith before the consistory with a number of others, and whose public profession had been scheduled and announced. Then it came to the consistory's attention that she worked at a confectionery store on Sundays. When the pastor visited the family concerning the matter, he was told that her employment was "an answer to prayer" and a "work of necessity," since this income was vital because it supplemented what the father earned from the Works Progress Administration in those Depression years. The consistory rescinded its approval of her for public profession and decided to make an announcement, which was initially deferred. Another visit with the young woman found her resolute, articulate, and mature. How could she, a sincere believer in the Lord, be denied access to his table? Her mother pointed out that wealthy members of the church had hired help that worked on Sundays. The father implored the pastor and consistory not to proceed in the planned way. But the announcement was ultimately made. H.J. withdrew from the "case." The young woman stopped attending church. She was cited for Sabbath desecration. She asked for a public apology from the consistory or she felt she could no longer worship at Neland. Later, letters were exchanged. The young woman was warned that persistence in her attitude and actions would lead to discipline. Finally, eleven months after she had appeared before the consistory to profess her faith, the consistory decided to ask the congregation publicly for their prayers for "an erring baptized member." Three months later she personally appeared before the consistory to inform them that she was resigning from Neland Avenue. It was a heart-wrenching outcome that left many in the congregation deeply troubled.

When a *Grand Rapids Press* article reported on a fraternity house homecoming dance at the University of Michigan, it named six of the church's young people as participants. The consistory immediately dispatched two elders to Ann Arbor to investigate this public blot on the congregation's reputation. Their report the next week at two special consistory meetings, held four days apart, yielded absolutions for four of the young people, confessions of wrong-doing by two others, and a warning against worldliness to the congregation.[1] The episode kindled Kuiper's and Neland's interest in matters at the state's premier university sufficiently that the consistory submitted an overture to the next classis meeting asking the classis to request the Phi Alpha Kappa fraternity not to schedule dances and to cease the practice of hazing, since so many Christian Reformed young men were members, and since

---

[1]   The matter was handled at consistory meetings November 6, 13, and 17, 1936. To what extent the worldly amusements decision affected the Calvin College community, see Harry Boonstra, *Our School: Calvin College and the Christian Reformed Church*, The Historical Series of the Reformed Church in America, no.39 (Grand Rapids: Eerdmans, 2001), 92-105.

these practices militated against the values of the Ann Arbor Chapel.[2] The classis prudently tabled the request. But it continued to monitor the campus scene, and several years later approved an overture from Neland Avenue asking for a more rigorous method of overseeing the campus chapel.

Military service was as spiritually dangerous an environment as the secular campus. Kuiper's editorials in the *Banner* repeatedly addressed the threat. Having completed service, some veterans joined the Ex-servicemen's Club of Grand Rapids, at whose functions movies were shown. Neland asked the classis to investigate and to advise the churches on how to deal with the matter. The classis committee judged that these activities "do not merit our approval," and classis advised every consistory in writing to discourage participation in them.[3] Concerned that the war effort during World War II required strategic Sunday labor in defense factories, the classis approved a position that "unanimously" affirmed the importance of the Sabbath, sanctioned work only that was essential for civil defense, and warned that this temporary concession should not be used to defend lax standards for Sunday activities once the war had ended.[4]

The Great Depression

The stock market crashed in October 1929, six months after Kuiper began his ministry at Neland. The first hint of economic downturn in the church's minutes was a visit to the consistory, in March 1931, of representatives from the Oakdale Christian School board. They outlined the financial struggle the school was having and appealed to the consistory for help. It was decided to give the school the loose offerings at the evening service every other week for two months. In May the consistory decided to continue the practice indefinitely.

The economy worsened. That September the consistory accepted—with thanks—the offer of a member to purchase and donate a lot in Comstock Park and to pay for the erection of a chapel on it as a City Mission board project. The next month the consistory deferred implementation, noting that the budget was in arrears and fearing that the project could not be sustained. The consistory also appointed a

---

[2]   Minutes of the consistory of the Neland Avenue Christian Reformed Church, 1/11/1937, art. 17.

[3]   Minutes of Classis Grand Rapids East, 5/14/1941, art. 18.

[4]   Minutes of Classis Grand Rapids East, 1/21/1942, art. 38.

committee to formulate an overture that would secure "better financial management" of denominational funds.[5] When the budget for the following year was considered in November, Kuiper voluntarily reduced his annual salary 10 percent, from $3,000 to $2,700. It was a deeply appreciated gesture—one made in many Christian Reformed consistory rooms that fall.

The slide continued precipitously. By the next July the consistory asked the bank's permission to pay only the interest on the church's recent building loan and to suspend temporarily payment on the principal. The interest obligation was met before fuel was purchased. That summer the pastor offered to pay personally for the clerical and teaching help for catechism classes; he received permission to cancel classes for six- and seven-year-olds. The consistory began making visits to families whose giving was anemic. That fall Kuiper took another voluntary salary reduction, to $2,250. At the congregational meeting approving the 1934 budget, he was given a "vote of appreciation." When economic conditions worsened that winter and spring, an all-out effort to canvass the congregation to encourage sacrificial giving was made. Kuiper reduced his salary yet again, to $1,800. Bills were now paid selectively, and prior year assessments were recorded as continuing obligations while denominational quotas were not.[6] A half-year later the congregation was meeting somewhere between 10 and 72 percent of its various ministry obligations, and it informed the City Mission board that it could no longer support the chapel ministry in Comstock Park and desired to turn it over to the board. By mid-1935, matters were beginning to improve and the consistory approved a request from the City Mission board that they be allowed to solicit gifts for a new building.

The Depression was deep and persistent. H.J. Kuiper regarded it as both a divine admonition and as an opportunity. It was an admonition against the secularism and worldliness that infected even the church. It was an opportunity to develop stronger faith, deeper dependence on the Lord, and more genuine service. It was also a time when churches could not meet or increase their budgets, when many Christian schools left

[5]   Minutes, Neland, 10/5/1931, art. 19.
[6]   Minutes, Neland, 5/1/1934, art. 12. Synodical assessments for the college and seminary were regarded as financial obligations; synodical quotas for other denominational causes were regarded as target figures, which if not met by a given congregation were usually made up by other churches in the classis after an acceptable explanation was given.

teachers' salaries unpaid, and when many missions and other kingdom causes had to scale back their programs. H.J. Kuiper reminded *Banner* readers that deeper spirituality is more important than institutional expansion. Such problems God allows in order to deepen our prayer life and to teach us to listen more faithfully to the Word, to assist one another, and to trust him more completely.[7]

He repeatedly offered very practical, helpful ideas for diaconal response to the Depression: canvass the wealthy for larger contributions; visit the destitute before they are forced to ask for assistance; change the name from "poor fund" to "benevolence fund" out of concern not to stigmatize poverty; help the unemployed find work—even temporary work; and understand and promote government relief and work programs. One of the most significant threats of the Depression was that it might heighten the appeal of fascism, communism and socialism—reason enough to pray fervently for restored prosperity. But Kuiper was also a severe critic of unregulated, unrestrained capitalism. He warned against the spiritual dangers posed by the idleness imposed by unemployment, especially for the young, whom he urged to be especially supportive of parents who were at risk of losing their homes and savings built up over an adult lifetime.

In the depths of the Depression, in November and December of 1934, the editor ran a five-part series, "The Position of the Christian in the Present Economic Crisis." He had been reading and thinking deeply on the subject for several years. The series, he admitted, would bring him into political, social, and economic territory that "has almost become a tradition" for the *Banner* to avoid.[8] His aim was to articulate and to apply biblical principles for constructing a Christian view of society and government.

Listing a dozen or so abuses of capitalism, he condemned them from a Christian perspective but warned against discarding capitalism as an economic system. The Republicans lost the elections in 1932 and 1934 because they failed to offer a way out of the country's economic problems, he instructed his readers. He doubted that a Christian could be "an enthusiastic supporter of the New Deal" or vote Democratic, but he praised the Roosevelt Administration for imposing restraints on Wall Street, abolishing child labor, addressing unemployment and economic stagnation, and advocating unemployment insurance. With Henry Ryskamp of the Calvin College Economics Department, he had

---

[7]   *Banner*, 66/1787 (5/29/1931), 501-502.
[8]   *Banner*, 69/1962 (11/2/1934), 932.

misgivings about the level of proposed controls on industries and on prices, which Kuiper saw as a form of socialism that both diminishes consumer freedoms and impedes investment. He considered the recent diplomatic recognition of atheistic Russia as a "betrayal" of the nation's commitment to religious freedom.

It is the Calvinist, he argued, who best protects the balance between individual and collective rights. Loss of this balance occurs when basic Christian doctrines are ignored and distorted. The creation of man in the image of God, with "certain inalienable rights," is one such doctrine. Socialism, communism, and "our present-day capitalism" enslave workers and violate their creation in God's image, he believed. The first two violate the rights of the wealthy, the last those of the worker. The Christian favors a regulated capitalism as the best system. It best honors the biblical doctrine of limited functions for civil government, Kuiper believed. Government's primary function is to restrain and punish evil-doers. For this purpose it can make and enforce laws, judge in disputes or criminal matters, levy taxes, bear the sword, promote morality, and provide public safety. Other systems encroach on spheres like the family, the church, the school, and private charities. It was not accidental, Kuiper held, that the trend toward collectivism was most pronounced in countries where Christianity was slipping.

Finally, he tackled the fallacy that social evils are rooted in systems and programs rather than in human depravity. Improvements in the system are necessary, admittedly. But human greed and selfishness were more to blame for the crash of 1929 than the weaknesses of capitalism, Kuiper stated.

His series also offered encouragement. All the ingredients for economic recovery are present, he wrote, but fear is impeding it. People are fearful because they do not trust in God.

Kuiper's editorials on the economic condition of the nation and the church display thoughtful reflection, balance, and compassion. He challenged his parishioners and his readers not to lose hope, to be patient and mutually supportive in adversity, and ultimately to trust in God's provision. His own self-sacrifice authenticated what he preached and wrote.

Worship Disputed

No denominational cause claimed more from Kuiper than the issue of public worship. The first August of his tenure at Neland the consistory decided, in the pastor's absence, to implement the controversial new standard order of worship approved by the synod the year before. Kuiper may have favored the move, but knowing firsthand the volatility of the issue, he probably encouraged or even proposed the motion at the September meeting to study the most propitious way of implementing the change. The new order of worship had been debated for a decade before being adopted in 1928 with more built-in flexibility than was originally proposed. Kuiper, now nine months into his role as *Banner* editor, where he had already tackled the subject in editorials that had elicited substantial resistance, was understandably cautious because of the potential for division in his own congregation. Reaction in the churches against imposed standardization had already set in.

Implementation was delayed at Neland. Sensitivities were heightened when Mr. Hoogsteen, the choir director, and Kuiper collaborated that fall to have the choir sit on the platform to alleviate overcrowding at worship services. A special consistory meeting was called to deal with what some interpreted as a surreptitious step toward introducing the choir in worship, an innovation allowed in 1926 and upheld by the synod of 1928, but discountenanced by Neland's leaders, including Kuiper. In December H.J. was mandated to preach a series of sermons on worship prior to implementing the new order. As presented to the congregation, the order omitted the controversial absolution and substituted an assurance of pardon and a penitential hymn after the stipulated reading of the Decalogue in the morning service. Even so, reaction was such that implementation was again postponed in March 1930, and a committee was asked to study the matter more deeply. Two weeks later a member appeared before the consistory to register his questions and list his objections to the new order; he asked the body to delay implementation until after the synod considered the overtures and protests accumulating on the issue. These delays can only have tested Kuiper's patience, as he had been convinced of the soundness and desirability of the changes for a decade.

During Kuiper's first year at Neland, the consistory authorized the purchase of fifty copies of *The New Christian Hymnal* for use in the Bible class and approved an overture asking synod to make significant revisions in the *Psalter*. Two years later it declined a request that the choral club be permitted to rehearse after the Sunday evening service, since this was inappropriate Sunday activity. That spring it also squelched the suggestion of singing hymns and employing choir anthems at the Easter service.

Minor liturgical issues creep into the consistory minutes with regularity: an alternative tune for the doxology, the length of the silent prayer, the use of a children's choir on special occasions, and when and where the minister should stand during the service. In April, 1936, the consistory asked the classis to overture synod on a more substantial, serious matter, namely to expand the denomination's creed, since a number of contemporary matters do not receive attention in the three forms of unity.[9] Two months later, ten years after synod removed the denominational ban on church choirs, the consistory of Neland Avenue went on record as not being opposed in principle to having a permanent choir.

The fact that early in Kuiper's ministry liturgical issues would be prominent in the congregation's life is no surprise. They were prominent in its pastor's life. In his first seven years at Neland, he monitored the public reception of *The New Christian Hymnal*, served on the synodical committee dealing with a uniform order of worship, was appointed to the new committee on the introduction of hymns into Christian Reformed worship, and for the last two years chaired the committee to produce the *Psalter Hymnal*. In his first eighteen months as editor of the *Banner*, from January 1929 until the synod of 1930, Kuiper wrote more than twenty editorials on worship. Most of them advocated implementation of the uniform order of worship approved by the synod of 1928. In his fourth issue as editor, he noted the considerable negative reaction to the new order of worship, especially in congregations in the West.[10] Much of it had been occasioned by the alarmist views contained in the pamphlet of the Reverend G.J. Haan, *De Kwestie van den Eredienst in Onze Kerken* (The Issue of the Worship Service in Our Churches), Kuiper believed. But articles criticizing it as "this new Roman menace" had appeared in *Missionary Monthly,* the *Standard Bearer*, and the new premillennial magazine, *Grace and Glory.* He invoked the names of Calvin, à Lasco, A. Kuyper, V. Hepp, and his fellow committee members W. Heyns, Y.P. De Jong, J. Van Lonkhuyzen, and D. Zwier to calm the waters. He also asked readers to think "soberly" and "sanely" about the work approved by "a large majority" of synodical delegates in 1928.

---

[9] The term "the three forms of unity" refers to The Belgic Confession, the Heidelberg Catechism, and the Canons of Dort, historic confessional statements to which all Christian Reformed office bearers are required to subscribe.

[10] *Banner,* 64/1667 (1/25/1929), 56.

In a long essay, he corrected Y. De Leeuw, who had written an article in *De Wachter* against the new order of worship. Kuiper was especially sensitive to this piece, since it had appeared in the official, Dutch-language, denominational magazine. De Leeuw took the position that if a local consistory disagreed with the new order of worship, it simply retained the order it had in place, since the synod's decisions cannot trump those of the local consistory if no principle is involved. Kuiper registered his surprise at such a congregationalistic statement. "The adoption of an order of worship is a matter which pertains to all the churches,"[11] he asserted. Therefore, the synod properly determines the elements in the service and the order in which they occur. Details belong to the local church within this framework, he clarified. Kuiper then went on to explain that denominational unity in the Reformed tradition applies to unity in doctrine, government, and worship. This had been the worship committee's stock answer since the early 1920s. If unity in worship is compromised, unity in doctrine and government are at risk also, for the three are interdependent. "Now that synod has adopted the new form every one of our churches is in conscience bound to introduce it, unless it can prove to the satisfaction of the synod that this new form is, in part or as a whole, contrary to the Word of God." He quoted Article 31 of the church order on synodical decisions as "settled and binding," and he reminded readers that this applied also to the 1928 decision on a uniform order of worship.

That Kuiper came out this strongly so early in his editorial career and in the face of mounting denominational opposition to the decision indicates how deeply invested he was in the matter. It also displays how he construed denominational unity and how fiercely he defended his understanding of it. He could not leave the subject of worship alone long enough for emotions to cool. In February he mended fences with the *Missionary Monthly* over an errant opinion he had expressed on missions and liturgy. In March he warned that unless uniform worship is implemented, churches would be swept in all sorts of incongruous directions by the rapidly advancing Americanization process. In April he listed and responded to a number of thoughtfully presented questions by an irenic colleague. In May he defended the absolution as based in sixteenth-century Reformed practice. That month he also asserted that Arminianism was galloping into the churches on the back of English and American hymnody; he pleaded for discernment in the hymns churches chose to use.

[11]   Ibid.

In his longest editorial on worship during his first five months, Kuiper made the case for the Reformed character of the uniform order of worship.[12] It is thoroughly Reformed, he claimed, because it introduces the Decalogue and retains the sermon as central. It emphasizes the seriousness of sin in an antinomian era by using the law as a teacher of sin, prior to confession and forgiveness, thus fostering a humility "essential to real worship." The absolution, which is the gospel in a nutshell, strengthens the assurance of the believer. The new order is more logically progressive and coherent than the older one. It involves more active, overt congregational participation. Also, the offertory prayer gives greater prominence to the offering as an expression of grateful love. He asked people to consider the new order thoughtfully, churches to try it genuinely, and both not to dismiss it summarily because it was new. Frankly, he concluded, it is very conservative and modest in the changes it makes.

By September Kuiper was becoming alarmed enough about the increasing opposition that he floated the suggestion that the study committee's recommendations rather than those of the advisory committee be voted on by the synod, on the grounds that the former had worked harder and longer on the matter than the latter.[13] He cited how demoralized the committee on public worship was becoming. It had worked for ten years and submitted two long, careful reports. He noted that the committee's 1928 report had received little public disapproval prior to that year's synod. Its recommendations had been approved. Now the dissent was mounting. Kuiper was concerned. He pleaded for a thorough review of the committee's reports prior to the next synod.

Kuiper continued the editorial drumbeat on liturgy in late 1929 and early 1930. The more attention he gave it, the more resistance stiffened. By the April before synod, he noted that a number of classes were submitting overtures. He had grown sufficiently concessive to allow that churches should not be forced to implement the new order, but that when they did make changes they must follow the 1926-1928 order approved by synod. It did his cause no good when in reviewing the synodical agenda, he predicted that liturgical issues would dominate and noted that Dutch Calvinists "are not strong in liturgical appreciation" and that in their churches there had been "practically no liturgical development" for three centuries.[14]

---

[12] *Banner,* 64/1685 (5/31/1929), 384-86.
[13] *Banner,* 64/1698 (9/6/1929), 597.
[14] *Banner,* 65/1737 (6/6/1930), 541.

Of the eight classical overtures on the new order of worship submitted to the synod of 1930, only the one from Kuiper's former classis urged that it be introduced speedily. One suggested some improvements. But six objected to its imposition on the churches. Even the two positive overtures acknowledged widespread suspicion and resistance.[15] Two major issues faced by the synod were procedural. The first was whether the synod had the right to impose a uniform order of worship on all congregations of the denomination. The second was whether the 1928 decision adopting the uniform order of worship could be rescinded without showing that it was contrary to scripture and/or the confessions of the church, as the church order stipulated.

Although he had been installed at Neland only thirteen months earlier, Kuiper was delegated to this synod by his new classis. His election was no doubt governed by his prominent role in crafting and defending the new order of worship. At the synod of 1930, he functioned on the important committee that proposed the advisory committee assignments, and when these were made, he was found on the one that dealt with the issues of introducing hymns and choirs into Christian Reformed worship. The debate on the uniform order of worship was substantial and is amply reported in the *Acta der Synode, 1930*. By the time the last gavel on worship fell, the absolution had been eliminated, the service of confession muffled, the Apostles' Creed eliminated from the morning service, and a psalm of response removed. Other items had been added. In conclusion, the advisory committee said, "The remaining elements form a beautiful, logical whole, coming very close to the old order now in vogue in most of our churches."[16] If the changes were reassuring to the majority of classes and churches, they irritated and discouraged Kuiper. Some harsh judgments had been made in the debates, most notably that the uniform order of worship risked moving the church toward "formalism," high church worship, and clericalism. For Kuiper the beautiful cohesiveness and liturgical rhythm that he and others had worked so hard for twelve years to develop was dismantled during parts of three successive sessions of synod. Kuiper registered his protest in the synodical record. Rescinding the 1928 decision without the required proof was contrary to Article 31 of the church order, he stated. Further, "Synod has utterly failed in this matter to safeguard the

---

[15] Cf. Carl Kromminga, 13 ff. for a summary of the synod of 1930's handling of these materials.
[16] *Acta der Synode, 1930,* 185.

peace and welfare of the churches which now use the order of worship adopted in 1928."[17] The synod countered simply with a recorded decision that 1928 had erred, since neither scripture, confessions, nor church order required that all churches follow the same order of worship.

The synod continued the committee on the improvement of worship because its advisory committee had misgivings about the order of worship proposed for the second Sunday service. It referred that item to the churches and asked that their reactions be directed to the committee. It also instructed the committee to consider those reactions in resubmitting the proposed order of worship for the second service to the following synod. Demoralized by the "catastrophe" of 1930, the committee put little effort into its assignment, presented a brief report in 1932, and asked to be discharged. Its request was granted; no action was taken concerning the second service. What uniformity of worship subsequently developed in the Christian Reformed Church happened by consistorial conformity to wider practices—many of them proposed, ironically, by the committee on public worship. D.H. Kromminga, by now one of Kuiper's pew-sitters, was as glum as his pastor about the outcome: "Thus our search for uniformity of worship had led to the loss of what uniformity we had,"[18] he wrote.

Church music proved to be a more satisfying area of Kuiper's endeavor. The Broadway consistory had informed its classis already in January 1928 that it was in favor of adding "some doctrinally sound hymns" to the *Psalter*.[19] That year synod created a committee on hymns. Kuiper was named to it. Kuiper's service on this new committee was not only gratifying and invaluable because of his experience editing *The New Christian Hymnal*, but it alerted him to the need to review the adequacy of the *Psalter*. Accordingly, he developed an overture approved by Classis Grand Rapids East that the 413 psalm versifications and harmonizations be evaluated with a view to recommending which ones should be dropped entirely, which ones revised, and which ones replaced with substitutes.[20] His overture was echoed by similar ones from classes Pella, Holland, Sioux Center, and Orange City. The synod approved, and it assigned responsibility for the review to its hymn committee. The same synod received the committee's thorough analysis of the

[17]   Ibid., 186.
[18]   D.H. Kromminga, *The Christian Reformed Tradition*, 141.
[19]   Minutes, Broadway, 1/3/1928, art. 12.
[20]   Minutes of Classis Grand Rapids East, 1/22/1930, art. 31.

history of hymnody, one that articulated good responses to common concerns about using hymns in public worship. In appreciation, the synod of 1930 mandated the committee to propose a revision of the church order article restricting the use of hymns. It also requested it to select the best of the 197 hymns it had circulated for review by the churches, to be guided in its choices by four considerations ("doctrinal soundness, New Testament character, dignity and depth of devotional spirit, and clearness and beauty of expression"), and to distribute its recommended selections to the churches nine months prior to the following synod.[21] The synod stressed that the use of hymns was not to be compulsory for the churches. It also carefully replied to concerns raised in a number of overtures.

The synod of 1930 also reflected H.J. Kuiper's position on choirs. While it took the position that the use of choirs was to be at the discretion of local consistories, it discouraged their use because choirs curtail congregational singing and because control of the musical selections is difficult. Where hymns are used, the churches were directed to use only synodically approved hymns or anthems that contain scriptural wording.[22]

By 1932 the "Committee on Hymns and Psalter Chorales" had evolved into the "Committee for a Psalter Hymnal." Led by R.B. Kuiper, now president of Calvin College, the committee had worked hard and submitted a thirty-five-page report. H.J. had kept the church abreast of committee progress in his *Banner* editorials. The synod commended the committee on its good work. It adopted, with only minor revisions, the proposed changes in the existing *Psalter*, including a number of new metrical versions and the elimination of numbers the committee judged inferior. It approved adding a number of Dutch chorales and made provision for hiring musicologists to improve several arrangements. Numbers from *The New Christian Hymnal* were included. Concerning the proposed hymn collection, the synod noted that it had been duly circulated nine months earlier, as directed, had been four years in the making, and was based on the prior decisions of two synods that the Bible is not in principle opposed to using hymns in public worship. The latter issue was not to be reopened, it dictated, despite several overtures attempting to do so. Both R.B. as a faculty advisor and H.J. were on the advisory committee and represented the positions of the hymn committee persuasively. The synod approved a

---

[21]   *Acta der Synode, 1930*, 97-98.
[22]   Ibid., 101.

proposed wording change in the church order. It stated that only the psalm versions and the hymns approved by the synod were to be used in Christian Reformed worship. It further stipulated that psalms were required, but that the singing of hymns was left to local discretion. Then it answered objections raised in overtures, eliminated more than a dozen hymns proposed by the study committee, made a few changes of wording in others, and approved the collection as amended. Finally, the synod entrusted the oversight for publishing its first *Psalter Hymnal* to the study committee, which it continued for that purpose. Revised liturgical forms, the work of a parallel committee, were to be included.[23] Two businessmen, H. Denkema and J.B. Hulst, both on the Christian Reformed Church's publication committee, were added to facilitate publication of the book.

Actual publication did not happen without problems. R.B. Kuiper dropped off the committee to assume the presidency of Westminster Seminary, and H.J. Kuiper became "acting chairman." William Heyns, committee stalwart and the professor who had taught public worship at the seminary, died. The committee realized that it had no legal standing that would permit it to copyright the book. The synod had made no provision for funding the project. In that vacuum, the committee was forced to make some assumptions and to take initiative. Led by H.J. Kuiper, the Reverend D. Zwier, and J.B. Hulst, who by then chaired the denomination's publication committee, which was the board that controlled both church papers, *De Wachter* and the *Banner*, the committee asked the publication committee to assume legal responsibility for publishing the *Psalter Hymnal*. It also requested it to underwrite the costs of production and to be responsible for advertising, marketing, and storing the product. It also judged that the synod would want updated translations of the three forms of unity and of the liturgical forms included in the volume. The synod of 1934 recognized that these decisions "exceeded the mandate" of the committee but approved such responsible initiative. That synod made final changes in the projected hymnal and approved a final recommendation: "We recommend that synod give a vote of thanks to the Psalter-Hymnal Committee for its

---

[23]   The decisions concerning this project are found in *Acts of Synod 1932 of the Christian Reformed Church* (Grand Rapids: Office of the Stated Clerk, 1932), 127-40. (Henceforth, *Acts of Synod* , with the appropriate year) This is the first year the titles are designated in English, although substantive parts of this record were published in English since the mid-1920s.

manifold labors, and in particular to the Rev. H.J. Kuiper and the Rev. D. Zwier."[24] The synod did.

A half-year later Kuiper reported that the first printing of one thousand copies of the *Psalter Hymnal* had just arrived.[25] The church in Purewater, South Dakota, had submitted the first order and would get the first copies shipped. Kuiper reviewed some of the final changes incorporated into the book in several successive issues of the *Banner*. In the March 15, 1935, issue he editorialized that this book was special. First, it was the first denominational praise book compiled entirely by competent Christian Reformed people,[26] he noted somewhat immodestly. Second, its numbers showed the creativity of Christian Reformed people in versifications, textual and musical editing, and musical composition. It also was a faithful, Reformed alternative to the theologically and musically inferior hymnody that dominated the American market. On March 29, Kuiper reflected knowledgeably on the rhythmic rearrangements of the chorales included. He wrote in technical detail, the kind of detail unusual for a magazine like the *Banner*, but the kind that reflected intimate involvement and immense satisfaction with the outcome.

The publication of the *Psalter Hymnal* marked the end of a seventeen-year preoccupation with liturgical transition for the denomination and for H.J. Kuiper. Thoughtfully selected hymns, reharmonized psalm tunes and chorales, freshly translated and updated liturgical forms as well as newly minted ones, the sanctioning of church choirs, and a deeper understanding of and appreciation for the components of the worship service gave the Christian Reformed Church its own liturgical character as a denomination. It was an identity that was both American and Reformed, one characterized by features of its Dutch-Reformed liturgical origin, but not a simple

---

[24] *Acts of Synod 1934*, 158.

[25] *Banner*, 70/1973 (1/18/1935), 53.

[26] The 1914 *Psalter*, the first English-language Christian Reformed worship book, consisted of a metrical version of the Psalms published by the United Presbyterian Church of North America in 1912, 52 hymns correlated with the Heidelberg Catechism and used by the congregations in Classis Hackensack of the CRC, and the translations of the psalms and liturgical forms largely from an earlier Reformed Church in America resource. It had a green cover. The 1934, 1959, and 1987 editions of the *Psalter Hymnal* had red, blue, and gray covers, respectively, and are often designated by the color of their covers. I am indebted to Dr. Harry Boonstra for helpful information on the sources of the 1914 edition.

replication of it. The volume shaped the church for the next generation and more. Its content was in turn defined and brokered by H.J. Kuiper more than by anyone else.

The Editorship

The dual responsibilities of pastor and editor, along with his many other commitments, affected Kuiper's health. The crisis was a long time coming, but not unforeseen. Already in September 1928, when he met with the publication committee, having told them a month after the synod appointed him that he was "not disinclined" to accept,[27] he confided that the more he understood what was involved, the more he saw the editorship as a full-time position. They assured him that he could structure his responsibilities in a way that made the dual arrangement manageable. By the mid-1930s Kuiper was feeling the pressure more intensely and had discussed with the publication committee a number of times the inevitability of making the editorship a full-time position. Finally, in its report to the synod of 1936, the committee admitted, "We have for some time considered the advisability of having a full-time editor for the *Banner*."[28] It articulated five arguments in favor of the idea and four reservations about moving in that direction. It concluded, rather limply, "We . . . herewith leave the matter to you hoping that you may see your way clear to appoint a full-time editor . . . ."[29] With Kuiper presiding, the synod followed the advice of its advisory committee, decided against the idea, and authorized the publication committee to make "such provisions for relief" of the editor's load as might be needed.[30] In its next action it elected Kuiper to his fifth consecutive, two-year term as editor-in-chief. The record discloses neither the level of synodical empathy for Kuiper's predicament nor the degree of his disappointment. He did ask the synod for a week's time to consult with his consistory before giving his answer.

When H.J. Kuiper informed the Neland elders of the synod's actions and asked for their advice, he left the room so they could discuss the subject freely. When he returned, they informed him that "in general" they agreed that he should continue as editor with the

[27] Minutes of the Publication Committee of the Christian Reformed Church, 7/10/1928, art. 5 (henceforth Minutes, Publication Committee).
[28] *Acts of Synod 1936*, 246.
[29] Ibid., 248.
[30] Ibid., 42.

understanding that "the burden can and should be made easier."[31] That fall the elders raised the problem of Kuiper leading the men's society, because it impinged on his catechism teaching and his family visiting responsibilities. Scheduling adjustments were made. The consistory also decided to request the publication committee for a subsidy of $1,200 annually to hire a part-time assistant pastor to share some of Kuiper's pastoral load.[32] The following year he was given one Sunday off every six weeks. These efforts relieved but did not resolve the workload problem, however, and the consistory devoted parts of four successive meetings in the spring of 1938 to crafting a letter of concern to the synod. Two elders were chosen to present it in person. The letter stated that while the Neland Avenue consistory was supportive of Kuiper serving as editor of the *Banner*, the arrangement "entails a great deal of effort on the part of our pastor and takes from our congregation time and energy which are greatly needed."[33] The decision of the synod of 1936 has not resolved our problem, it said, despite several adjustments the consistory has tried. The consistory also assured synod that Kuiper had no responsibility for initiating and no hand in formulating its letter. It was signed by Tony Noordewier, Neland's clerk, who also served as the denominational treasurer. The synod appointed a committee to study the problem and to propose a solution the following year. Publication committee members met with the consistory to gain a clearer understanding of the problem. In their report the committee offered three possibilities to the synod of 1939: (1) appoint a full-time editor, (2) appoint a managing editor to relieve the part-time editor-in-chief of administrative responsibilities, (3) continue the present arrangement with added relief for the editor. The synod approved the third option, despite the misgivings of the Neland Avenue consistory. It urged the consistory to work closely with the publication committee, which was now in a more accommodating mood, to determine the actual shape of the relief.[34] After several protracted discussions, the consistory hired the Reverend Ralph Bolt, a recently retired pastor, for four hundred dollars a year, to provide pastoral relief on a part-time basis. Financial arrangements stipulated that the publication committee, which did not wish to get involved in contractual arrangements with either the church or Bolt, would increase Kuiper's honorarium and he would

---

[31]   Minutes, Neland, 6/22/1936, art. 4.
[32]   Minutes, Neland, 10/23/1936, art. 5.
[33]   *Acts of Synod 1938*, 71.
[34]   *Acts of Synod 1939*, 56-58.

in turn contribute to Bolt's salary. The committee also honored the editor's suggestion that he be relieved of the column commenting on correspondence with readers and of the magazine's young people's department.

The relief measures remained in place for the next five years. Kuiper's extensive work on producing and revising the *Psalter Hymnal* was virtually finished. After 1937 he was never again delegated to synod, although twice in the early 1940s he was chosen as an alternate. He also remained the alternate synodical deputy from his classis. His days of serving on synodical committees were behind him. But he did not relinquish, nor is there evidence that he was asked to relinquish, his involvement with the City Mission board, which will be discussed at some length in the following chapter. And about the time the relief measures were implemented, Kuiper assumed intensive new involvement with the launching of the Reformed Bible Institute, which will be considered in chapter 8. This politically sensitive and taxing new commitment was an added drain on his time and energy. He was in his mid-fifties, and his energy and stamina were waning. Just as significant was the added work imposed by the success of the *Banner*. The report of the publication committee to the 1944 synod noted that in 1917 the magazine had 3,275 subscribers, 11,100 when Kuiper took over in 1929, but now 31,000.[35] Kuiper was now also handling between sixty and eighty pieces of correspondence a week. The negative criticism of several pet Kuiper projects was increasing, and staff differences had intensified. The load was crushing. He was crumpling.

H.J. Kuiper missed the September 1943 meeting of the classis due to illness. A delegation was dispatched to pay him a visit of support and concern.[36] The following January he was well enough to attend the classis meeting, at which the group charged him with drafting an overture to the synod concerning the work of synodical deputies with respect to calling ministers from other denominations. He unwisely accepted the assignment. By then the editor had reached the decision that he could no longer maintain his dual responsibilities as both pastor and editor. On February 15, 1944, Kuiper served the publication committee with a document discussing the full scope of the editor's responsibilities and making the case for a full-time editor, whether that would be himself or another. He and the committee met and reviewed their options.

[35]   *Acts of Synod 1944*, 264.
[36]   Minutes of Classis Grand Rapids East, 9/15/1943, art. 17.

By March Kuiper was hospitalized. For three months he was in recuperation, absent from consistory meetings, and under doctor's orders to curtail his activities significantly. The Reverend Richard Frens came to the City Mission board meeting that spring directly from the hospital and announced Kuiper's resignation from the board. By the May classis meeting his classical assignment lay uncompleted. Nor was he in attendance. The classis tabled its earlier decision to overture synod concerning synodical deputies. It also accepted Kuiper's written resignation as their synodical examiner or deputy and as a member of their student fund committee. It also honored his request to be relieved of another assignment related to the supervision of the Ann Arbor Chapel.[37] Kuiper did retain his position on the Reformed Bible Institute board.

That June synod took the publication committee's extensive report on the editorship of the *Banner* to heart, declared it a full-time position, and re-elected Kuiper by ballot from a slate of seven nominees.[38] It was the afternoon of June 19. Kuiper wasted no time. That same evening he met with his consistory and informed it that he felt compelled, in light of his physical problems, to accept. The consistory members congratulated him and thanked him for his years of service as their pastor.[39] The next morning he informed the synod that he accepted its appointment as full-time editor.

On July 31 his fifth and longest pastorate ended. On August 1 his full-time editorship of the *Banner* began.

[37] Minutes of Classis Grand Rapids East, 5/10/1944, arts. 9 and 15.
[38] *Acts of Synod 1944*, 20.
[39] Minutes, Neland, 6/19/1944, art. 16.

CHAPTER 5

Keeping Covenant through Christian Schools

Concurrent with his pastorates, H.J. Kuiper devoted himself to several emerging ministries that his leadership shaped and guided. In time they became significant expressions of what it meant to be Christian Reformed. As editor of the *Banner* he often gave them strategic exposure, which magnified their impact on the wider church. One of these ministries was the Christian day-school movement.

Kuiper himself was a product of the Christian day schools in the 1890s, attending the Williams Street School in Grand Rapids at a time when Abraham Kuyper's influences were redefining and revitalizing the Christian school movement through new immigrants. In his Luctor charge, as noted earlier, he advocated making the Christian school a year-round program rather than just a summer effort that supplemented public school education. He recruited his sister, Dena, to teach for a year in the expanded program, and he himself taught in the school until he accepted the call to Holland. The school flourished during his ministry in Luctor and closed down only some years after he left.

His support of Christian education continued in his second and third charges. In Chicago the Ebenezer and the Englewood Christian School boards had advocated a Christian high school early during the second decade of the twentieth century. It was not until Kuiper was established in Englewood that the movement for a Christian high school gained momentum, however.

In the latter half of 1915, a series of meetings was scheduled to discuss the possibility seriously. At a meeting of the Alliance of Christian Schools of Chicago and Vicinity on September 15, the Ebenezer group was asked to initiate steps toward the first year of a high school and to spearhead the organizing of a Christian high school society. Because of his facility in English and his organizational aptitude, Kuiper is the probable author of an eight-page promotional brochure circulated in the Chicago area later that year and summarized extensively in the *Banner* the following March.[1] He supported and promoted the Christian high school movement enthusiastically, and the Chicago Christian High School Association was born April 24, 1916, in Englewood.

When the first board was elected that July, H.J. Kuiper was the only ordained minister to serve on it.[2] His interest in secondary Christian education and his service on the Chicago Christian High School board made him the natural choice in September 1917 to visit the Southern Normal and Industrial Institute in Alabama as the classis's delegate when the school appealed for financial support from Classis Illinois and its churches.[3]

The Chicago Christian High School opened in September 1918 with twenty-eight students in two rooms of the Bethel Mission at 72nd Place and Loomis. The Reverend J.M. Lumkes, pastor of the First Reformed Church in Englewood, gave the opening address to a full house in his church on the night before the school opened, September 3. On the rostrum were H.J. Kuiper, who made remarks on behalf of the Chicago Christian Education Association, and Mark Fakkema, first

---

[1]   *Banner*, 3/30/1916, 211.

[2]   Others elected were J.J. De Boer, often regarded as "the father of Chicago Christian High School" and the board's first president, G. Ottenhoff, H.G. Dekker, A.S. De Jong, F.J. Vos, A. Blystra, and J. Meeter. De Jong was principal of Englewood Christian School. For an account of the emergence of Chicago Christian High School and the roles of J.J. De Boer, A.S. De Jong, and others, see Robert P. Swierenga, *Dutch Chicago: A History of the Hollanders in the Windy City*, The Historical Series of the Reformed Church in America, no. 42 (Grand Rapids: Eerdmans, 2002), 392-404.

[3]   Minutes of Classis Illinois, 9/25-27/1917, art. 31 and art. 35. Kuiper made a visit in January 1918. The classis supported this school for a time, but support was withdrawn in January 1919. Cf. Minutes of Classis Illinois, 1/21-22/1919, art. 36. Editor Donald Bruggink alerted me to the fact that Southern Normal was, however, supported by the Reformed Church. Cf. Donald J. Bruggink and Kim N. Baker, *By Grace Alone, Stories of the Reformed Church in America*, The Historical Series of the Reformed Church in America, no. 44 (Grand Rapids: Eerdmans, 1992), 105-110.

principal and Kuiper's life-long friend and comrade in the cause of Christian education.

Less than a year later Kuiper moved to Grand Rapids, where he assumed the pastorate of the Broadway Christian Reformed Church. His heavy involvement in the birth of Chicago Christian High School positioned him strategically to give leadership in the founding of Grand Rapids Christian High School, the third in the country.

President J.J. Hieminga of Calvin College had contended in 1919 that the time had arrived to close the college's academy program. The school was about to become a four-year, state-certified, degree-granting liberal arts college. It was time to dispense with the high-school-level courses. He challenged the people of Grand Rapids to establish their own Christian high school. He argued that it was unfair to ask the people of the entire denomination to support this portion of the Calvin program when the people in New Jersey and Chicago had created and were supporting their own Christian high schools. The curators agreed and announced that they would so recommend to the synod of 1920.

Anticipating the synod's approval, some Christian Reformed leaders in Grand Rapids, including H.J. Kuiper, scheduled a planning meeting at the YMCA for the evening of February 11, 1920. At that meeting, a Christian high school society was formed, and H.J. Kuiper was selected to chair the committee to draft a constitution and by-laws and to propose a plan for opening the school in September. That work accomplished, Kuiper was elected to serve on the first board, which he also chaired.[4] The board tendered an offer of twenty thousand dollars to purchase the Theological School and Calvin College building on the corner of Franklin and Madison, since Calvin had recently moved to its new campus further east on Franklin Street. That June's synod accepted the offer.

Also that summer, an ad appeared in the *Banner* announcing the opening of Western Academy in Hull, Iowa, with Garrett Heyns as principal. The August 25 issue of the magazine contained a report of a meeting of Christian high school principals in Chicago, where a common curriculum was planned and accreditation was discussed. Heyns and Fakkema, who had just been appointed as the first director of the new National Union of Christian Schools, were assigned to plan

---

4   Serving with Kuiper on the first board were K. Bergsma, Y. Feenstra, John Hekman, Eerde Hoogsteen, R. Postma, G.J. Stuart, J.M. Vander Wal, and John Vanden Berg.

The Grand Rapids Christian High School faculty, 1921-1922. Frank Kuiper is seated third from the left.

the following meeting of the group. Frank J. Driesens, just named as principal of the about-to-open school in Grand Rapids, was chosen as secretary. That spring J.J. Hieminga had editorialized on the strategic relationship between Calvin College and the emerging Christian high school movement; his ideals were taking shape.

On September 7, Grand Rapids Christian High School opened its doors to 284 students, 130 more than earlier estimated. Unable to handle that many with the appointed staff, the board scrambled late in the summer, then quickly identified and hired three additional teachers. Frank J. Kuiper, H.J.'s younger brother, was on the faculty of six and taught commercial courses for two years, until he enrolled in dental school. Students came from as far away as California, Iowa, Minnesota, New Mexico, and South Dakota as well as from Michigan beyond the immediate Grand Rapids area. The ninth and tenth grades commenced that month. The budget for the first year was $19,050. The eleventh grade was added in 1921; the twelfth in 1922. The school offered four programs: a regular high school program, a college preparatory program, a teacher education program, and a business program. By November, the board had decided that a single, central high school was preferable to several branches scattered around the city and its surrounding areas, as initially envisioned. The board authorized four basketball games that year, later grudgingly increased the number to six, but stipulated that games could be played only against other Christian organizations. At the first graduation, in the spring of 1923, board president H.J. Kuiper presided. He gave the welcome and offered the invocation; Louis Berkof delivered the commencement address; and fellow board member and vice president, the Reverend Herman Hoeksema of the Eastern Avenue Christian Reformed Church, closed in prayer.

As board president, Kuiper wrote a two-page "Introduction to the Grand Rapids Association for Christian Secondary Education" for the first edition of the school's *Memoirs*. "A Christian education is not only an indispensable means for promoting the spiritual and moral welfare of their children and for the preservation of the church," he wrote, but by supporting it Christian parents provide a "safeguard of the moral soundness of the home, the state and the entire fabric of social life."[5] These deeply held convictions were themes which he would later revisit in his *Banner* editorials. During the second year of the school's history, he countered an article by R.B. Kuiper in *Religion and Culture* suggesting that a lackluster response to a financial campaign could be corrected by involving non-Christian Reformed people in the movement. We leaders, said H.J., have to work harder to convict our people of the importance of the school, and then the support will come.[6] His leadership in the wider Christian school movement was expressed about this time in an exceptionally insightful series of articles written for the *Witness* entitled, "The Task of the Christian School Teacher." In another article he argued for appointing a superintendent for all the Christian schools in Michigan.[7] In one of the last actions taken during Kuiper's tenure as board president of Grand Rapids Christian High School, the board decided at its June 1923 meeting not to proceed with a building expansion, since three of the seven local Christian grade schools had embarked on building programs and would add the ninth grade to their programs in the fall. This would alleviate overcrowding at the high school.

That summer Kuiper did not begin a second term on the high school board, as he was by then heavily engaged in denominational endeavors. The school had made a good beginning and had met with

5   *1923 Memoirs*, Grand Rapids Christian High School, 10.

6   *Witness*, 1/2 (January, 1922), 30-32.

7   *Witness*, 2/1 (December, 1922), 13-14; 2/3 (February, 1923), 44-45; 2/4 (March, 1923), 59-61 on the former, and 2/4 (March, 1923), 61-62 on the latter.

the enthusiastic acceptance of Christian Reformed Grand Rapids. Others were willing to serve and were capable of guiding the flourishing new movement. So H.J. Kuiper, one of the founding fathers of Grand Rapids Christian High School, stepped aside. But his contribution was not forgotten. When the association rented the Grand Rapids Civic Auditorium April 3, 1946, to celebrate the school's twenty-fifth anniversary, Kuiper, as president of the first board, was invited to open the event with prayer.

After he became editor of the *Banner*, Kuiper wrote his opening editorial on Christian education in March 1929. It was addressed to Christian school board members. It encouraged them to hire teachers who exude personal piety, are deeply convicted of the Reformed world view concerning the child and their subject matter, create a wholesome atmosphere, come from sterling families, and honor and respect the synod's stance against worldly amusements. These qualities are more important to the well-being of Christian schools than the crucial matters of finances and facilities.[8] Two months later he featured on the cover of the *Banner* the proposed new building of Grand Rapids Christian High School.

That summer Kuiper embarked on a year and a half of sustained attention to Christian education matters. It was to be the most concentrated writing on the subject of his editorial career. Unacknowledged initially, the precipitating cause for this attention was a series of twelve articles in *De Wachter* in late 1928 and early 1929 urging a temperate, pragmatic approach to establishing Christian schools. They were written by the Reverend John Vander Mey, an older minister who had served five congregations, mostly in rural western communities, and who since 1913 had been the educational secretary for Calvin College and Seminary. He wrote his series near the end of his career, for he retired in 1932, and it obviously reflected his experience with churches that had struggled to maintain their ministries and had few financial resources for Christian schools. Kuiper and others regarded Vander Mey's position as far too temperate and unprincipled.

So in mid-August of 1929, on the threshold of a new school year, Kuiper commenced a three-part series of editorials on the vital importance of Christian schools. In the first, he lauded the growth of the Christian school movement, which had increased from fifteen

---

8   *Banner*, 64/1673 (3/8/29), 172-73.

schools in 1900 to eighty-six, including six high schools.[9] Christian Reformed people had really caught the vision, he noted, despite the fact that some do not yet see that high schools are essential, when in fact they serve young people at the most crucial stage in life. An improved curriculum in biblical subjects and better training of teachers at Calvin College were further causes for thanks. He posited the thesis that where Christian schools flourish, the churches will also.

His second editorial in the series introduced a caveat.[10] Unfortunately, he wrote, there had been a "slump" in the Christian school movement for the last six years. Only six new schools had been started in that time, none of them high schools, he observed. Kuiper attributed this to a slowdown in immigration, the internal church controversies, hard economic conditions in agricultural communities, growing materialism among the church members, a lack of covenantal emphasis, and some leaders who espouse Christianizing the public schools through Bible reading or taking illegal advantage of the *de facto* Christian character of many local public schools. Here he had Vander Mey's articles particularly in mind. In some communities, he noted, there has actually been regression in the percentage of families sending children to the Christian school.[11]

The third and last editorial in the series called for a "more distinctive" Christian school system. The rhetoric of some who espouse the improvement of public school instruction now that our schools are "flourishing" confuses a civic with a covenantal obligation, he contended. He quoted excerpts from an address by the Reverend J.K. Van Baalen pleading that Christian schools be opened to others, and he called them the church's greatest evangelistic asset. He concluded by making a case for more Christian textbooks, against too much dependence on secular textbooks, and for a deeper, fuller, and more thoughtfully Reformed theory of Christian education.

The next week Kuiper quoted extensively from an article by Mark Fakkema, in which Fakkema developed the ideas that a Christian public school is a "self-deception," constitutes an "educational loss" to the covenant community, and poses a "moral question." When Kuiper

---

9   *Banner,* 64/1696 (8/16/29), 564-65. As a member of the Eastern Avenue Christian Reformed Church, Vander Mey had understandably protested Herman Hoeksema's stand on common grace in the spring of 1924. See Hoeksema, *The Protestant Reformed Churches,* 32-37.

10 *Banner,* 64/1697 (8/30/29), 580-81.

11 *Banner,* 62[*sic*]/1698 (9/6/29), 596-97.

received a letter the following month advocating Bible reading in public schools and supporting the improvement of public education, he overrode it with an editorial arguing that the state has no more business establishing education than it does establishing religion. Neutrality in the educational arena is a myth. Bible-reading and even the removal of evolution will not correct the public schools. Advocating these initiatives is "pernicious dualism," the editor snorted. The first issue in the month of November included an extensive review of the Christian school teachers' annual convention, a report that Kuiper included every year during his editorial career.

Meanwhile, Vander Mey, unhappy with the treatment his ideas had received, approached the publication committee, which directed Kuiper to publish his rebuttal. Vander Mey responded in two pieces entitled, "Extreme Views."[12]

In the first he affirmed six principles: (1) Parents owe full, covenantal instruction to their children. (2) "As a rule" this cannot be done through public schools, which is why in fidelity to our baptismal vows and church order Article 21 we should establish Christian schools. (3) Love for Christian schools should not yield to fanaticism or exaggeration, however; these are just as dangerous as indifference. (4) As Calvinists, not separatists, we have a great calling and duty to be engaged in improving and reclaiming the domain of public education. (5) Unlike the Netherlands, public schools here are favorably disposed to moral instruction and are antisectarian as an expedient for keeping public peace. (6) In our 130 communities where no Christian school exists, parents ought to foster Christian leadership and instruction in public schools, as is widely tolerated despite laws to the contrary.

In the second article, Vander Mey pleaded for not making an either-or issue of this matter and for being constructively engaged with public as well as with Christian education, noting that many Christian Reformed parents and even teachers were involved with public schools. Vander Mey's articles were irenic and temperate. But they did allege extremism regarding some of Kuiper's examples and affirmed the desirability and priority of Christian schools, but not at the expense of dismissing public education.

One of the features of Kuiper's editorial style was that he always ensured that he held his editorial advantage. The publication

---

[12]   *Banner,* 64/1704 (10/18/1929), 756-57, and *Banner* 64/1705 (10/25/1929), 780-81.

committee may have instructed him to print Vander Mey's two articles, but he would not do so without comment. In the issue in which Vander Mey's first installment appeared, Kuiper placed an editorial that was a deeper critique of the movement advocating Bible reading and moral instruction in the public schools.[13] He said that this movement violated the formal principle that children belong to parents—not to the state, which is the implication when parents accept, use, and defend the public school system as it exists in the United States. The movement also violated the material principle that the Word of God must permeate and illumine all subject matter and all educational relationships, a principle which this movement could not and did not espouse. Further, it put the Bible in the hands of profane teachers, and this constituted religious instruction that perforce will be critical and modernistic. Further, as a recent book and court case revealed, this movement would lead to all kinds of community conflict between differing religious constituencies—Jewish, Protestant, Catholic. Will the New Testament be used, Kuiper asked rhetorically? Which version of the Bible? The Roman Catholic Douai version? The Protestant King James version? And will the apocryphal books be read? His probing questions were designed to discredit the workability of the movement and to expose the weakness of Vander Mey's support of it.

But Kuiper was not finished. Two weeks later he engaged Vander Mey by name for the first time and referenced his twelve articles in *De Wachter.*[14] He let readers know that it was he and Fakkema that Vander Mey was accusing of "extreme views." Kuiper contended that Vander Mey's position was that the public school was the norm and that Christian schools were the exception under less than desirable circumstances. He repeated and reapplied his formal and material principles in response, alleged that Vander Mey came to his position because of an unbalanced overemphasis on common grace, and pointed out that "he has *in principle renounced the stand of our church* on the matter of Christian instruction" (italics Kuiper's), since the synod and the church order had both declared in favor of Christian schools.

In his editorial the following week, Kuiper rejected the allegation that he and others were "separatists and fanatics," as Vander Mey suggested.[15] "Separatism is unnecessary separation," Kuiper defined.

---

[13]   *Banner,* 64/1708 (11/15/1929), 836-37.
[14]   *Banner,* 64/1711 (12/6/1929), 908-909.
[15]   *Banner,* 64/1712 (12/13/1929), 932-33.

And he added, "We deny the charge with indignation!" He then answered three questions Vander Mey put to him in a private letter. First, Christian school supporters do have a civic obligation to public schools, as he had said before. We should seek to make them safe, good, and devoid of teaching the false religion of evolution. Second, what can be done for those communities that cannot afford a Christian school? Many that do not have a Christian school can afford one—at least they can afford several teachers at the outset. Others could hire underpaid Christian school teachers to give a six- or eight-week summer school, and efforts in the home and through catechism could be strengthened. Third, what do we do with the surplus of normal school or teacher-education graduates? Kuiper answered that we would not have the surplus if we had been establishing new Christian schools at a responsible rate rather than "resting on our laurels" for five or six years. Personally, he concluded, he would never recommend that these graduates seek positions in the public schools, as this would inhibit them from being responsibly Christian in their teaching and would compromise their convictions.

Following a two-month lull, the exchanges resumed.

At the end of February 1930, Vander Mey submitted the first of two articles responding to Kuiper. The articles were again printed by directive of the publication committee and were entitled, "A Happier Medium."[16] In them Vander Mey insisted that he had not accused the Christian Reformed Church or anyone personally of being fanatic on this subject. He asserted that he did not disagree with Article 21 of the church order but with Kuiper's interpretation and application of it. He went on to rebut three objections to his appeal to take advantage of and to use public schools, especially country public schools, wherever possible. Often public schools were expedient in fulfilling the parental obligation to provide Christian instruction to covenant youth, he argued. This was so since the state would not and had not interfered with Christian instruction in public schools, where the community consensus supports it. Second, state money for public schools is community money—the money of Christian parents, who are taxed for these schools. Third, Kuiper's acknowledgment that public education could be but a "temporary expedient" in some unique situations unfortunately minimized their contribution, for in a number of communities fully two generations of children have received Christian

---

[16]   *Banner,* 65/1720 (2/28/1930), 204-205, "The Readers' Page."

education through the community's public schools, he concluded.

In his second installment, Vander Mey insisted that the only difference between his position and Kuiper's was in regard to communities where parents were able to implement Christian education through the public school system.[17] The editor's insistence that even here independent Christian day schools should be promoted is "an extreme and even ridiculous interpretation of Article 21." He turned Kuiper's assertion that he was treading "dangerous ground" back on Kuiper as "treading on the dangerous ground of separatism." Further, Kuiper offered no word of encouragement to the many parents who were compelled to send their children to public schools. By God's common grace, many fine things happen in many public schools, he said. How lamentable when visitors to our churches never hear a prayer of thanks or of intercession for our public institutions. In the Reformed Church, the public schools are too uncritically affirmed, but let us not fall into the opposite extreme, appealed Vander Mey. He cited Clarence Bouma's lament that too many Christian Reformed people seem to join ranks with agnostics and atheists in rejoicing over the godlessness and secularization of public schools. How sad was the editor's inability to support our young people teaching in public schools, where their Christian influence could be felt. "We should consider it a distinct achievement to get our young Calvinites appointed in grade schools, in high schools, in colleges, in state universities, and in all positions of influence and importance. This is Calvinism, a militant Calvinism, going out to battle and to conquer." He noted how the Reformed Presbyterian Church had lost its hold on its people because it had succumbed to "narrow-mindedness and separatism." This should not happen to the Christian Reformed Church. This, promised Vander Mey, was his last word on the subject. He would not respond further.

But in an editorial entitled, "Unhappy Compromising," Kuiper felt compelled to rebut.[18] He found Vander Mey's choice of terms characterizing his position to be inflammatory and unhelpful. Further, Vander Mey minimized the differences between them. First, the two differed in their assessment of the public school system, which Kuiper reminded readers was in a sorry moral and spiritual state, as also leaders in many other denominations lamented. Second, they disagreed on the fundamental, principled obligation of parentally established and

---

[17]   *Banner*, 65/1721 (3/7/1930), 227.
[18]   *Banner*, 65/1723 (3/21/1930), 268-69.

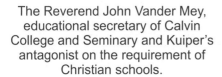

The Reverend John Vander Mey, educational secretary of Calvin College and Seminary and Kuiper's antagonist on the requirement of Christian schools.

controlled Christian schools. Vander Mey's position that we should create Christian schools "as a last resort," when Christian instruction is impossible or impeded in public schools, Kuiper caricatured as untenable and in opposition to church order Article 21. Vander Mey "virtually admits" that he concedes the principle of parental obligation, Kuiper further stretched. Vander Mey's position, he argued, was no different from that of the majority in the Reformed Church, and as such it undermined the Christian school movement. If pioneers in Christian education had held his views, we would not have a Christian school movement today, Kuiper asserted. How can we pray for a system that structurally opposes Christian instruction and thereby jeopardizes the spiritual formation of our children? Would Vander Mey really give Roman Catholics, Mormons, and modernists permission to teach their religious views in the public schools of communities where their views enjoyed majority support? If, in communities where a Reformed consensus exists, an unbelieving family complained, would Vander Mey and his followers yield to the state law and cease religious instruction? The really hurtful result of this extended debate, Kuiper concluded, is that in many Reformed communities "the opposition to the Christian school movement has appreciably stiffened."

In a stroke of editorial genius and prowess, Kuiper began publishing in the summer of 1930, without announcement or forewarning, the West Michigan Christian school graduation pictures. Whereas the magazine had always published pictures of new church and

Picture of the Baxter Street Christian School graduates in the July 4, 1930, issue of the *Banner.*

school buildings, this was an innovation. The pictures were published in a generous size, often three columns wide and a third of a page deep, and always with every face identified by full name. The effect was a repeated, visual reinforcement of the essential and prominent part of Christian schools in the Christian Reformed ethos. Every graduate, every parent of every graduate, every relative of every graduate, and every Christian school community pictured became emotionally identified with the movement represented in the faces of their young people. These were the fruits of the covenant harvest! Young, committed, equipped Reformed young people ready to serve the Lord and glorify his name. The impact was strong, and it hit unrelentingly week after week after week. That summer graduation pictures appeared of

> Oakdale Park Christian School graduates, 65/1740 (6/27/1930), 624;
> Baxter Street Christian School graduates, 65/1741 (7/4/1930), 643;
> Grandville Avenue Christian School graduates, 65/1742 (7/11/1930), 672;
> East Paris Christian School graduates, 65/1744 (7/25/1930), 693;
> Cutlerville Christian School graduates, 65/1745 (8/1/1930), 715;
> Moline Christian School graduates, 65/1746 (8/8/1930), 732;

Baldwin Street Christian School graduates, 65/1746 (8/8/1930), 733;
Kelloggsville Christian School graduates, 65/1748 (8/22/1930), 749;
Allendale Christian School graduates, 65/1748 (8/22/1930), 760.

The summer's last issue culminated with an editorial flurry on
Christian education in preparation for the new school year just ahead.[19]
Kuiper wrote a three-pronged editorial. In "Which Pasture for the Little
Lambs," he contended that covenant lambs could graze healthfully only
in the pastures of Christian schools. In "Love for Christian Instruction
Put to the Test," he challenged constituents not to use the onset of the
Great Depression to withdraw their children from Christian schools
but to sacrifice not only luxuries, but even necessities to make this
crucial commitment a reality. In "The Annual Meeting of the National
Union," he gave a preview of the convention in Holland, Michigan, to
be held August 26-28. He invited the public to attend and promised
that he would take in as many of the fine addresses as he could. To
add heft to his assault, he printed "The Value of Christian Education
in a Christian School," by the esteemed Dr. Garrett Heyns, principal of
Holland Christian High School and president of the National Union,
and an article by the widely popular Dr. Edward Masselink entitled
"Why We Need Christian High Schools." It was a frontal assault with
heavy artillery.

Two weeks later, Kuiper wrote the editorial "What the Church
Has the Right to Expect of the Christian School."[20] In it, he contended
that no institution profits more from healthy Christian schools
than does the church; similarly, the schools cannot flourish without
the full, generous support of the church. Without meddling in the
schools unless corrective measures are needed, the church can expect
the teaching of all subjects to reflect Christian, especially Reformed,
principles. It can expect no compromise with modernistic premises in
the areas of pedagogy and psychology, and no tolerance of the theory
of evolution. Other expectations are a thorough grounding in biblical
studies, exemplary conduct, and full staff loyalty to the Christian
Reformed stand on worldly amusements. Two weeks later he produced
a four-part editorial reviewing the National Union convention and
published a picture of visitors and delegates. The Christian school
movement is "marching on," he wrote. Louis Berkhof's address
demonstrated powerfully that both scripture and natural revelation

[19] *Banner,* 65/1748 (8/22/1930), 750.
[20] *Banner,* 65/1750 (9/5/1930), 788-89.

make parents responsible for raising their offspring. The public school cannot provide the religious training needed by covenant youth. Finally, the United States' legal system makes it well nigh impossible to provide robust Christian education in public schools, even in communities that are completely Reformed. Another two weeks passed before Kuiper took to task his former Broadway parishioner, Judge A. Dykstra, as he had in his exchanges with Vander Mey, for advocating the allegedly tepid practice of Bible-reading in public schools.[21]

Never before or since has a more overwhelming campaign for Christian education through the Christian school system been mounted in the official Christian Reformed press than H.J. Kuiper waged in 1929 and 1930. Pictures of graduating classes did not run in subsequent years.

Both in tone and in duration, H.J. Kuiper's debate with John Vander Mey and its aftermath solidified his reputation as an unrelenting and uncompromising champion of Christian schools. He returned to many of the themes and emphases in this exchange subsequently. Almost every summer he ran an article or two in support of Christian schools prior to the opening of the new school year. He reported on Christian school meetings and Christian school building programs. Fakkema and other leaders in the movement published pointed pieces in support of Christian education on the pages of the *Banner*, and the alliance of Kuiper and Fakkema was deepened and strengthened by their joint service on the newly formed board of the Reformed Bible Institute a decade after the Vander Mey debate. Noteworthy is that after 1930 the preference for Christian schools as a covenant obligation was never again challenged seriously or debated during Kuiper's editorship of the *Banner*.

The deepening Depression was especially hard on Christian schools. Kuiper's attention turned to possibilities for giving them economic relief. At one point he suggested that without compromising sphere sovereignty, the churches might temporarily take over Christian schools to help them through the financial crisis.[22] It would also help, he noted, if more ministers served on Christian school boards, as was true earlier. The next year he promoted the first Christian school field day in Grand Rapids. An expected crowd of between four and five thousand listened to the speakers, engaged in recreation, contributed funds for

[21]   *Banner,* 65/1754 (10/3/1930), 886.
[22]   *Banner,* 67/1863 (11/25/1932), 1020.

the schools' support, and demonstrated to the entire community their vigorous support of Christian education.

A few weeks later J. Gresham Machen, a gifted champion of Reformed orthodoxy who had recently resigned from the Princeton Seminary faculty over alleged modernism and begun Westminster Seminary as a biblically faithful alternative, gave the opening address to a packed house at the National Union of Christian Schools convention in Chicago.[23] Machen praised the movement highly and concluded by saying that it was his honor and privilege to be in the presence of a constituency so sacrificial in so noble a cause.

Kuiper seized the initiative; he summarized the speech fully, amplified Machen's commendation, and only mentioned the addresses of Louis Berkhof and Cornelius Van Til in passing. In 1934 he assessed Garrett Heyns's proposal, which he called "the Holland plan," whereby the churches would assume responsibility for that portion of the tuition of their members' children that parents could not pay. The plan went further than Kuiper thought responsible. However, he endorsed a recently proposed "education plan" that every church create an education fund to support local Christian schools, and that collections for it be a regular cause along with the budget, quotas, the mission fund, and the benevolent fund. He expressed regret that some opponents of Christian schools had used his earlier proposal that churches temporarily take over Christian schools until they survived the Depression to disparage the Christian school cause. In 1934 he also contended that ministers must help in two ways: first, by preaching the principles of Christian education repeatedly, since each generation of young parents must be educated and won to the cause; second, by winning the whole Christian Reformed constituency to its support, since support by only half the church's population was not good enough.[24] In another segment, he challenged communities and boards to hire teachers that are truly Christian educators.

By the time the Depression ended, the Christian school movement had survived, thanks in part to Kuiper's encouragement. In August 1935, he ran an article by Fakkema assessing the state of Christian schools.[25] Before the Depression there had been fourteen thousand students in schools belonging to the National Union of Christian

---

[23]   *Banner,* 68/1901 (9/25/1933), 692-93.
[24]   *Banner,* 69/1929 (3/9/1934), 212.
[25]   *Banner,* 70/2003 (8/23/1935), 751.

Schools, currently there were thirteen thousand, a loss of 7 percent. Seventy of the eighty-seven schools showed an enrollment decline; four had closed. New Jersey was hardest hit, where the population in the four schools had dropped 21.5 percent, while Christian Reformed Church membership there had risen 4 percent. But, he pointed out, the Christian school movement was alive and poised to move into another phase of its existence.

That phase was the addition and strengthening of Christian high schools. In 1938 Kuiper wrote a series on the topic. For many years there had been five Christian high schools, he observed. Now it was time to add them in places like Pella, Kalamazoo, and Muskegon. He noted that this initiative would build on the dedication of the founders of Christian elementary schools and would recognize that a high school education was becoming much more common and necessary. He developed eight reasons in three successive editorials.[26] (1) Christian grade school education can be weakened when it is followed by a public high school program. (2) The high school age group needs wholesome, Christian exposure to all subject areas. (3) The high school years find young people at an age of strong social ties, many of which even lead to marriage. (4) These young people are covenant children and need to be spiritually separated from the world. (5) The children need more advanced Bible and religious instruction as they mature. (6) The children need protection from the moral corruption in many high schools. (7) Untapped financial resources exist to support new high schools. (8) They will strengthen and complete the Christian elementary schools.

Kuiper returned to this initiative for the next several years, reporting with thanks on the opening of each new Christian high school. By September 1943, Fakkema reported that the movement had made more progress in the last two years than in any previous period. Nine Christian high schools were in operation, and other schools had added one or two high school grades. Both he and Kuiper celebrated.

Characteristically, H.J. Kuiper's attention to Christian schools was nontheological. His writing on the subject was almost always either practical or polemical. He made an exception in 1944, when he wrote "The Two Pillars of Christian Education."[27] Here he produced his most

---

[26] *Banner,* 73/2170 (12/1/1938), 1108-1109; 73/2171 (12/15/1938), 1132; 73/2172 (12/29/1938), 1156-57.

[27] *Banner,* 79/2466 (8/25/1944), 796-97; and 79/2467 (9/8/1944), 803.

Mark Fakkema, a leader in the Christian school movement, toward the end of his career—Kuiper's ally in promoting the cause and one of the founders of the Reformed Bible Institute.

theologically developed basis for Christian schools. Grateful that in the last few years the movement had caught fire and was expanding in communities where it previously existed and was emerging in new ones, he reminded readers that they establish Christian education because their children belonged to the covenant of grace and in order to prepare them for a lifetime of kingdom service. He developed both ideas at length. He said, in summary,

> Our Christian schools therefore might be called covenant schools and kingdom schools. There is a difference of emphasis here. Our schools are covenant schools. Their purpose is to train the children of God's people by imparting to them *the rich spiritual heritage* which is theirs by virtue of their covenant relationships. Our schools are kingdom schools because their purpose is also to prepare the children of the kingdom *for the service of their King in every sphere of life*. In the former case, the emphasis is especially on what the Lord will do for them; in the latter, on what they should be for the Lord.[28] (italics Kuiper's)

These reflections led to a covenantal problem in Kuiper's mind. As the flourishing movement attracted non-Christian Reformed families and students, he grew concerned. So, in 1945 he wrote a

[28] Ibid., 803.

three-part series, "A Christian School Problem." The large number of "outsiders" enrolling their children or wanting to enroll their children in Christian schools, either because of their dissatisfaction with public schools or their desire for quality or value-based education, was redefining the schools. The financial side of this problem was that Christian Reformed people would end up subsidizing the children of such families, since outside families would not want or be able to pay the full cost. The spiritual side of the problem was that the influence of these young people from outside Christian Reformed circles would dilute the beliefs and behavior of the covenant children and would yield "mixed marriages."[29]

Like churches, schools can lose their distinctiveness, he said in the second installment. This can happen in three ways: through the teachers, through fellow students, and through the association itself. Christian school boards and administrations must be vigilant and diligent in hiring and overseeing dedicated, Reformed teachers. Because students are influenced as certainly and as greatly by their peers as by their teachers, many parents have objected to letting the children of outsiders into the Christian schools. We must hear this very real concern and keep faith with our parents, he admonished. Third, board and association members must control the membership and direction of the school by enforcing good constitutions with proper safeguards and by electing board members faithful to them. In his final editorial on the matter he said, "We strongly incline to the thought that our Christian schools should NOT accept pupils from non-Reformed homes." If they did, he said, it would be very difficult to maintain a limit on the percentage of students from other churches. Kuiper suggested this limit should be no more than 5 percent. Also, it would be very difficult to screen outside parents, since terms like "Reformed" and "evangelical" are elastic and many churches are "honeycombed" with modernism. Non-Christian Reformed students should pay the full cost of education, he advised, and this must include not just the cost of current-year operations but also a prorated share of capital investments and new hires.[30] By the end of the Second World War, Kuiper recognized that the Christian Reformed world was becoming much less self-contained and that this trend was also evident in the Christian school movement.

[29] *Banner,* 80/2505 (5/25/1945), 484.
[30] *Banner,* 80/2507 (6/15/1945), 532.

During the last decade of his editorship of the *Banner*, Kuiper wrote about as much on Christian schools as he had in the first sixteen months that he held the position. He repeated his opinions about what makes for good schools and teachers, how the schools strengthen the churches, and the need for higher salaries. But he sounded new notes, too. He responded to what he considered a pernicious pamphlet produced by a Reformed Church in America pastor in 1949 and which, to his dismay, was commended by that denomination's synod. It accused the Christian school movement of undercutting public education.[31] Kuiper also championed the initiative of the National Union to develop Christian textbooks, and he observed that he knew of "no worthier cause" needing support than that. But by the end of his editorial career, he believed that the hearts and minds of the Christian Reformed constituency had been substantially won over to Christian schools. The schools were flourishing, bulging with baby boom children, and Kuiper directed his attention elsewhere.

---

[31]   *Banner,* 84/2714 (6/24/1949), 773.

CHAPTER 6

With Pen in Hand

From early in his ministry, H.J. Kuiper crafted and submitted numerous overtures to his classis for eventual synodical consideration. His writing for other venues was incidental until he assumed his fourth pastorate, at the Broadway Christian Reformed Church in Grand Rapids. His written contributions to the life of the church by way of synodical committees have been reviewed in earlier chapters of this study. In this chapter his major extra-ecclesiastical publication is reviewed.

The *Witness*

In December 1921, the *Witness* made its appearance. Louis Berkhof was the editor, Y.P. De Jong assistant editor, and H.J. Kuiper, Herman Hoeksema, Henry Danhof, Samuel Volbeda, Richard Postma, Daniel Zwier, and John M. Van De Kieft were associate and department editors. In addition to the men already identified in this study, Zwier was the minister at the Maple Avenue Christian Reformed Church in Holland, Michigan, and Vande Kieft was serving the Fourteenth Street congregation in the same city. Postma, principal of Grandville Avenue Christian School and later director of the Young Calvinist Federation, was the only layman among them. Kuiper was responsible for covering higher education. The monthly magazine ran for five years, folding in 1925. Its purpose was to apply the confessional Reformed faith to issues of the day and to emphasize the centrality of the institutional church, particularly the effective and pure preaching of the gospel, for the believers' welfare.

The magazine differed in focus from *Religion and Culture*, which had begun three years earlier and was edited by E.J. Tuuk, with editorial help from William Harry Jellema, R.B. Kuiper, and H.J.G. Van Andel. It also wanted to bring Reformed principles to bear on issues of the day, but it was decidedly more academic and less ecclesiastical in orientation. Both magazines gave guidance to a Dutch Reformed subculture grappling with how to be both American and Reformed. The two publications complemented one another and overlapped in conviction and intention as much as they differed from time to time on specific issues and emphases. *Religion and Culture* was engaged intellectually with the academic issues and forces of the era, often from a position of empathy and appreciation nurtured by a predilection for common grace. The *Christian Witness* was born in the context of the Janssen controversy and out of the conviction that the antithesis between church and world should not be lost, but safeguarded and applied.

H.J. Kuiper's contributions on higher education began in the first issue with three brief articles. The first, in Dutch, argued that denominational issues and institutions should not be above scrutiny. Removing the Janssen controversy from discussion in the church papers would not resolve anything, he contended. A second, English, essay noted how "grave" the Janssen issue was for the well-being of the seminary, no matter whether Janssen was justly or unjustly accused. Either way the church would have to make some changes to keep its most vital institution healthy. A third entry, also in English, wondered whether Calvin College was "losing its distinctiveness," since its glee club had sung a Roman Catholic number at the last commencement and the school had invited to speak a prominent political figure who was also a high ranking Mason.[1]

In the second issue H.J. tangled with R.B. Kuiper. Writing in *Religion and Culture*, R.B. had used the weak results of a Grand Rapids Christian High School financial drive to argue for involving other evangelical Christians in the cause rather than to challenge Christian Reformed ministers and people to a deeper and more generous commitment to it.[2]

---

[1]   *Witness*, 1/1 (December, 1921), 12-14.
[2]   *Witness*, 1/2 (January, 1922), 30-32.

H.J.'s defense of the Calvin curators' narrow majority decision to recommend termination of Janssen without hearing him personally drew fire in the spring of 1922. So did his examination of President Hiemenga's emphasis on academic excellence rather than on distinctively Reformed teaching and the cultivation of campus spirituality. He responded to criticisms of both essays. When R.B.'s brother, Professor B.K. Kuiper, defended Calvin College and its president against the H.J. essay questioning whether the college was fulfilling its Reformed mission adequately, he answered in detail.

But Kuiper's greatest effort that first year was poured into a three-installment rebuttal of R.B. Kuiper's attack on the synod of 1922's handling of Janssen. R.B. leveled his charges in the summer of 1922 in *Religion and Culture*. With surgical precision H.J. dissected R.B.'s critique, dismantled his arguments, gave the church a masters-level lesson in logic and synodical procedure, and painted Janssen as ecclesiastically belligerent. He cut R.B. no slack and accused him of reacting viscerally to his brother-in-law Janssen's deposition by defending him against perceived board and synodical injustice. Having personalized the exchange, H.J. claimed he would stick strictly with the issues!

The Kuiper battles of 1922 were not blood feuds; H.J. was not related to R.B. and B.K. But these were intense exchanges, and when R.B. extricated himself by accepting a call to the Second Reformed Church in Kalamazoo shortly thereafter, it provided the cooling off that both men needed for working together constructively when R.B. later rejoined the Christian Reformed Church.

By the November 1922 issue of the *Witness*, the names Danhof and Hoeksema had disappeared from the masthead. It was testimony that the allies in the Janssen controversy were divided on other matters of consequence. In the following years, H.J. Kuiper wrote in the *Witness* on themes dear to his heart, ones that he would amplify in his later *Banner* editorials: the need for godliness in Christian school teachers; the importance of training for Sunday school teachers; support for the infant National Union of Christian Schools; the importance of the antithesis in scientific theorizing; the dangers of indifferent orthodoxy; advocacy of a balanced and discerning doctrine of common grace; the qualifications for seminary professors; the strength of denominational distinctiveness; consistorial enforcement of catechism attendance; the meaning and force of the synod's decisions on common grace; the prevalence of worldliness; and the need for reformation and the importance of Sabbath observance. Simply listing the topics constructs a profile of H.J. Kuiper, one that came into sharper focus in later years but did not vary in basic contours. The magazine folded abruptly and without explanation in mid-1925, in the middle of a two-part series Kuiper had begun. He was so deeply involved in his pastorate and in denominational projects at the time that the demise of the publication must have come as a relief.

The *New Christian Hymnal*

In the mid-1920s, Kuiper immersed himself in producing a hymnal. The *New Christian Hymnal* made its debut within months after Kuiper became editor of the *Banner*. The hymnal was a collection of "popular sacred song" and had been the vision of William B. Eerdmans, Sr., its publisher, and H.J. Kuiper for a number of years. Its purpose was to put into peoples' hands hymnody that reinforced and was compatible with the Reformed faith. The collection of 451 numbers, responsive readings, and indexes was intended for use by church groups, including choral societies, and in Christian homes and schools. It was created as a deliberate antidote to the Arminian music widely popular and indiscriminately used in many Christian Reformed settings. Eerdmans had invited five musical and theological experts to serve on the committee that would select the book's content after critical review. As the project dragged out beyond the publisher's desired timeline, Kuiper assumed the role of editor.

In the preface, dated January 1929, Kuiper articulated five "distinctive features" that justified the appearance of yet another Christian hymnal on the glutted market. Scrutinized for "doctrinal purity," its hymns "glorify God's grace in Jesus Christ as the sole cause of man's salvation," rather than giving some credit to the believer."[3] They were chosen for popular, nonliturgical use. Compelling tunes of warmth and quality were selected. A collection specifically designed for children was included. Some chorales were provided for those who appreciated the revival of that musical idiom then in vogue. Kuiper's responsive readings at the end of the volume were selections from or blends of biblical passages.

Kuiper announced and commended the hymnal in the *Banner*. He had earlier introduced the project when he used it in devotions he led at the synod of 1928, a practice he continued in years thereafter. He

---

[3]   H.J. Kuiper, ed., *New Christian Hymnal* (Grand Rapids: Eerdmans, 1929), "Preface."

438   Jesus, Savior, Thou Art Mine

CALVIN COLLEGE   7 8 7 8 8 8 7 7

Henry Van Andel, 1928   Henry Van Andel, 1928
Free translation of "Jesu, Jesu, du bist mein"

Moderato

1. Je - sus, Sav - ior, Thou art mine, While I wan-der un - be - friend-ed;
2. Je - sus, Sav - ior, Thou art mine; E - ven though in pain and sor - row
3. Je - sus, Sav - ior, Thou art mine; When the waves of doubt are surg-ing,

Let my life be whol - ly Thine, Ev - er by Thy grace at - tend-ed.
I should feel my faith de - cline, I would find Thee on the mor-row;
I cling to that Word of Thine, Till I, from the depths e - merg-ing,

Unison if preferred   Parts   rit.

Thou art my De-fense and Tow-er, When the storms of e - vil low - er;
With Thy Spir-it's light to guide me, And Thy wings of love to hide me;
By its light re-gain Thy fa - vor, For Thy truth can nev - er wa - ver;

a tempo   rit.   rit.

I will trust, for I am Thine, Je - sus Sav - ior, Thou art mine.
I will trust, for I am Thine, Je - sus Sav - ior, Thou art mine.
I will trust, for I am Thine, Je - sus Sav - ior, Thou art mine.

Copyright, 1928, by Henry Van Andel

A chorale arrangement by Professor Henry Van Andel of Calvin College that Kuiper included in the hymnal's collection of chorales.

fostered its use whenever and wherever he could. The hymnal caught on quickly, was disseminated widely, and shaped the spirituality of two generations of Christian Reformed faithful. It appeared just as the synod was sanctioning the wider use of hymns and choirs in worship. Its music was generally harmonious, lively, and easy to sing. The texts were experiential, while reinforcing the Reformed faith. The book was used and appreciated beyond Christian Reformed circles, where it became a witness to the faith that lived in the denomination and a "pass" for the church's representatives into the wider evangelical arena. It was also a window into the soul of a man who left little behind by way of personal papers, correspondence, memoirs, or journals.

Heidelberg Catechism Sermons

At the peak of his career, in the mid-1930s, when he served consecutive synods as president, H.J. Kuiper embarked on a publication project that complemented his substantial contributions to liturgy and hymnody. He persuaded the young Zondervan brothers, Bernie and Pat, nephews of Eerdmans who had recently begun a new publishing and book-selling business of their own, to publish a series of Heidelberg Catechism sermons by the most illustrious Christian Reformed and Reformed Church in America pulpiteers of the day. The plan called for one sermon on each of the fifty-two Lord's Days into which the document is divided.

The first volume appeared in 1936, was entitled *Sermons on Sin and Grace*, and covered the first seven Lord's Days. In its preface, Kuiper asserted: "In an age teeming with religious oddities and doctrinal vagaries, there is great need of a systematic, though popular treatment of the fundamental doctrines of our faith."[4]

The series aimed to be good devotional literature for individual growth and reflection, a resource for those who led reading services, and a guide for pastors in preparing catechism sermons. Kuiper confessed how he, who seldom heard colleagues preach on the catechism and often wondered how they approached it, was delighted by the creativity and the methodological variety shown by the seven contributors.

---

[4] H.J. Kuiper, ed., *Sermons on Sin and Grace: Lord's Days I—VII* (Grand Rapids: Zondervan, 1936), [7]. For an analysis of catechism preaching in the Christian Reformed Church and the debates about it during this era, see Carl E. Zylstra, "God-Centered Preaching in a Human-Centered Age," Ph.D. Diss., Princeton Seminary (Ann Arbor: University Microfilms, 1983), 223-35.

The first sermon was contributed by the Reverend Dr. Harry J. Hager, popular pastor of the Bethany Reformed Church in Roseland, Illinois, which was the largest Reformed Church in America congregation in greater Chicago and featured a widely followed radio program.[5] Sermons by professors Kromminga and Schultze of Calvin Seminary were included. So were contributions by the Reverends Peter Hoekstra, Henry Triezenberg, and Emo Van Halsema of the Christian Reformed Church as well as one by the Reverend John Ter Louw of the Reformed Church.

Sermons on the Apostles' Creed: Lord's Days VIII—XXIV followed the next year. Its twenty-two sermons were contributed by six Reformed and sixteen Christian Reformed ministers. *Sermons on Baptism and the Lord's Supper: Lord's Days XXV—XXXI* was published in 1938 and contained only one message by a pastor from the Reformed Church in America. The project then experienced a hiatus, as the fourth volume, *Sermons on the Ten Commandments: Lord's Days XXXIV—XLIV*, did not appear until 1951; Christian Reformed contributors exceeded Reformed by ten to one. *Sermons on the Lord's Prayer: Lord's Days XLV—LII*, 1956, completed the series of five books, covered the final eight Lord's Days, and featured sermons by Professor Richard Oudersluys and the Reverend H. William Pyle of the Reformed Church in America and by six Christian Reformed pastors. No one contributed more than one sermon to the series, and, deferentially, Kuiper did not include one of his own.

The five volumes not only achieved the editor's three stated purposes, but they also provided both a useful cross section of Dutch-American homiletical approaches to the Heidelberg Catechism and an expression of significant confessional solidarity between two Reformed denominations in the second quarter of the twentieth century. The project also reflects an H.J. Kuiper capable of ecclesiastical statesmanship.

Editor of the *Torch and Trumpet*

At the end of his career, after laying down his editor's pen at the *Banner,* H.J. Kuiper joined the editorial committee of *Torch and Trumpet.* His name first appears on the masthead in the February 1957 issue. This magazine had begun in 1951, at the same time as the *Reformed Journal.* The two publications had similar profiles to the *Witness* and *Religion and Culture* thirty years before, although the tensions and antagonism

---

[5]   On Hager and Bethany see Swierenga, *Dutch Chicago*, 318-25.

CONTRIBUTORS

REV. HARRY J. HAGER, PH.D., Minister, Bethany Reformed Church, Chicago, Ill.

REV. PETER A. HOEKSTRA, Minister, Second Christian Reformed Church, Cicero, Ill.

REV. DIEDRICH H. KROMMINGA, TH.B., Professor of Church History, Calvin Seminary, Grand Rapids, Michigan.

REV. JOHN S. TER LOUW, Minister, Reformed Church, South Holland, Ill.

REV. HENRY SCHULTZE, B.D., Professor of New Testament, Calvin Seminary, Grand Rapids, Michigan.

REV. HENRY J. TRIENZENBERG, Minister, Christian Reformed Church, Rochester, N. Y.

REV. EMO F. J. VAN HALSEMA, Minister, Northside Christian Reformed Church, Passaic, N. J.

List of contributors to the first volume in the sermon series.

between the two were sharper in the 1950s than had existed between their predecessors in the 1920s. Kuiper's sympathies lay clearly and decisively with *Torch and Trumpet*. From the time he joined the editorial committee until his death six and a half years later, Kuiper wrote more than fifty articles and editorials for the magazine. By the July-August issue of his first year, he was identified as "managing editor," a position he held until his unexpected death in December 1962. In that capacity he contributed several short editorials in each issue under the rubric, "Timely Topics"; it was a format he had used as editor of the *Banner*.

What catapulted Kuiper into the editorship of the magazine was a two-part article replying to one by Henry Stob entitled, "Mind of Safety," in the April 1957 issue of the *Reformed Journal*. Stob was a figure of denominational stature.[6] He had been runner-up for the presidency

---

[6]   On his early life and his career through his service in the Calvin College Philosophy Department, see Henry J. Stob, *Summoning Up Remembrance* (Grand Rapids: Eerdmans, 1995). His account of the origin of the two magazines appears on pages 290-91 and 299.

of Calvin College in 1952 and for the presidency of Calvin Seminary in 1956. He was on the editorial committee of the magazine in which his article appeared. Stob's article profiled three attitudes toward the world allegedly present in the denomination: safety, militancy, and love. The first produces world flight and the second combativeness; both exhibit fear. He proceeded to illustrate the mind of safety by pointing to a number of widely expressed Christian Reformed practices, attitudes, and values—many that Kuiper had championed in twenty-seven years of editorializing. Stob's alternative was to put on the "mind of love." "We can not at present recall any article with which we disagree so completely as the one now under consideration," Kuiper opened in his response.[7] In the issue in which his first installment appeared, Kuiper was welcomed prominently as a "champion for the doctrinal and spiritual integrity of the church he has served so well."[8] By the issue carrying the second, he was identified as the magazine's "managing editor."

Kuiper wrote that Stob's characterization of the mind of safety as anxious, humorless, stifling, isolationistic, externalistic, legalistic, and racist was an uncharitable caricature. While he acknowledged some truth to some of Stob's characterizations, others were erroneous or exaggerated in his judgment. Stob's portrayal was, therefore, divisive— Kuiper's second objection to it. In the third place, he pointed out, it was illogical, since being concerned with confessional and theological safety is not incompatible with the attitude of love, nor is wholesome fear of evil or standing in awe (fear) of the Lord less than what the Bible requires. Stob's argument might have some force if those in the church who put the safety of orthodoxy and faithful living first made safety their *only* concern. "The very reason why we should make the safety of the church our first concern is that *the church cannot properly discharge its task in this world unless it clings with might and main to the truth which it has embraced*," Kuiper rejoined (italics Kuiper's). Both the New Testament warnings against false doctrine and immoral living and the history of churches that had let down their guard reinforced the need to put "safety first."[9] Wholesome safety is essential for maintaining a healthy church and theological progress. Stob's "nonchalance" on this score was misleading and dangerous, in Kuiper's estimation.

---

[7] "Safety First," *Torch and Trumpet*, 7/2 (May-June, 1957), 3. The entire article appears on pages 3-6, the second in 7/3 (July-August), 15-21, and is entitled "The Safety-First Principle Tested."

[8] Ibid., 5.

[9] Ibid.

The second article examined all of Stob's specific examples of the mind of safety. On the fear of sending seminary graduates to liberal graduate schools, Kuiper pointed to many who were shaken in the faith or who discarded it in such contexts. On the National Union of Christian School's Christian textbook program as sheltering students from alternative positions, Kuiper noted that anyone who knows the material realizes that that judgment is unfounded. On opposition to sponsoring Dr. Lever, the Dutch advocate of theistic evolution, to speak in Christian Reformed circles, Kuiper stood by his published opposition to the Calvin board appointing him to a lectureship, since his views in print were in dissonance with Genesis. On lowering such standards for church membership as thorough knowledge of the Reformed faith and nonmembership in secret societies, Kuiper stated that he knew of no one who defended the view that a convert with "incomplete faith" ought not be admitted to membership, but that all denominations expected a rudimentary understanding and support of their distinctive emphases. On maintaining policy on divorce and remarriage, Kuiper argued that verbal penitence alone over broken marriage vows must not become a gateway for allowing people living in "continuous adultery" (people remarried after an "unbiblical divorce") to belong to the church. On advocating Christian labor unions, Kuiper noted corrosive effects on the church through members who belonged to corrupt, spiteful, secular unions. On worldly amusements, Kuiper noted that they were still regarded as spiritual contaminants that the synod held might require admonition and discipline. On theological advance, he repeated that it was fostered by orthodox commitments and undermined by liberal relativism.

What Henry Stob cited as expressions of a crippling attitude of safety and fearfulness, Kuiper claimed as high standards of biblical fidelity and spiritual vitality. Stob had diminished causes long championed editorially by Kuiper; Kuiper met the challenge, and it launched him into the editor's chair of *Torch and Trumpet*. While the exchange had a five-year pre-history,[10] the lines between the men and their respective publications were never more clearly and widely drawn than in this exchange. What the exchange accomplished was to set forth

---

[10]   On previous tensions and disagreements between the two leaders, see Stob, 300-301, 315, 319, 324, and 333. Bratt's reflections on the exchange occur within a broader characterization of the two approaches to the calling of the church in the world. Bratt, *Dutch Calvinism*, 194-95.

APRIL 1957

The Reformed Journal

A PERIODICAL OF REFORMED COMMENT AND OPINION

Contents of
the issue of the
Reformed Journal
containing Stob's
article.

with clarity and in detail the polarities within Reformed confessional loyalty concerning the living of the faith in the modern world.

The issue of *Torch and Trumpet* that followed immediately after Kuiper's second installment was the first containing the column, "Timely Topics." Kuiper announced department changes. He produced the magazine in a larger, 8 ½ by 11-inch format, and he introduced a column entitled, "As Our Women See It." The latter continued an innovation he had made some years before in the *Banner*. The first contribution to the new column was written by his younger daughter, now known as "Claire" rather than her baptized "Clara," on developing children's talents through excellent Christian education. In subsequent years, a phalanx of talented women wrote on a variety of subjects. Using women writers was part of his strategy to increase readership, and it indicated the respect he held for their opinions.

Safety First!

A Reply to Dr. Henry Stob's
"Mind of Safety" in
The Reformed Journal
of April, 1957

H. J. KUIPER

THE ARTICLE mentioned above states that there are in our Church three different attitudes toward the world which enjoin three very different courses of action: the mind of safety, the mind of militancy, and the mind of love. The first, we are told, leads to world-flight, the second to world combat; but "neither has any right of existence except in so far as they are subordinated to the mind of love." Dr. Stob adds that governing the first two minds, as they actually exist among us, is the mind of fear.

We can not at present recall any article with which we disagree so completely as the one now under consideration.

Our first objection is that it is a misrepresentation, a caricature or distortion, of the attitude which we have labeled *Safety First*. Those who have this attitude are said to be motivated by fear rather than love. The "mind of safety" is so anxious about the purity of the Church that those whom it characterizes are unable to laugh at themselves; they have lost their sense of humor. They stifle theological growth and block the way of theological advance. Their attitude encourages isolation, and therefore it ignores large social evils such as prostitution, segregation, tenement housing, tyranny, and the like. It encourages externalism, legalism, and individualism. This is not a description but a distortion of the attitude: Safety First.

The "mind of safety" is further characterized in a very practical way according to certain recent manifestations; for example, as being opposed to sending our young men to Union or to Princeton. It is opposed to inviting Dr. Lever of the Free University to Calvin Campus as a short-term lecturer in biology. It insists that "outsiders" who are converted should stay in the chapel until they have a complete(!) understanding of Christ. It fights the admission of negroes into our congregations. It wants Christian textbooks from which "everything anti-Christian or even non-Christian is excluded." It is reflected in the synodical decision of 1945 which urged our people to establish Christian labor unions in view of the moral and spiritual dangers of membership in non-Christian organizations. It is legalistic because it wants the church to publish bans against worldly amusements. Because of it we cannot look for a definitive Reformed ethic any more than we can look to it for a vigorous Reformed dogmatic.

Some of these allegations are correct; others are incorrect or exaggerations. Our judgment stands that the article as a whole is a caricature of the attitude which it labels as "the mind of safety."

* * * *

Our second objection to Dr. Stob's presentation is that it is *divisive*. Its implication is that those who have this "mind of safety" are motivated only by fear, not by love. In being zealous for the preservation of the purity of the church they do not have love as a governing motive — love for the world round about us which we are commanded to win for Christ. Perhaps without intending it, the writer is passing judgment on the hearts of those whom he

Kuiper's reply in *Torch and Trumpet* the following month.

Kuiper enlisted contributions from recognized thinkers and leaders both inside and outside Christian Reformed circles. Several men from Calvin Seminary and from Westminster Seminary wrote in the magazine. Rousas John Rushdoony, an Orthodox Presbyterian pastor and lecturer, began to appear on the pages in 1958. R.B. Kuiper, with whom H.J. had contended strenuously over the application of common grace and the antithesis and over the Janssen issue when each was identified with other magazines, weighed in against Harry Boer's views on evangelism and church membership.[11] Through years of confronting the forces of liberalism, R.B. had traveled into H.J.'s camp, and by 1961 the two old warriors were seated side by side on the magazine's editorial committee. William Hendriksen wrote continuously on the second coming of Christ and eschatology, themes on which he had built his reputation. Leonard Greenway, an irenic and popular minister, provided monthly meditations. Extensive Bible studies suitable for use in societies were introduced and enhanced the magazine's circulation. Ralph Danhof, stated clerk of the denomination, wrote extensively and conservatively, even paternalistically, on apartheid in South Africa and race relations in the United States. A young James Packer reflected on Calvinism in Britain; Leon Morris and Klaas Runia on its prospects in Australia; Synesio Lyra, Jr., on the health of the Reformed faith in Brazil.

In the summer of 1960, Kuiper discontinued "Timely Topics" and introduced "Pointed Paragraphs." The latter featured up to a half-dozen brief editorials by regular contributors and people on the editorial committee. Until that time, Kuiper had been the editorial voice of the magazine; afterwards, he relinquished that status in favor of shared responsibility for the paper's positions. It was the beginning of the end of his long editorial career.

His editorials in *Torch and Trumpet* were of the same style and length, though not as wide-ranging, as his had been in the *Banner*, but he had to produce them only once instead of four times a month. He took positions that were predictable by those who knew him and had read him for more than three decades. He stoutly opposed evolution, the welfare state, and worldliness. He urgently advocated Christian schools, spiritual reformation in the home, the antithesis, and effective doctrinal instruction of young people. When the Russians launched the first space satellite, and later when they sent a dog into orbit, he editorialized that man had been mandated to subdue "the earth" and had best keep his feet on the ground and out of space. On the question of an ecumenical seminary or a distinctively Reformed seminary in Nigeria, he argued for the latter. He sounded the alarm and provided thorough analysis when the Hoogland brothers appeared to stretch inspiration and infallibility beyond Reformed parameters in their

[11] "Is Dr. Boer Right?" *Torch and Trumpet*, 7/7 (December, 1957), 11-14.

Calvin Seminary student paper, *Stromata*, and when the seminary president, John H. Kromminga, seemed overly concessive to their views in his efforts to explain the issue to the church. He inveighed against membership in the World Council of Churches. He was apprehensive at the end about developments in the Dutch mother church and wondered whether it would "drag our own Christian Reformed Church along with it into the muddy waters of unsound doctrine."[12]

Kuiper's work ethic kept him involved and productive until his death, and it was articulated in an editorial shortly after his own retirement that bluntly opposed retiring to Florida to wile away winter days at shuffleboard and evenings visiting with similarly disengaged but misguided believers over board games. In fact, he never really retired. He died still actively managing the editorial responsibilities of *Torch and Trumpet.*

In a posthumous tribute, H.J. Kuiper was praised for being exactly the expert editor and staunch defender of the Reformed faith that the magazine needed. He was seen to possess the qualities of courtesy and congeniality—even in disagreements on the board—as well as industriousness, focus, and Reformed conviction transcending denominational boundaries.[13]

[12] "Doctrinal Disturbances in a Sister Church," *Torch and Trumpet*, 12/6 (November, 1962), 10. A second article on the subject appeared the next month, the month that Kuiper died. See *Torch and Trumpet*, 12/6 (December, 1962), 12-14.

[13] Edward Heerema, "The Reverend Henry J. Kuiper, 1885-1962," *Torch and Trumpet*, 13/1 (January, 1963), 5-6.

CHAPTER 7

Every Church's Calling

A third area of H.J. Kuiper's sustained activity and interest beyond the institutional church was evangelism, especially through city mission work and chapels. He was formed in large part by the *Afscheiding's* spirituality, which emphasized personal conversion, a daily communion with the Lord through prayer and Bible reading, and heart-felt concern for the lost. He was raised when the denomination was making its initial missionary overtures to Native Americans and to urban Jews in New York and Chicago and when it had a vigorous, intentional, and successful church planting program underway among Dutch immigrants in many communities. Furthermore, his student days in the preparatory and theological programs of the theological school included lively campus interest in the vigorous Student Volunteer Movement devoted to missions.

As a youngster, Kuiper would have been aware of the effective ministry of the Reverend Sipke Sevensma, pastor of the Eastern Avenue Christian Reformed Church, whose experiential preaching fostered a series of revivals and numerous conversions in his church in the 1880s and 1890s and who used the American Sunday school movement as an outreach tool. Sevensma's preaching was close in emphasis to that of his own pastor, J.H. Vos. During Kuiper's Calvin days, the La Grave Avenue church began a program of evangelistic outreach to patients in the Kent County Infirmary. When Kuiper was in his early pastorates, Christian Reformed congregations in his home town initiated several evangelism projects: Franklin Street's Grant Street Missionary Sunday

School in 1909, Eastern Avenue's Way of Life Mission, and Oakdale Park's Madison Square Gospel Mission. The last was sparked by the Reverend William P. Van Wyk's influential 1913 pamphlet appealing for evangelism by mission chapels: *"Statsevangelisatie: Waarom en Hoe?"*[1] At the turn of the century, a dynamic convert from a life of alcohol dependency named Mel Trotter established his highly successful City Rescue Mission in Grand Rapids and began to promote this type of ministry nationally and internationally.[2] Trotter generated Christian Reformed interest in and support for his work. Missions and evangelism were in the ecclesiastical air Kuiper breathed. He caught the vision and became a life-long leader in the cause.[3]

Mobilizing Churches

In Luctor, Kuiper's interest in outreach is evident from the decisions to give missionary Cora Hartog an opportunity to address the congregation about her work among Native Americans and to take offerings for the Chicago Tract Society.[4] In Holland, Kuiper devised and presented to the classis a strategy for community-wide involvement in a day of prayer. It called for participation by businesses, all the local schools, Reformed Church leaders and congregations, and even the city council.[5] The event was held as proposed, but afterwards communications to the classis strongly suggested that the next year

[1]   John Knight, *Echoes of Mercy, Whispers of Love: A Century of Community Outreach by the Christian Reformed Churches in the Greater Grand Rapids Area* (Grand Rapids: Grand Rapids Area Ministries, 1989), 20-21. Remarkably, the book does not mention H.J. Kuiper's central role in the Grand Rapids City Mission .

[2]   See Melvin E. Trotter, *These Forty Years*, with an introduction by G. Campbell Morgan and an endorsement by Harry Ironside (London and Grand Rapids: Marshall, Morgan, and Scott; Zondervan, 1939).

[3]   If Harvey Smit's conclusion that "the evangelistic outreach of the church appeared to be a secondary thing, almost peripheral to the true being of the church," has validity for some in the Christian Reformed Church prior to 1915, the sources indicate that it does not hold true for Kuiper nor for those who rallied to his vision and behind his efforts. See Harvey A. Smit, "Mission Zeal in the Christian Reformed Church: 1857-1915," *Perspectives in the Christian Reformed Church*, ed. Peter De Klerk and Richard R. De Ridder (Grand Rapids: Baker, 1983), 240. Smit does not mention or deal with Van Wyk's appeal and its significant influence.

[4]   Minutes of the consistory of the Luctor Christian Reformed Church, 2/21/1908, art. 13 and 2/2/1910, art. 9.

[5]   Minutes of Classis Holland, 1/3/1912, art. 3.

the service be held in the evening, and businesses indicated that they would not again close their doors early for the event.[6] Undeterred in his initiative to make a Christian impact on Holland, Kuiper outlined for the following meeting of Classis Holland a proposal for beginning an evangelistic outreach on the north end of the city by means of an English-language Sunday school. A committee to study the feasibility of the idea reported favorably. A steering committee consisting of one representative from each consistory was appointed, and by the spring of 1913, forty-three youngsters were in regular attendance.

A half year before H.J. Kuiper moved to Chicago and assumed the pastorate of Second Englewood, the first pastor, John R. Brink, presented the consistory there with a draft of the by-laws for a collaborative home mission effort in that city. The consistory approved, stipulating that all documents be produced in "the American language."[7] Because Brink that summer accepted the call to be the home missionary or church planter for the joint home missions committee of Classis Grand Rapids East and Classis Grand Rapids West, it was left to others to carry the venture forward. Brink's acceptance was a continuation of the ministry he had done for the two Grand Rapids classes between 1905 and 1907.[8] Then he had basically been a circuit rider among eight fledgling congregations and evangelistic centers in new Dutch communities. The new model called for Brink to spend two consecutive Sundays in each location preaching, advising, celebrating the sacraments, and moving each group toward organization as a congregation. The work was exhausting, but during his brief tenure he had the support of committee members such as Louis Berkhof, when he was the pastor of Oakdale Park Christian Reformed Church, and Jacob Noordewier, pastor of the Christian Reformed church in Jenison. As a result of the work of Brink and others who preceded or followed, the committee was involved in the organization of a remarkable number of Christian Reformed churches: Goshen, Indiana (1904); and, in Michigan, Byron Center (1902); Burton Heights (1905); Plainfield (1906); Ada (1909); Walker (1912); Detroit (1914); Dutton (1915); Neland Avenue (1915); Portland (1915); Wyoming Park (1919); Coopersville (1920); Battle Creek (1933); Lansing (1935); and Dorr (1938). Work that did not yield an organized congregation until much later or not at all was done in South Bend, Indiana (1959), and Lowell (1968), Sunshine (1971),

6   Minutes of Classis Holland, 5/27/1912, art. 6.
7   Minutes, Englewood, 4/15/1913, art. 5.
8   Minutes, Joint Home Missions Committee, 8/14/1905.

Bowen, Bradley, Talmedge, Otsego, and Gun River—all in Michigan. Brink's second stint with the two classes extended from 1913 to 1928, after which he took up similar work for Classis Illiana. In 1921, Kuiper joined the joint committee as a representative of Classis Grand Rapids West.

The month after Brink left Englewood in the summer of 1913, the five consistories involved[9] established what was to become the Helping Hand Mission, a work to which they called the Reverend Peter J. Hoekenga of Lynden, Washington. Two weeks later, Second Englewood called H.J. Kuiper.

Hoekenga and Kuiper arrived in Chicago almost simultaneously. The former joined Second Englewood, where he was welcomed as a participating member of the consistory. The two men cooperated in launching the mission.[10] When the parameters of the work were still under discussion during the winter of 1913-1914, the Second Englewood consistory asked Hoekenga to consider whether work on State Street really belonged within the scope of what the churches had envisioned, and it directed Kuiper to accompany Hoekenga on an exploratory visit of the neighborhood in question.[11] The leading role of Kuiper and the Second Englewood consistory in this mission is evident from the fact that it located and rented a home for the Hoekenga family, appointed a support committee for the missionary, and welcomed into its fellowship the next year John Vande Water as the unordained superintendent of the mission.

The latter event was the beginning of a twenty-five-year partnership in city missions between Kuiper and Vande Water. Within a half year, tensions arose between Hoekenga and Vande Water,[12] and by the following year Hoekenga had left to become a denominational home missionary and church planter in California. Meanwhile, the work in Chicago expanded. The Second Englewood consistory assumed responsibility for recruiting Sunday school teachers for the Bethel Mission in Englewood. It deputized Kuiper to leverage the local Christian school teachers to assist with catechism teaching at the South End Mission, as the joint mission board had directed.[13] It

9   The five sponsoring churches were First Chicago, Douglas Park, Third Chicago, and First and Second Englewood.
10   Swierenga states, "Kuiper took a leading part in the founding of the Chicago Helping Hand Mission." Swierenga, *Dutch Chicago*, 263.
11   Minutes, Englewood, 2/3/1914, art. 3.
12   Minutes, Englewood, 7/2/1915, art. 12.
13   Minutes, Englewood, 11/23/1915, art. 22.

proposed modifications in the mission constitution that granted two seats per church on the joint board. Just prior to Hoekenga's leaving, it facilitated reconciliation between him and Gerrit Haan, pastor of First Englewood, because Hoekenga had accused Haan of undermining the work of the mission.

The Helping Hand Mission and its expanded sites were not the congregation's or Kuiper's only involvement in local outreach. In May, 1917, the Second Englewood consistory overtured Classis Illinois to investigate whether the Chicago Hebrew Mission was an interdenominational project in which Christian Reformed churches could legitimately continue to participate, or whether they ought to begin their own, Reformed work in Jewish evangelism.[14] The overture bore Kuiper's fingerprints. When the classis committee did not respond in a timely manner, Second Englewood overtured the classis again, this time asking that "synod discontinue giving financial support to the Chicago Hebrew Mission and establish a Christian Reformed Hebrew mission," because the former was not sufficiently Reformed.[15] The classis approved. The synod of 1918 considered the matter, agreed, asked Classis Illinois to undertake the work of Reformed Jewish evangelism on behalf of the whole denomination, and pledged at least four thousand dollars a year for the new work and a similar amount to Classis Hudson and Classis Hackensack, where Jewish evangelism had been underway for several decades. The decision marked the inception of the Chicago Jewish Mission, later named the Nathaniel Institute.[16] Kuiper's case for a distinctively Reformed approach to Jewish evangelism had carried the day.

By the end of Kuiper's tenure at Second Englewood, the Chicago City Mission was conducting work at four sites. He had been an architect and motivator for the expansion. Classis Illinois had also implemented the synod's request that it craft a constitution and implement a Christian Reformed ministry of Jewish evangelism. Kuiper's gifts and reputation as a Reformed apologist with a missionary's heart and zeal had been established among his contemporaries, although this appears to have eluded succeeding generations.

The Broadway Christian Reformed Church in Grand Rapids, Kuiper's fourth charge, was both large and generous towards missions

---

[14]   Minutes of Classis Illinois, 5/22/1917, art. 34.
[15]   Minutes of Classis Illinois, 1/22/1918, art. 36.
[16]   *Acta der Synode, 1918,* 23-24.

John Vande Water,
pioneer of city missions
in Chicago and later in
Grand Rapids.

and evangelism. It took frequent offerings for many outreach ministries, as noted earlier. In addition, it was deeply engaged in the denomination's first overseas mission effort, the China mission begun in 1920. It sent gifts to Wilhemina Kalsbeek. The young Reverend J.C. De Korne, a son of the congregation, was one of the denomination's first ordained missionaries to China and the recipient of special gifts from the church. Its fondness for China missionary Harry Dykstra, whom it also supported, further extended the congregation's commitment to foreign missions.

The level of the congregation's involvement in outreach suited Kuiper well. He built on it. He was undoubtedly behind an overture sent to Classis Grand Rapids West that the denominational mission board be strengthened to include a pastor and an elder from each classis.[17] It was an early but failed effort to give lay members parity with ordained pastors on denominational boards. Dissatisfied with inadequate salaries paid to missionaries, Kuiper fostered the idea that the four west-side consistories protest to the mission board,[18] and

[17] Minutes, Broadway, 5/1/1022, art. 30.
[18] Minutes, Broadway, 11/27/1922, art. 9. The four were Broadway, Alpine Avenue, West Leonard, and Twelfth Street.

thus began a sustained interchange between the consistory and the board on the sensitive subject that really amounted to a test of wills for ultimate control—local consistory or denominational board.[19] The following spring Kuiper came with a proposal, patterned after his Chicago experience, for united evangelistic work in Grand Rapids, led by a full-time, nonordained person able to train others, to visit unchurched families, and eventually to supervise and coordinate all the Christian Reformed evangelistic work in the city. His suggestion was that the work be governed by a board composed of representatives from each supporting church. The consistory liked the idea and authorized its pastor to present it to the three other pastors west of the Grand River.[20] Before long, Kuiper won his three colleagues' support. Next, the consistories indicated theirs. A board structure was proposed. But when the Alpine Avenue consistory balked at appointing a full-time evangelist before a site had been selected, John Vande Water was brought in from Chicago to advise the joint consistories. He recommended the Bridge Street-Stocking neighborhood.

Meanwhile, the idea of coordinated, city-wide evangelism spread beyond the four congregations on Grand Rapids' west side. When city mission workers made a case for this expansion at a pastors' *internos*,[21] a committee of ministers, chaired by the Reverend Benjamin Spalink of the East Leonard church, investigated and presented a plan. Finally, on September 26, 1928, a constitution was approved by delegates from the twenty-nine participating consistories.

Expenses for a full-time worker were to be shared on a pro-rated, per family basis. The joint endeavor did not preclude individual churches from engaging in their own work, but it was understood that this would be coordinated so that the entire metropolitan area would be covered. A board for governing the work was elected, and Kuiper, still considering whether to accept his recent appointment as editor of the *Banner*, was chosen as chair. It had been almost five years since Kuiper had first broached the idea in the Broadway consistory room. The following January, the month Kuiper commenced his duties as editor, the board offered the position of director of the West Fulton

---

[19] See Minutes, Broadway, 9/24/2923, art. 15, and 1/18/1924, art. 20.3.
[20] Minutes, Broadway, 4/9/1923, arts. 11 and 33.
[21] *Internos* (literally, "among us") meetings were monthly or quarterly gatherings of Christian Reformed ministers and their spouses in a given classis for fellowship and discussion, sometimes based on presentation of a formal paper.

Street Mission to Vande Water. He accepted. His mandate was to train evangelistic workers, to promote the work of evangelism among the churches, to provide strategic guidance and city-wide coordination of evangelism, to recruit the participation of churches that were not involved, and to be personally involved in evangelism at the West Fulton Street Mission.[22] His family joined Broadway, as they had joined Second Englewood when Kuiper was pastor there. Less than three months later, Kuiper accepted the call to Neland Avenue. But his move did not impede the renewal of his effective partnership with Vande Water in city missions.

Kuiper chaired the City Mission board from the time of his election in November 1928, until he submitted his resignation for health reasons to the April 1944 board meeting. He was not at that meeting, for he was hospitalized, exhausted from fifteen years of simultaneously pastoring the Neland Avenue church and editing the *Banner*. The Reverend Richard Frens, secretary of the board, went to the meeting directly from the hospital and reported that Kuiper had received "doctor's orders to limit his activities as much as possible."[23] That June the synod relented after years of dithering and made the editorship a full-time position. Frens took over as chairman of the City Mission board. Kuiper's decision may have been influenced also by his friend John Vande Water's decision that January to accept an offer to become the superintendent of city missions in Paterson, New Jersey. For fifteen years the two had worked side by side to develop one of the most robust, comprehensive, coordinated, congregation-based, urban evangelistic efforts in the country.

A Bold Plan

In one of his earliest editorials, the *Banner* editor christened the new era of city mission work in Grand Rapids with a blueprint for evangelism in which he regarded evangelism as the work of every believer and every mature congregation.[24] It was written a month after he became editor, three months after he assumed leadership of the City Mission board, and the month Vande Water moved into town. Entitled "Our City Mission Work Just Begun," it unpacked the term

22   See "Report of the Committee Regarding the Origin and Scope of the West Fulton Street Mission," Grand Rapids Area Ministries (hereafter GRAM) materials, Box 1, Folder 12, Archives, CRC.

23   Ibid., Folder 13.

24   *Banner*, 64/1670 (2/15/29), 1120.

"evangelization," noting that it really covers all missionary work. "City missions" would technically include work in foreign cities, which he did not intend. Professor Hepp of the Free University of Amsterdam thinks of evangelization as "re-Christianization," Kuiper instructed. This was a useful idea in the European situation. He admitted that a lot of mission terminology was "inexact and confusing."

He then reviewed the Christian Reformed track record in a way that showed that for him missions and evangelization were more than planting Dutch Reformed congregations in immigrant communities. Sixteen years earlier, he reminisced, five Chicago churches had started mission work in the slums and called the Reverend P.J. Hoekenga for it and then hired John Vande Water as his assistant. That same year the Reverend W.P. Van Wyk printed his brochure *Statsevangelisatie*. The Helping Hand Mission evolved out of the Chicago work and had even become recognized by the University of Chicago Sociology Department, Kuiper celebrated, as one of the best in the city. More importantly, he continued, the leaders had developed a Reformed approach to the work that was noteworthy and worth emulating. He reported that similar work had been started in Hammond, Indiana, and in Holland and Grand Rapids, Michigan. He emphasized that "our churches have just begun to do their duty" in this area.

Kuiper's opening editorial on evangelism proposed a bold plan. He contended that every Christian Reformed congregation that was large enough to support a program of local evangelization should start one and should hire either a competent full-time or a part-time person, ordained or nonordained, for this work. Kuiper's vision, evangelistic heart, and organizational aptitude came to expression when he dissected the denomination and argued that nine communities—Grand Rapids, Muskegon, Holland, Kalamazoo, Grand Haven, Zeeland, Passaic, Paterson, and Chicago—had enough churches and resources to support such a concerted effort. Only in Zeeland and Grand Haven might there not be enough unchurched people to keep a full-time evangelist busy. He identified thirteen additional urban areas where the denomination had a presence but insufficient numbers to support a full-time person. However, in these places motivated volunteers, with some training by a person like John Vande Water, "would be of unestimable value" to their communities and would be a powerful antidote to the un-Reformed evangelistic methods rife in North America. Even rural churches should become involved in urban evangelism through prayer and financial support, as a number already have with respect to the work in Chicago.

"Nearly every church or group of churches has a mission field in its own community *and not until every one of these fields is occupied by a salaried missionary or volunteer workers or both are we able to say we are making serious business of our missionary task*" (italics Kuiper's).

Kuiper became personally involved in locating the site of the West Fulton Street mission. He accompanied Vande Water in scouting possible sites for the work.[25] He endorsed publication of the *Gospel Herald*, a four-page bimonthly newsletter on the work that soon was issued monthly. Consistent with a Reformed, holistic approach, the mission added an industrial department its first year as a means of occupational training and a source of revenue.

In September 1929 the City Mission board initiated its "training school" with a course in personal evangelism taught by Vande Water, and another in Reformed doctrine. The next year the board added two additional courses taught by seminary professors Clarence Bouma and Henry Schultze and advised the synod that the denomination needed such a school. In the mid-thirties, when the synod instituted Bible school courses on an experimental basis, the board vacillated on whether to terminate its efforts, but it finally opted to maintain control of training its own workers. It urged the churches of Grand Rapids to require their evangelism workers to use its program. It sought the guidance of Samuel Volbeda, the seminary's professor of practical theology, on how best to help converts bridge the gap between mission chapel and sponsoring church. It also adopted the guideline that professing converts should attend the mother church once a Sunday. After 1940, the board made extensive use of Reformed Bible Institute students in the expanding work and supplemented their education with training sessions led by Vande Water.

All did not go smoothly, however. The Great Depression curtailed programs dramatically, but it also strengthened resolve to press forward. When staff member Peter Winter, one of the fathers of the industrial department, felt slighted and unrecognized by Vande Water, the board facilitated reconciliation by clarifying titles and lines of accountability. A fund was established to help the families of converts meet the cost of Christian day-school education for their children.

---

[25] John Vande Water, *Miracles in Forgotten Streets* (Grand Rapids: Eerdmans, 1936), 15. Vande Water writes, "On January 29, 1929, we arrived in Grand Rapids. After spending a few days putting things in order, we started out, in company of the president of our city mission board, to find a location in which to open a mission."

When churches slacked in promised support, they were approached and their enthusiasm rekindled. Sometimes the board stumbled, as it did regarding work among an expanding black population composed of people moving north from the South. It did not recommend establishing work among these migrants, noting the unspecified "special difficulties" of whites working among blacks.[26] In the early 1940s it contended with the denominational education committee over the inadequacy of its Sunday school materials for a mission population, and the board finally produced its own lessons.

But any problems and failures were eclipsed by successes and satisfactions. Kuiper's own congregation, Neland Avenue, became a strong supporter of city missions. When political turmoil in China made the work there a poor investment, the congregation redirected its resources to city missions.[27] An anonymous member offered to purchase a lot and to pay for the construction of a City Mission chapel in Comstock Park. The consistory could not refuse and accepted the offer with thanks.[28] Neland became the major supporter of this work, even when the Depression forced it to solicit financial help with the effort from other churches. The church maintained its Boston Street mission through the Depression and closed it only when population changes forced this action. Neland Avenue was as explicitly preoccupied and innovative regarding missions and evangelism as Broadway had been, and its undeniable commitment to the cause can be attributed in no small measure to its pastor's leadership.

After his opening editorial on evangelism, Kuiper continued to promote outreach in the *Banner*. That fall he summarized the fifth annual meeting of the Union of Mission Workers of the Christian Reformed Church held September 25-26.[29] The organization was then five years old. Vande Water was president and Spalink was vice president. Kuiper predicted that the event would grow from year to year. He also endorsed Vande Water's *Sunday School Newsie* as superior

[26] Minutes of the board of the City Mission, 9/30/1943, art. 6; GRAM materials, Box 1, Folder 13. Archives, CRC.

[27] Minutes, Neland, 6/17/1929, art. 11 and 1/6/1930, art. 20. [Subsequent events revealed that those churches that continued in the task in China reaped rich rewards, establishing a strong indigenous church. Cf. Gerald F. De Jong, *The Reformed Church in China, 1842-1951*, The Historical Series of the Reformed Church in America, no. 22 (Grand Rapids: Eerdmans, 1992). —Ed.]

[28] Minutes, Neland, 9/21/1931, art. 3.

[29] *Banner*, 64/1702 (10/4/29), 1692-94.

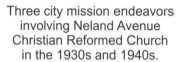

Three city mission endeavors involving Neland Avenue Christian Reformed Church in the 1930s and 1940s.

to the International Sunday School Lessons a half dozen years before the synod decided to produce its own Sunday school materials. The next week he applauded the synod's sympathy for a Christian Reformed training center for those without high school or college who wanted to be evangelists or church school teachers. He emphasized that the denomination's approach to evangelism had not been distinctive enough. Nor had the church stressed sufficiently the importance of the family or its own role in nurturing faith in young people. It had too uncritically capitulated to Arminian emphases in the transmission of the faith, Kuiper alleged.

Distinctively Reformed Evangelism

By the spring of 1932, Kuiper's reputation as a leader in the city mission or evangelism movement was such that the synod that June appointed him to a study committee on evangelism. The committee was mandated "to make a careful study of the methods which should be used by our churches in evangelistic work, in order that this may proceed along sound Reformed lines."[30] Despite a similar report to

30 *1932 Acts of Synod,* 21, and *1934 Agenda for Synod, I,* 4. The synod of 1924 had appointed W.P. Van Wyk, E.J. Tuuk, and John Vande Water to prepare

the synod of 1926, subsequent interest in creating a denominational Bible school or a training school for lay evangelists had influenced the decision to take another look at the subject. The Reverend David D. Bonnema, pastor of the First or Bates Street Christian Reformed Church of Grand Rapids and a fellow City Mission board member, chaired the new committee. Kuiper and Vande Water were appointed to it along with the Reverend Martin Monsma—then pastor of the Detroit Christian Reformed Church—the Reverend John Dolfin, and the Reverend Dr. Samuel Volbeda of the seminary faculty.

The committee took its mandate seriously, and its thirty-seven-page report submitted two years later featured prominently the five doctrines of the Canons of Dort.[31] Because of the "rampant neo-paganism" of American society and the pervasiveness of Arminian methodology in evangelistic work, all-out efforts in Reformed evangelism were needed, the report asserted. Every congregation should give priority to evangelism by hiring, in addition to the minister, a full-time "ordained minister especially for this evangelistic work." This work must be under the aegis of the church—consistory, classis, and/or synod—since it is a ministry of the Word. It can employ a variety of strategies, depending on the local situation: week-day evangelistic meetings, Bible and doctrine classes for adults, Sunday school and catechism for children, annual canvassing of the neighborhood, face-to-face witnessing, tract distribution, and fellowship with interested persons in their own homes. These strategies were all discussed amply.

At the outset, the committee emphasized, evangelistic work must make a strong and clear case for the Bible as inspired revelation authoritative for all of life. The gospel must be presented in its distinctive, Reformed character, which the committee illustrated

---

a report that would guide the churches in their increasing involvement in city mission work. As Kuiper's successor at Englewood, Tuuk was heavily involved in the Helping Hand Mission. Their ten-page report on Reformed principles and methods of evangelism was recommended to the churches for their guidance. *Acta der Synode, 1926*, 88.

31   *1934 Agenda for Synod*, 4-40. M. Monsma attached a three-page qualification objecting to the report, which, he believed, gave the synod too much authority for evangelism. Volbeda wrote an introduction to Vande Water's account of the Helping Hand Mission: *The Street of Forgotten Men* (Grand Rapids: Eerdmans, n.d.). Bonnema later wrote the introduction to Vande Water's 1936 book. While no indexed record exists of the synod's action, its approval appears in *1934 Acts of Synod*, 135.

biblically and doctrinally. Total depravity and human inability to earn salvation make the gospel compelling and evangelism urgent. Election is a doctrine of assurance and comfort to be addressed once a convert has begun to grow in faith. Limited atonement makes salvation precious and certain in all its aspects. Irresistible grace and perseverance of the saints bring assurance to the convert and magnify the greatness of God's work. The call to believe and to begin a new life of trust and obedience must be clear and forceful.

The report identified unbiblical phrases and practices to be avoided in evangelistic witnessing. Sensationalism, emotionalism, altar calls, and personal testimonies were to be avoided. A covenantal approach compelled the evangelist to address the family, to speak to people in a way that recognizes their social context, and to explain the implications of conversion for all of life. With commendable ecumenical sensitivity, the report called for churches not to duplicate the work of or to compete with the evangelism of other, Bible-believing churches. But Christian Reformed churches should not hesitate to begin evangelism in areas where none exists or where modernistic churches are present, the report counseled.

Reformed evangelism is forthright about the church's stands on the lodge, Christian schools, worldly amusements, and Sabbath observance, because these distinctive strengths of the Christian Reformed Church provide an opportunity to explain the full implications of discipleship and biblically rooted values and the beauty of the Reformed lifestyle. When properly presented and understood, these matters of distinction become "points in our favor, and inducements for the seeking of membership with us," the committee concluded. Because the faith is so full and deep, on-the-spot conversions and rushing people into profession of faith and church membership should give way to a process of encouraging and schooling people in the faith, it emphasized.

The report was explicit, thoughtfully Reformed in approach, and a clear alternative in the North American context. The committee produced what the synod had mandated and what D.H. Kromminga considered "a valuable report."[32] The report reflects the understanding and work of evangelism prevailing in Christian Reformed city mission work at the time. When it was considered, the synod accepted the report "as information," thanked its committee "for its splendid work," urged

---

[32]   D.H. Kromminga, *The Christian Reformed Tradition*, 142.

churches to study it and the minority report seriously, and ordered its printing "for distribution among our people at cost price."[33]

Expanding the Movement

In an editorial written a month after this committee had been appointed in 1932, Kuiper praised that same synod's vision in creating the emergency committee and an emergency fund to receive gifts that would enable the oversupply of candidates for ministry to be placed in evangelistic settings or smaller, economically dependent churches.[34] Kuiper depicted America as having forsaken the gospel, its churches as either closing their doors or compromising pure biblical teaching, and the Christian Reformed Church as one of only a few faithful churches that, through every congregation, should be devoted to reaching the great American mission field. He lamented that as yet the denomination did not have one full-time home evangelist who was ordained. He applauded the statistic that every Sunday the Christian Reformed Church, according to a recent study, had two thousand unchurched children in its Sunday schools. That synod, he said, the synod of 1932, of which he had been vice president, had transformed a problem into a challenging opportunity. In its almost three hundred congregations, only seven pulpit vacancies existed in churches with more than twenty-five families. Yet, the Lord had blessed the denomination with forty-four seminary students. Kuiper urged generous support of the new committee and its emergency fund as God-given instruments of outreach and growth. The committee, with its three members, was one that he chaired and that he may well have proposed.

That same year the City Mission was featured in a theme issue of the *Banner* that Vande Water helped Kuiper prepare.[35] The magazine's cover announced, "Home Evangelization Issue." It featured two photographs—one of mission Sunday school students and the other of a tenement house near the West Fulton Street Mission in Grand Rapids. Kuiper reported that there were twenty-eight places where the denomination was doing city mission work. Involvement has been a blessing to the supporting churches, he stated, since souls are being saved and our people are experiencing the spiritual growth of leading others to the Lord. He paid tribute to the workers for their dedication

---

33   *1934 Acts of Synod*, 135.
34   *Banner*, 67/1846 (7/29/1932), 668-69.
35   *Banner*, 67/1860 (11/4/1932), 949.

and modesty. Short reports on their work and the pictures of a number of them were included in the issue. Vande Water had reviewed synodical attention to home missions in 1928 and 1930, and he did so again in 1932. The editor highlighted the two committees scheduled to report in 1934. This was not to be the last time Kuiper touted the Grand Rapids City Mission in the pages of the *Banner* or that he enlisted Vande Water's expertise in doing so.

With special satisfaction, Kuiper reported that on May 7, 1933, eleven people had become members of the Broadway Christian Reformed Church. They were the first converts of the West Fulton Street Mission.[36] Six adults joined by profession of faith, among whom was one who also received adult baptism. Kuiper commended their thorough preparation in the faith by Vande Water. He complimented the consistory's wisdom in giving permission for the converts to continue attending one service a week at the mission, since this policy would enable them to make a good transition to the congregation. He stated emphatically that keeping mission and church separate was important. "It will never do to convert our city missions into churches by ordaining the missionary and permitting him to maintain a membership roll and to administer the sacraments," Kuiper pronounced. But our churches are too formal and cold to assimilate converts easily, he acknowledged in a moment of refreshing candor. They must become warmer, more welcoming, and more hospitable, he added.

When Vande Water's book *Miracles in Forgotten Streets* appeared in print, Kuiper described its appearance, purpose, and contents in the *Banner*.[37] He capitalized on the event to update readers on the West Fulton Street Mission and its industrial store, and he promoted the book's purchase by reporting that William Eerdmans was publishing it at cost so that all profits would be directed to construction of a new mission building. Five years later, Kuiper highlighted *Good News*, a Sunday school lesson system for mission Sunday schools. It was edited by fellow City Mission board member Richard Frens under synodical auspices.[38]

By 1945 the editor of the *Banner* announced that Christian Reformed congregations were supporting more than one hundred city mission programs. Yet, true to form, he urged more churches

---

[36]   *Banner*, 68/1887 (5/12/1933), 437.
[37]   *Banner*, 72/2082 (3/5/1937), 220.
[38]   *Banner*, 77/2375 (11/27/1942), 1068-69.

to become involved in city evangelism and expressed gratitude that Reformed Bible Institute now existed to prepare people for this work. In a follow-up piece, he commended a forty-six-page pamphlet entitled "Neighborhood Evangelism," produced by the City Mission board, as helpful in expanding interest and involvement in city missions.[39] It reported that twenty Grand Rapids locations, involving 253 workers, were engaged in outreach to the unchurched. Of the workers, eleven were full-time employees, five were part-time, and the rest were volunteers. Kuiper then listed the twenty locations and again commended Reformed Bible Institute's vital role in the work.

H.J. Kuiper's vision, drive, and organizational genius as well as his promotional editorials contributed immeasurably to an era of unparalleled local engagement, before or since, in Christian Reformed urban evangelism. While some of his assumptions and strategies were critiqued vigorously by later denominational leaders, it is noteworthy that a number of the largest and most dynamic Christian Reformed congregations in Grand Rapids a half century later began as chapels under the City Mission board in Kuiper's day.[40] The initiatives demonstrated, in an era of militant orthodoxy, that vigorous and dedicated contending for the faith need not be an impediment but can rather be the driving force behind evangelistic outreach.

[39] *Banner*, 80/2499 (4/13/1945), 340.
[40] The Sunshine, Madison Square, Ivanrest, and Grace congregations are several of the most notable examples.

CHAPTER 8

Reformed Bible Institute

The impetus toward creating a Reformed center for training Christian Reformed people for evangelism, mission work, or other forms of lay leadership within and outside the church began in the second decade of the twentieth century. During the First World War, the five Chicago churches sponsoring the Helping Hand Mission began such an endeavor. In 1922 their classis overtured the synod to recognize it, assume responsibility for it, and appoint trustees or directors to oversee it. The synod declined. Similar overtures from Classis Muskegon, the First Fremont Christian Reformed Church, and again from Classis Illinois were considered later in the decade. When John Vande Water moved to Grand Rapids, the Chicago churches terminated their program and so reported to the synod of 1930. Vande Water apparently had been the moving force behind it. With him gone, the program had been difficult to sustain. Similar work was being conducted in Holland, Michigan.

Classis Illinois was not to be deterred, however. Recognizing a wider interest in such training, Classis Illinois once again approached the synod. This time it asked that the training of mission workers be assigned to Calvin College and Seminary and adduced practical arguments for this strategy. Not coincidentally, a companion overture from Grand Rapids East asked that a denominational training school for mission workers be created.[1] The synod appointed a committee to study the matter, and Vande Water was named to it.

The synod of 1932 took a further step by making interim arrangements for evangelistic and Bible training for interested consistory members, lay missionaries, church educators, evangelists, and anyone else desiring to study the faith more deeply. As reviewed in the last chapter, this synod also established a second committee and mandated it to articulate the principles of Reformed evangelism and to serve synod with the results. Both H.J. Kuiper and John Vande Water were named to the second committee, which submitted its extensive report in 1934.

That same year the synod approved an experimental Bible school on Calvin's campus that satisfied the needs for training lay evangelists and others.[2] The experiment encountered opposition from Calvin's faculty driven by the concern to protect academic standards and accreditation. Although the synod of 1936, which Kuiper served as president, continued the Bible school experiment for two more years,[3] the synod of 1938 terminated the denominational project. However, it commended for prayer and support the local training programs that already existed. It did so based on the advice of the board that had been selected to guide the synodical experiment.

Meanwhile, in Chicago, the Helping Hand Mission board had resumed a part-time teaching program in 1937, at what it called the Reformed Bible Institute—an alternative to the Moody Bible Institute. The superintendent, the Reverend George Weeber, Mark Fakkema, and the Reverend Henry Evenhouse, a young Bible teacher at Chicago Christian High School, taught courses as part of the effort.[4] The synod's endorsement of the several local programs and its acknowledgment of the need for such training in the church rekindled interest in taking the next step. It also gave Kuiper and others added incentive to work toward the creation of an independent Reformed Bible institute that would offer a more complete program for full-time students.

---

[1]   *Agendum, 1930,* I, 27-29; *Acta der Synode, 1930,* 25-26. The overture originated in the Bates Street Christian Reformed Church, with the Reverend D.D. Bonnema.

[2]   *1934 Acts of Synod,* 78-79.

[3]   *1936 Acts of Synod,* 117-19. These pages contain the most succinct, comprehensive review known to me of the various efforts to establish a Reformed Bible school and missionary training center.

[4]   See Swierenga, *Dutch Chicago,* 288-89.

After two informal meetings, the first minuted gathering of the board of what would become the Reformed Bible Institute (RBI) was held March 28, 1939, in Kuiper's living room in the Neland Avenue parsonage. Present were the Reverend Dr. John C. De Korne, secretary of the Christian Reformed Foreign Mission board; Mark Fakkema, still director of the National Union of Christian Schools; the Reverend Oren Holtrop, pastor of the Eastside Christian Reformed Church in Cleveland; the Reverend Cornelius M. Schoolland, pastor of the Harderwyk Christian Reformed Church in Holland; the Reverend John C. Schaal, pastor of the Milwood, Kalamazoo, Christian Reformed Church; the Reverend William Van Peursem, pastor of the Sherman Street Christian Reformed Church in Grand Rapids; Johanna Timmer, dean of women at Calvin College; Albert Reitsma; George J. Stob; G.B. Van Heyningen; and Agnes Vellinga. Stob and Reitsma were active promoters of the Chicago initiative, and Van Heyningen had served as a leading elder at Second Englewood with Kuiper and subsequently with E.J. Tuuk. Absent, according to the first set of minutes, were the Reverend John Vander Ploeg, pastor of the East Paris Christian Reformed Church in Grand Rapids, and P.J. Zondervan, the Grand Rapids publisher. The group was dedicated to establishing a full-fledged Bible institute. To calm anticipated fears in the church, it recorded that it was "unalterably opposed" to the ordination of its graduates as ministers.[5]

The four Chicago board members proposed hiring Timmer as field agent and as the school's first full-time instructor. She left the room while the others discussed the motion, and when she returned, she was offered the position. Those present agreed to underwrite initial expenses, and each committed forty dollars to the fledgling school. That the board's subsequent meetings were usually held at the Neland Avenue church is an indication of both Kuiper's leading role in the cause and probably also of Neland's moral support.

At the second board meeting, a month after the first, the board agreed to meet quarterly. It directed Timmer to begin her promotional work among Chicago-area ministers. It also discussed the advantages and disadvantages of locating the school either in Chicago or in Grand Rapids. Timmer began her work in June. It was daunting—promotions,

[5]   Minutes of the board of the Reformed Bible Institute (RBI), 3/28/1939, art. 6. Henry Beet's short review of Christian Reformed Bible school endeavors does acknowledge Kuiper's central role. Henry Beets, *The Christian Reformed Church: Its Roots, History, Schools and Mission Work* (Grand Rapids: Baker Book House, 1946), 127-30.

1

2

Early homes of the
Reformed Bible Institute:
Wealthy Street (1),
Eastern Avenue (2), and
Robinson Road (3)—all in
Grand Rapids.

3

fund-raising, planning the curriculum, drafting policies, recruiting part-time instructors, locating facilities, and preparing for the arrival of the first students. Kuiper, who chaired the group, and a small executive committee were available as resources, but the initial work was essentially hers. By the fall, sufficient progress had been made that the board decided to hold several evening classes beginning in January. It rented the second floor of a building on Wealthy Street for this purpose, and it decided to use space there for a girl's dormitory as well. The program would be open to all qualified high school graduates.

By the next June, Kuiper reported that he had been criticized severely by the publication committee of the *Banner* for printing several articles promoting the new institute. The committee believed this to be inappropriate, since the school had not been approved by the synod. Thereupon Kuiper had taken up the matter with the synodical committee, which took a more lenient stance and endorsed such exposure until the synod convened.[6] Nonetheless, he advised against giving the school more "free space," and the board approved purchasing a full-page ad in the magazine. Kuiper was delegated to represent the cause at synod, where he asked the synod to "provide moral and financial support" for the school. The synod listened to Kuiper for fifteen minutes and referred the request to its advisory committee. Six days later the committee presented a lengthy review of previous synodical consideration of a possible Bible school, concluded that previous synods had heartily encouraged local training programs but did not approve creating its own school, and recommended that a committee be appointed to study how the Bible institute fitted into the church's system of education and to present its recommendations the following year.[7] Until then, the synod believed it could not provide the requested endorsement. It did permit the school to report receipts from the churches in the church papers, but "without making any propaganda" for the school. As a concession, it suggested that the Grand Rapids consistories consider providing interim financial support, if such should be needed. This was consistent with the endorsements of local training initiatives given by previous synods. Kuiper dutifully reported to the board at its next meeting that although he noted "a favorable undercurrent" of support among delegates, for the next year "propaganda" for the school in church papers would be more harmful than helpful.[8] The board asked Kuiper and Van Peursem to maintain contact on their behalf with the synodical committee.

Appropriately, the board selected Kuiper to speak at the opening festivities of the first, full academic year of the Reformed Bible Institute that September. Timmer, still the only full-time staff member, ran the school, taught, and relied on the part-time instructional services of pastors Rolf Veenstra, William Hendriksen, and William Van Peursem. The *Beacon* appeared as the school's news organ. By January 1941 the board had prematurely formed a nomination of three for president of the school: John Vander Ploeg (first choice), Rolf Veenstra (second choice) and H.J. Kuiper (third choice). It intended to present the

---

[6]   Minutes, RBI, 6/3/1940, art. 5.
[7]   *1940 Acts of Synod*, 120-23.
[8]   Minutes, RBI, 6/26/1940, art. 5.

trio at the association's first annual meeting in June. Just before the association met, however, the board wisely postponed action on naming a president. The first association meeting was held, strategically, at the West Fulton Street Mission. Vande Water and Kuiper both had strong interests in forging a close link between the mission and the school. Twenty-three people attended and nineteen others submitted absentee ballots. Reports were distributed and discussed, the constitution was approved, and Kuiper was elected board president—a position he retained throughout his active ministry and until he died. The board was disappointed when the synod of 1941 deferred action on the status of the institute. The study committee had recommended the institute and similar schools in Christian Reformed circles for prayer and financial support and had suggested steps for keeping the school Reformed as well as keeping it from becoming a competitor with existing denominational schools. But the advisory committee recommended a thorough study of the history of the whole Bible school movement before the synod acted. The synod agreed with the advisory committee. Kuiper, who had been given floor privileges, then rose and pointedly asked whether the board could promote the school in the church papers. The synod deftly responded that it left this in the hands of the publication committee and the editors of church papers. Sentiments were obviously keen on both sides of the issue. Three successive synods had withheld endorsement of what Kuiper and his allies in the cause had in 1939 considered straightforward and obvious, given the 1938 synodical affirmations.

The cause was not helped that fall by an exchange between Fakkema and Calvin College's professor of education, Lambert Flokstra, in the pages of the *Banner*. Fakkema had written an article appealing for a more thoroughly Christian collegiate or "normal school" training of Christian school teachers, particularly at Calvin. Flokstra requested and was given editorial space to respond.[9] He noted that it would have been better for Fakkema to come to the college directly with his request and critique, and it would have been better for the editor not to have published it. Also, as an RBI board member, Fakkema should have known that his published suggestion that future teachers spend a year at the institute in order to strengthen their Christian teaching perspective was unworkable, since RBI's purpose did not include

---

[9]   *Banner*, 76/2323 (11/28/41), 1108.

teacher training. The exchange confirmed fears of RBI encroachment on Calvin turf.

Kuiper mediated. He pointed out that he did not share the perspective of some that denominational ministries should be above review and critique in the church papers. It would be the "worst thing" that could happen, he asserted, if we made our denominational institutions "immune to public criticism."[10] He pointed out that the synod of 1934 had adopted guidelines for the publication board defending this very position. As president of the RBI board, he expressed regret both over Fakkema's suggestion and over Flokstra's rebuttal. He assured readers that Fakkema's proposal had never been discussed by the board, and he agreed that courses there could not be taken for credit in teacher training. RBI has no desire to be a competitor with Calvin, he continued, and he reminded readers that the school was founded only because neither Calvin nor the synod wanted to implement Bible training for lay evangelists and other lay-workers. It is unfair to judge the school out of the misguided fear some have concerning what it might become, he ended.

Despite Kuiper's assurances to the church, the synodical committee that was mandated to provide a recommendation on the status of RBI in light of a comprehensive review of the genesis and history of Bible schools disappointed the board. It communicated before the synod convened that it found its mandate impossibly broad, the needed resources for its work nonexistent, and the time frame of one year inconsistent with the synod's recent policy of giving study committees two years to complete their work. It communicated that it had no report or recommendation for the synod of 1942.

Kuiper was incensed. The delay of four synods in endorsing the school would hurt enrollment, inhibit funding, and maintain a muzzle on the church papers regarding the school. "We are in need of Christian layworkers. If our day school course suffers, some of our future kingdom workers will obtain their Bible institute education at places like Moody," Kuiper read into the school's board minutes.[11] Furthermore, the claim that Calvin would suffer by such endorsement is "unfounded." Meanwhile, the people sponsoring the evening classes in both Paterson and Chicago were petitioning RBI to give credit in its program for the courses they were teaching. A committee with

[10]   Ibid., 1109.
[11]   Minutes, RBI, 4/21/1942, art. 9.

representation from all three places and chaired by Timmer was appointed to work out the details. The board must have judged that a softer voice than Kuiper's would suit its cause better, for it designated board member J.C. De Korne to speak on behalf of the institute at the synod of 1942.

This time the synod turned the tables on both its study committee and its advisory committee, which expected that a routine request for a reasonable extension would be granted. But on the synod's table were three freshly minted, detailed, and thoughtful overtures in favor of granting RBI its simple but stagnating request for synod's blessing for moral and financial support. All three were read on the floor and included in the record.

One, from Classis Illinois, argued simply that it was unfair to a growing institution engaged in work cordially applauded by previous synods to delay action a third time. The synod had had ample time; the work was suffering; it was time to act.

The second overture was from the Rochester, New York, church, where charter RBI trustee Oren Holtrop was serving. It documented (1) that previous synods urged churches to do local mission work, also through lay workers; (2) that they had recognized the importance of proper preparation of these workers; (3) that RBI was providing that training; (4) that the esteemed committee reporting in 1941 had provided a thorough review supporting its recommendation for the requested endorsement; and (5) that the people through their giving were demonstrating their readiness to support RBI. The synod should extend to RBI the endorsement the synod of 1938 gave local, evening Bible school programs.

The third overture was from the Sherman Street congregation, which was attended by a number of RBI students who were doing effective work in Grand Rapids city missions. The overtures were reinforced by an articulate minority report from the advisory committee. The next morning the synod approved the Reformed Bible Institute for moral and financial support. No indication appears in the synod's record that De Korne ever had to speak on behalf of the school or that the majority report of the advisory committee ever reached the floor. RBI had finally been granted its coveted synodical endorsement.

Sounding like the proud father he was, Kuiper wrote a glowing report for the synod of 1943.[12] The school had deployed its first

---

[12]   *1943 Acts of Synod*, Supplement XXII, 350-52.

eleven graduates the previous December, and all but one who desired placement were now serving in strategic ministries. Another seven were scheduled to graduate that June; he listed the positions four had already accepted. He also listed the full- and part-time teaching staff. He reported that the board had purchased its own property on Eastern Avenue for $6,000, spent $4,000 on renovations and had a remaining indebtedness of only $1,700 that he predicted would be liquidated before the end of the summer. He invited synodical delegates to tour the facilities and thanked the synod for its endorsement that would open the way for ordained ministers to accept appointments as teachers and administrators.

With the synod's endorsement in hand, the board set in motion the search process for RBI's first president. The Reverend Dick H. Walters, pastor of the Central Avenue Christian Reformed Church in Holland, Michigan, soon received and accepted the appointment.

The following year, after protracted debate, the synod again endorsed the Reformed Bible Institute for moral and financial support. In a slightly condescending tone, it stated that the matter of the place of RBI in the whole Reformed educational enterprise can best be judged when its standards have improved and it has demonstrated in peace-time conditions to what extent it can attract and retain male students. The synod went on record that the RBI board had neither sought nor been given synod's endorsement of a rather ambitious capital campaign it had launched under its new president. It neglected to acknowledge that previous synods neither required requests for nor gave campaign endorsements for other nonecclesiastical organizations approved for support.

With an administration in place and the school recommended for the prayers and support of the churches, Kuiper's work as president of the board assumed a more routine character. He worked with Walters from time to time on constitutional revisions. He designed strategies for fund-raising efforts, was active in staff recruitment and appointments, and served on the educational policy committee. Once synodical endorsement had been achieved, and despite the synod's expressed interest in keeping a watchful eye on the organization to be assured that it remained Reformed and that it did not compete with Calvin College, Kuiper and the board soon stopped sending annual reports to the synod.[13] Whether due to neglect or by deliberate intent, the absence of informative, courtesy reports to the synod was uncharacteristic of organizations approved for support by the churches. The reports resumed in 1968, with a change in board and administrative leadership.

Meanwhile, though it was never large, the school flourished and demonstrated that it could attract and hold male as well as female students once the Second World War had ended. The Reformed Bible Institute was a natural result and an extension of H.J. Kuiper's commitment to city missions as well as an institutional expression of the importance he placed on a deeply devotional knowledge of scripture for the life of faith. The school remained his cherished cause, and he its esteemed board president until his dying day.

---

[13]   Kuiper and Fakkema signed a report that stated the RBI case for a "national Bible day school" in the Christian Reformed system of education, *1944 Acts of Synod,* 301-10. Treasurer George Stob for several years submitted financial reports to the synod. Kuiper wrote a report in 1947, *1947 Acts of Synod,* 404-406. Frieda Monsma, an RBI secretary, submitted reports in 1949 and 1950, *1949 Acts o f Synod,* 260-64 and *1950 Acts of Synod,* 386-88, after which they disappear from the synodical record.

CHAPTER 9

The Editorship

The Reverend Henry J. Kuiper is known most widely for his editorship of the *Banner*, the weekly inspirational and informational magazine of the Christian Reformed Church. He held the post longer than anyone in its history—longer by a little than the Reverend Dr. Henry Beets, his immediate predecessor. The paper achieved a level of denominational prominence and influence under his leadership unknown before or since his tenure.[1]

Beginnings

If Kuiper reluctantly and after considerable soul-searching accepted the appointment as *Banner* editor, after a year on the job he admitted to readers that "the work has been more pleasant than we anticipated, and not as hard as we feared."[2]

At the outset he assured subscribers that he had no hobby horses to ride and no axes to grind. He merely wanted to "speak the truth in love." In italics he promised that when he disagreed with someone on controversial issues before the church, he would articulate his position, then give the editorial page to a spokesperson for the opposing view. The policy was too generous editorially and he never implemented it. He did adhere consistently to the conviction that full and frank discussion is a

---

[1] For a recent, brief review of Kuiper's editorship see Schaap, *Our Family Album*, 273-83. He is also cited regularly in Schaap's subsequent narrative.

[2] *Banner*, 64/1714 (12/27/1929), 980.

The Christian Reformed Publishing House on Eastern Avenue in Grand Rapids, Michigan, home of the *Banner* and *De Wachter* for all but the last several years of Kuiper's editorship.

"safeguard" of denominational peace. He also used his pen unswervingly to promote denominational ministries, defend denominational values, and inform people of denominational developments. Two dangers which he aimed to avoid were "provincialism" and "metropolitanism," a quirky term that connoted too amicable an attitude toward the broader American culture.

When Kuiper began his work as editor, the *Banner* had been the Christian Reformed Church's English-language weekly for almost fifteen years. The synod had purchased it for five thousand dollars in 1914 from a group of individuals called The Banner of Truth Publishing Company. The magazine had originated in and been identified with the True Protestant Reformed Dutch Church, or Classis Hackensack. The churches of Classis Hackensack had joined the Christian Reformed Church in 1890, and some Christian Reformed members had been reading the magazine, then a monthly, for several decades by that time. Henry Beets led the group that formed the company and purchased the publication in 1903. It then had only three hundred subscribers and was almost defunct. He became its editor and succeeded in reviving it, soon transforming it into a weekly magazine and giving it a Christian Reformed identity. Kuiper had been a strong advocate of bringing the paper under synodical control in 1912 and again—this time successfully—in 1914, since by that time it was perceived as the English-language voice of the denomination.

Putting his predecessor's picture on the front cover of his first issue, Kuiper wrote that Beets had been a remarkable editor, noted for his diligence, energy, vision, and broadmindedness. This public praise was a different posture from the one Kuiper and the Second Englewood consistory had taken a decade earlier in their communication to the publication committee asking for Beets's removal. Then they argued that the church needed a more distinctively Reformed, less culturally accommodating editor, and had proposed suitable replacements. Now, however, Kuiper recognized that by the time Beets's twenty-five-year career as editor had ended, the magazine had grown to 11,500 subscribers—a remarkable record of success. It was received and read in half of all Christian Reformed homes.[3]

Organization

Both the *Banner* and *De Wachter,* the widely read Dutch-language organ of the denomination that had originated in 1867, were under the supervision of the synod's publication committee. The chairman of the committee when Kuiper began was the Reverend Peter A. Hoekstra, who had recently moved from western Michigan to become pastor of the Second Christian Reformed Church of Cicero, Illinois. J.B. Hulst, the Grand Rapids publisher and churchman already encountered in this narrative, was vice president and a licensed exhorter in Christian Reformed churches. Professor William Heyns ably served as committee secretary. Other members were the Reverend E.F.J. Van Halsema, pastor of the Fuller Avenue Christian Reformed Church, and G.J. Rooks, H. Denkema, and M. Hoffius. The laymen were all from the Grand Rapids area and were prominent denominational, civic, and business figures. The committee was unusual in that the nonordained members outnumbered the ministers. Denkema, Heyns, and Hulst had been on

---

[3] John Kromminga reports that in 1917, "the earliest figure available," there were 3,275 subscribers and 30,000 by 1947, based on a letter he had received from business manager J.J. Buiten. *The Christian Reformed Church,* 165.

the publication committee continuously from the time the *Banner* had been taken over by the synod; Heyns had been on the *De Wachter* committee even before 1914.

Sometime between January 1, 1924, and December 31, 1925, revenues from subscriptions to the *Banner* overtook those from sales of *De Wachter*; the financial report for those two years showed they came to $30,409.54 and $29,427.29 respectively.[4] The disparity widened rapidly in the next few years, and it is a reliable indicator of the pace of Americanization in the church. Four years later the totals were $46,239.04 and $29,488.58 for the two papers.[5] The cost of a subscription for either publication remained a uniform $2 per year in the late 1920s. Kuiper's counterpart at *De Wachter* was the Reverend Henry Keegstra, who had moved from Holland, Michigan, to Allendale, Michigan, the month before Kuiper became editor of the *Banner*.

About the time Kuiper was named editor, the *Banner* was undergoing significant revision and the publication committee was reassessing its role. The size of the magazine had been increased by the 1926 synod because it had been judged to be the more prominent of its two publications. The committee and Henry Beets had discussed strategies for using the new space to serve a constituency increasingly engaged with the wider culture. They had tried several new departments but were not entirely satisfied with some that mimicked those in *De Wachter*. Three prospective department editors had turned them down when asked to contribute. Noting that a number of other church periodicals were successfully introducing columns by and for women, and certain that the talent for producing one of their own existed in the church, Beets persuaded the lukewarm committee to introduce it. "Vera" wrote an experimental series, which was not continued. More enthusiasm and success attached to the introduction of monthly reports on the college and the seminary. The committee also desired that professors write feature articles more frequently in order to expose both them and their fields of expertise to readers. The college professors pleaded problems with writing short, popular pieces on complex matters; seminary professors participated more willingly. "Least of all, our magazines must not be colorless. They must illumine and esteem our principles, and they must state our positions clearly and faithfully,"

---

[4]   *Acta der Synode, 1926,* 289.
[5]   *Acta der Synode, 1930,* 287.

the committee stated[6] (translation mine). When Kuiper assumed the position of editor-in-chief, therefore, the *Banner* was still looking for a more effective format and a contemporary, more serviceable identity.

The synod that appointed Kuiper also adopted a substantially revised set of "Rules and Regulations Governing the Publication Committee." The previous ones had been in place since 1910. Since then the *Banner* had been acquired by the denomination, subscriptions had increased, a printing plant and its staff had been added, and other printing projects had been undertaken. The committee proposed the revisions after careful review, deliberation, and formulation. The synod approved them as submitted and ordered them translated into English.

The various articles or regulations called for the incorporation of the publication committee as a legal entity in the state of Michigan. They set terms for the seven members at four years, and made them renewable with no limit on the number of consecutive terms that could be served. They called for a minimum of one meeting a month, which made it desirable that committee members have convenient access to Grand Rapids. They provided that the editors of the two papers and the business manager might attend meetings in an advisory capacity "if necessary and desirable." They defined the work of the committee as supervising the work of the editors, giving advice to the editors and coeditors when asked or when necessary, settling any disputes over placement of material, appointing and supervising a business manager, setting the salary of the same, making interim appointments between synods, and providing reports to the synod. The regulations also stipulated that the committee might nominate editors-in-chief to the synod and that the committee might appoint the coeditors or department editors, "in consultation with the editors-in-chief." Finally, the regulations required annual auditing of the books, directed that profits after the needs of the magazines had been met were to be given to the college and seminary, and limited the work of the printing shop to jobs done for the denomination.

The effect of the "Rules and Regulations" was to create a small, geographically limited, virtually self-perpetuating committee that determined the broad shape of the magazines, both in terms of departments and department editors. The committee curbed

---

[6]   *Acta der Synode, 1928,* 256. The committee report to the 1928 synod, 251-62, gives a good review of the new initiatives.

involvement of the two editors in policy making, and it accorded the department editors freedom from editorial intrusion by the editors-in-chief. Furthermore, the new policies did not clarify the relationship between the business manager and the two editors. For their efforts, the editors of the two denominational magazines were given two-year, renewable appointments, a stipend of six hundred dollars a year for 1929, and the certainty that come reappointment time they would stand in nomination against a number of other denominational lights. The committee and the synod kept them on short leashes. The stipend for producing fifty-two issues of a twenty-four-page paper was equivalent to less than 20 percent of Kuiper's Broadway salary. Given the realities of the offer, it is not difficult to understand why he first withdrew his name when nominated, then took a half year and successfully negotiated several concessions before accepting his appointment as editor-in-chief. Several ambiguities and lacunae related to the editorship as presented in the regulations would become problematic, if not matters of contention, in years to come.

Division of Labor

The coeditors and the departments of the *Banner* during Kuiper's first term were

Zachary J. Sherda, "Our Doctrine";
Jan Karel Van Baalen, "The Sunday School Lesson";
Edward J. Tanis, "Timely Topics";
Leonard Trap, "A Word a Week";
Henry Beets, "Mission Work of Our Denomination";
James M. Ghysels, "Meditation."

All were ordained ministers. Sherda was a pastor in Evergreen Park, Illinois, a charge which afforded him the opportunity to pursue courses at the University of Chicago and post-graduate studies at McCormick Theological Seminary. He was a thoughtful, studious, and discerning man with a fine library and an inquiring mind. In 1930 he accepted a call to the church in Cutlerville, Michigan, his third charge, from which he retired in 1953. Sherda's department was phased out within two years of Kuiper's arrival.

Van Baalen, four years younger than Sherda and five years Kuiper's junior, had continued his theological studies at Princeton, arriving there from the Netherlands in 1914. When the First World War made his return problematic, he sought ordination in the Christian Reformed Church. The author of seven books, including a widely appreciated study on the cults, he was for seventeen years in charge of the Sunday school lessons that were published weekly.

The career of Edward J. Tanis most closely interfaced with that of Kuiper. He preceded Kuiper as pastor of the Broadway church and was the minister of Second Englewood when Kuiper became editor. He was American-born, taught for a year at Grand Rapids Christian High School, wrote several books, and took graduate courses at the University of Chicago and Northern Baptist Theological Seminary. He was a mainstay at the *Banner*, to which he contributed his keen insights on contemporary life from 1919 until his death in 1958.

Born in 1885, ordained in 1914, Leonard Trap was pastor of the Second Roseland Christian Reformed Church in Chicago when Kuiper assumed the editorship. He had been a camp pastor and army chaplain during the First World War, which gave him a wider than usual perspective for his wide-ranging column.

Henry Beets, after yielding the editorship of the *Banner*, wrote the column on missions in his capacity as full-time director of denominational missions. The directorship had become a full-time position in 1920, the year the denomination embarked on overseas missions in China. Beets had been converted as a young immigrant living in Luctor, Kansas; had studied under Geerhardus Vos at the seminary; and had encouraged Americanization in his pastorates at the La Grave Avenue and Burton Heights congregations. He served as stated clerk of the denomination from 1902 to 1942. Outgoing and civic-minded, Henry Beets had an enormous circle of friends and contacts and more than anyone in his day became the public face of the Christian Reformed Church outside the denomination. Muskingum College in Ohio awarded him an honorary doctorate of letters in 1911, which title he thereafter used without hesitation or apology. He was sixteen years Kuiper's senior.

James M. Ghysels, like Kuiper, was born in Grand Rapids in 1885. He graduated from Calvin Seminary and was ordained a year after Kuiper. Then, while in his first charge, he studied for a year at Princeton Seminary, from which he like many other Christian Reformed pastors of the era received the B.D. degree. By the time Kuiper became editor, Ghysels was in his last and longest charge, Lafayette, Indiana, from which he retired in 1951. For thirty-six years he wrote the weekly devotions for the *Banner*; a number of them were collected and published in two volumes.[7]

This cadre of department editors was a remarkably gifted group of colleagues for Kuiper. Most of them had broader theological exposure in the American context than he did. All of them were competent in English as well as Dutch. They were balanced, discerning, substantive, and principled in their commitment to the Reformed faith. If they were not accountable to him as editor-in-chief, they complemented him confessionally and intellectually. If he thought some of them were more culturally accommodating than was healthy, as he certainly did regarding Henry Beets, he respected them to a man. Beets was the oldest, at sixty; the others were all experienced, effective pastors in their early to mid-forties, like Kuiper. Together they produced a meaty denominational magazine whose impact on the Christian Reformed membership for the next several decades was enormous.

Neither the editor-in-chief nor the coeditors, as the department editors were called, ran the magazine. In fact, they were watched closely by the publication committee, all having to be reappointed every two years. The same arrangement obtained for *De Wachter*. Occasionally a coeditor was not reappointed. The day-to-day operations of both publications were in the hands of Jacob Buiten. He was assisted by Jacob Van Ess as field agent.

Van Ess had begun his promotional work on the magazine's staff in 1907,[8] when he was employed to sell advertising space and subscriptions. He became the field agent for both *De Wachter* and the *Banner* when the latter was purchased by the denomination in 1914, and he in effect became a denominational employee under the supervision of the publication committee.

As early as 1912 the publication committee had proposed hiring an administrator for *De Wachter*, but the synod had refused. In 1916 it failed to approve the publication committee's recommendation to subcontract the responsibility for printing and administration to an outside source, while protecting the church's control of the magazines.[9] Finally, urged by the newly formed business subcommittee of J.B. Hulst and Henry Denkema, the publication committee had retained a

---

[7]   Most of the biographical material in these paragraphs was garnered from the sketches and tributes published in the Christian Reformed *Yearbook* the year following the death of each man.

[8]   *1947 Acts of Synod*, 225.

[9]   *Acta der Synode, 1916*, 22.

consultant, studied the problem, and hired Buiten in January, 1917, to administer the business affairs of the denomination's publications.

Buiten introduced a new system of record keeping. Van Ess gained new advertisers and subscribers for both magazines. "At the same time, many other improvements were introduced, too many to mention, but of great significance for the good operation of our church papers," the committee reported[10] (translation mine). The result was that by the synod of 1918 the remaining indebtedness on the *Banner* had been paid off, a cash surplus of five thousand dollars had been created, and "a larger contribution than ever before" had been distributed to the theological school.

We could do even better, the committee promised, if we created our own small printing operation that printed our two church papers. The synod that year gave its approval, admonishing that the operation was to be used only for church projects. It obviously did not desire to compete commercially with the several Dutch printing and publishing houses in Grand Rapids, or to put itself in the compromised position of giving the contract to Hulst. It also raised the stipends for the editors and coeditors, eliminated the subscription discount for ministers and professors, and approved rate increases.

By the time Kuiper became editor of the *Banner*, therefore, the administration of day-to-day operations was well established and in the capable hands of Buiten and Van Ess, supervised by the business subcommittee of the publication committee. Any disagreements about the placement of material were referred to an editorial subcommittee for resolution. In 1929 the editorial subcommittee consisted of Hoekstra, Heyns, and Van Halsema—the ordained members of the publication committee. The business committee was composed of Denkema, Hoffius, Hulst, and Rooks—the nonordained members.

Scope of Authority

As Kuiper began his editorial work, he had a fairly clear idea of the scope of his authority. The fall before, as he was negotiating with the committee, it had told him it was disinclined to formulate a list of the editors' duties because the editor was an appointee of the synod and should have the freedom to develop the position as he judged best, within the broad framework of the "Rules and Regulations."[11] It also

[10] *Acta der Synode, 1918*, 127.
[11] Minutes of the Publication Committee of the Christian Reformed Church, 7/10/1928, art. 5.

gave him liberty to assign book reviews to others and to have someone else write the brief notes on Grand Rapids events and news and the obituary notices, if he so chose.

He gauged the committee's authority when it sided with Van Ess in refusing to add a second full-time field agent and to expand the territory of a part-time agent in Chicago, and when it supported Buiten over Professor Schoolland, who wanted his column to run weekly instead of biweekly in *De Wachter*.[12] Kuiper noted with satisfaction that the committee at the same meeting deferred action on the request of Henry Beets and the mission board that a column on missions be added to both papers, because this was *de facto* to add a new department and needed the approval of the editors. Kuiper willingly gave his consent. In Kuiper's second month as editor, however, the committee disapproved of his suggestion to reprint editorials from other magazines and to make changes in the placement of letters and comments on them because they required too much additional space.[13] A month passed, then the committee reacted favorably to his suggestion for a new department on "spiritual life," provided Kuiper could identify a competent coeditor for it. Meanwhile, he should write the articles from time to time, the committee directed.[14] When he sought the committee's advice on resolving a dispute between Clarence Bouma, who had written a negative review of an Eerdmans book, and William B. Eerdmans, it counseled him to run the review and to give Eerdmans space for rebuttal.[15] But the editorial subcommittee intervened when Kuiper returned three articles by John Vander Mey responding to Kuiper's critique of his position on Christian schools. As reviewed earlier, it directed that Vander Mey be allotted space for two articles.[16]

In the spring of 1930, sixteen months into his first term, Kuiper raised a fundamental question. "Who actually manages the publication of the magazines?" he posed to the business subcommittee[17] (translation mine). The subcommittee discussed the issue. It reported to the full committee that a situation had developed in both the position of business manager and the position of the editor that was "not entirely proper." The publication committee discussed the situation and

[12]   Minutes, Publication Committee, 12/4/1928, arts. 4 and 5.
[13]   Minutes, Publication Committee 2/6/1929, art. 5.
[14]   Minutes, Publication Committee, 3/5/1929, art. 12.
[15]   Minutes, Publication Committee, 7/10/1929, art. 13.
[16]   Minutes, Publication Committee, 2/4/1930, art. 8. See pp. 98-101.
[17]   Minutes, Publication Committee, 4/2/1930, art. 5.

referred it back to the business committee for "further consideration." Buiten said the problem was that the coeditors submitted more copy than could be used. He was deciding what to run and when. The magazine was paying for material it could not use. Buiten was *de facto* making editorial decisions. Both Buiten and Kuiper asked to be heard and were invited to submit suggested plans for resolution. The committee drew from both and limited the size of articles and their frequency for the various departments. It also drafted and approved more explicit regulations on the relationship of the two editors to the business manager. Having gained some ground, Kuiper pressed further. He wondered whether the editor-in-chief shouldn't have some responsibility for the content of the material submitted by coeditors. The publication committee responded emphatically that he was free to offer his opinions and suggestions to coeditors, but no more.[18] Might he then edit or abbreviate material in the "Calvinalia" column? he countered. He was granted permission to do so on the grounds that this column was news, and the person submitting it on behalf of the college and seminary was not a coeditor. He was admonished to use restraint, however, since the committee had found it difficult over the years to find someone on campus to provide good copy.

In its report to the synod of 1930, the publication committee glossed over some of the extended discussions of the previous several months and their outcomes. It gave a positive account of subscriptions, staff relations, and editorial developments. They reported that the "Our Doctrine" column had been discontinued, and the editor had introduced "special articles" to inject more variety into the *Banner*. He had expanded his "Timely Topics" rubric to include more church news. The committee signaled this change as important for developing in the younger, more Americanized reader a principled outlook on Reformed faith and life. The quality of articles in general had improved, and the committee liked the column on readers' questions and reactions that Kuiper had started.[19] When the synod voted, he was elected for a second term from a nomination that included himself and Clarence Bouma.

Editorial Style

Kuiper's editorial style included interacting with his readers. Frequently in his editorials he would quote extensively, with their

---

[18]   Minutes, Publication Committee, 6/3/1930, art. 9.
[19]   See *Acta der Synode*, 1930, 277-87 for the full report.

permission, from letters readers had written him. Often he would editorialize on subjects they raised in communications with him or in response to specific requests. In the early years he ran a column next to his editorials entitled, "Comments and Correspondence." Here he would give short responses and comments to two or three letters he had received. Sometimes these responses would precipitate a series of editorials.

A case in point is a series of two longer editorials responding to issues readers raised about a very short paragraph he had written on the "haphazard" way in which consistories created trios for calling ministers.[20] The editorials covered points he had made in earlier ones, but which deserved revisiting in the light of the new interest and questions regarding the matter.[21]

Kuiper's engagement with his readers and his responsiveness to their questions and interests contributed to his longevity as editor. Even when he disagreed with his correspondents, he usually did so respectfully and appreciatively. But he could become acerbic and manipulative when he perceived that influential leaders in the church were less than genuine, presented doctrinally dangerous views, or were condescending or inept in approach. That he was courteous and responsive toward the general reader and not intimidated by intellectual leaders whom he judged threatening to Christian Reformed values made him the champion of many. His approach won him multitudes of devoted, appreciative readers in the constituency. As editor, he was a populist.

Another prominent feature of Kuiper's style was his spiritual concern for readers and for the church. He considered the editorship a ministry of the Word. Look at the magazine as "your assistant pastor," he wrote in 1931.[22] It "brings messages of spiritual information, consolation, guidance, and inspiration." He saw the whole denomination as his congregation. With this perspective, he tried to keep people close to the Bible, doctrinally faithful, and obedient to the Lord. A high ideal in this regard was his desire to foster denominational identity, loyalty, pride, and obligation. He solicited prayers for himself and the magazine as servants of the Lord and the church.

---

[20] *Banner,* 87/2875 (9/5/1952), 1086.

[21] *Banner,* 87/2887 (11/28/1952), 1444-45, 1469; and *Banner,* 87/2888 (12/5/1952), 1476-77, 1501.

[22] *Banner,* 66/1796 (7/31/1931), 692.

In his closing editorial, Kuiper confessed that throughout his career he had felt a "duty" to write about "spiritual, theological, and ethical" dangers, since a church paper is the most effective medium to counteract these threats. The Bible and their ordination vows compel ministers to do this from the pulpit, and they compelled him to do the same with his pen. This approach makes an editor of a church paper vulnerable to the charge that he is trying to dictate to the church, he noted, but he believed deeply that he was called to be a watchman against the wolves that threaten Christ's sheep. "The chief concern of every church should be to cling with might and main to its heritage of truth and to preserve its best traditions. This is not easy. In fact, nothing is harder than to prevent its gradual, almost imperceptible slipping away from its moorings."[23] Keen spiritual discernment is needed to distinguish between healthy changes and religious compromises, he said. Kuiper was not a compromiser.

In the same piece, the editor expressed his appreciation—his amazement—for the vitality in Christian Reformed congregations for benevolence, Christian schools, and missions. One thing, however, made him "very apprehensive." With all the emphasis on pure doctrine, Christian Reformed people lacked doctrinal discernment, in his opinion. This left him "disillusioned." Thirty years before, Janssen, whose lectures "showed clear traces of higher criticism and liberalism," found many defenders, even after the synod of 1922 "unanimously condemned his views."[24] Kuiper referred with surprise to a recent dissertation by "one of our prominent ministers" that alleges that since then "the forces of reaction" have prevailed in the denomination. The last half century had produced "other instances" of heretical teaching and of following popular figures when their teaching should have been rejected. He identified several instances.

It was the year of the denomination's centennial, and it was important in that setting to engage "in penetrating self-examination and confess that we have not been as faithful as we should have been in contending for the faith." The most important concern should be that people do not strive for a closer walk with God, for this is "the root of all the worldliness that plagues the churches of our day, of all the doctrinal indifference and of the prevailing laxity in discipline." Many who are deeply concerned about "external unity" are indifferent

---

[23]   *Banner,* 91/3076 (8/31/1956), 1060.
[24]   Ibid.

to "spiritual and doctrinal unity," which are more basic and important. With apologies for where he may have failed to speak the truth in love, Kuiper concluded that he hoped that his service may have contributed to the "spiritual uplift" of Christian Reformed people and to the "preservation of our precious Reformed heritage."[25]

Kuiper's pastoral concern for the spiritual strength and well-being of the church had always been obvious. It had never been stated as fully, explicitly, or sincerely as in his closing editorial. A substantial portion of the denomination respected him deeply for it. It more than anything was the hallmark of his editorial style.

Pet Projects

H.J. Kuiper had a penchant for launching pet projects from his editor's desk. He was not content merely to reflect on the need for important initiatives in the church. He frequently created the organizational structures for addressing those needs, then used the editorial page to enlist support for the endeavors. The Reformed Bible Institute is the most notable example. Sometimes he trumpeted causes in which he had been involved before becoming editor, such as Christian schools and city missions. As editor he initiated several pet projects.

One noteworthy innovation early in his tenure was the sponsorship of correspondence courses by the *Banner*. A reader taking such a course from a Bible institute wrote asking whether Christian Reformed leaders could not provide such courses for interested church members.[26] Kuiper liked the idea. It appealed to his core value of developing a biblically informed, unapologetically Reformed faith in readers. He explored the suggestion with others, and he requested readers' reaction to it. He suggested four possible categories of courses that might be offered.

When the response proved encouraging, a committee, chaired by Heyns, was created, and the Reverend William Stuart, Bible instructor at Grand Rapids Christian High School, offered the first course. It was called "The Bible Book by Book," and it was first offered in the fall of 1931. Interest was overwhelming. Stuart reported that 335 people had enrolled.[27] He structured the course in such a way that students could proceed at their own pace, guided by materials he had developed and

---

[25]   Ibid., 1061.
[26]   *Banner,* 66/1782 (4/24/1931), 381.
[27]   *Banner,* 67/1804 (10/2/1931), 861-62.

by Davis's *Dictionary of the Bible,* both available at a reasonable price, postpaid. By the next spring 460 correspondence students were involved for a fee of $5 each. The project grossed $2,300 that first year—in the depths of the Great Depression.

The publication committee sanctioned two additional courses: one on the books of Genesis and Matthew, also taught by Stuart, and one on "Predictive Prophecy" taught by Professor Henry Schultze of the seminary faculty. Later in the Depression, interest slipped. Only a fifth as many people enrolled in 1933-1934 as in the first year, and by 1937 the publication committee reported to synod that only thirty-six had signed up that year.

But Kuiper resuscitated the program at the end of the decade. Stuart taught until his death in 1941. Schultze continued to offer his course even after he assumed the presidency of Calvin College in 1940. And the Reverend Dr. John Bratt, a young minister, taught a course on Paul's epistles and in 1943 was planning a second on the other New Testament letters when the publication committee sold the program to RBI. Its new president, the Reverend Dr. Dick Walters, intended to expand it.[28]

Editor Kuiper proposed or added other initiatives that were beyond the scope of editing the *Banner.* Some the publication committee countenanced; some it did not. It liked his idea of sending the magazine free of charge to Christian Reformed young men in the Civilian Conservation Corps during the Depression.[29] As acting chair of the psalter-hymnal committee, Kuiper urged the publication committee to assume responsibility for copyrighting and marketing the book in the absence of any arrangements by the synod of 1932.[30] The venture was highly successful. The first twenty thousand copies sold out in thirty days, and the committee made arrangements to have another twenty thousand printed immediately.[31] They sold for $1.10 per copy—hardcover.

On the other hand, the publication committee judged that Kuiper's proposal to create a marriage bureau would move them beyond its synodically mandated jurisdiction.[32] At the same meeting

[28] *Banner,* 78/2414 (8/27/1943), 701.
[29] Minutes, Publication Committee, 1/2/1934, art. 4.
[30] See pp. 85-86 for Kuiper's leadership on this project. Also, Minutes, Publication Committee, 1/29/1934, art. 3.
[31] *1936 Acts of Synod,* 244.
[32] Minutes, Publication Committee, 12/3/1935, art. 3.

the committee responded to his letter asking that the *Banner* promote the work of the City Mission board, which he chaired, by noting that other organizations paid for advertising space and that the board should also. The board countered quickly with a letter requesting the publication committee's compliance with the synod of 1934's directive to publish in pamphlet form the report on Reformed evangelism which Kuiper and John Vande Water had helped write.[33] It asked that it be done within a month so that the pamphlet could be used at a forthcoming convention of city mission workers. The business subcommittee was reluctant to do so, judging that the market for it was slim and that mission agencies that wanted it could have it printed in quantities. But, under synodical orders and almost two years after having received the assembly's directive, it ultimately complied with the request.

In the late 1930s and early 1940s Kuiper initiated and sponsored the program called "Know Your Bible League." It reflected his conviction that thorough and correct biblical knowledge was the basis of everything important and good in the church. The program enlisted people through his editorials for a program of memorizing seven Bible texts a week for seven weeks. Those who achieved the goal had their names published in the *Banner.*

With the help of readers, a second, third, and fourth cycle of texts were added. Buiten cooperated in soliciting money to pay for awarding a copy of *The Psalter Hymnal* to those who reached a designated goal. This helped sales, which Buiten liked. It got good religious music into more homes, which Kuiper liked. But the publication committee challenged the frequency with which the editor was writing on the program, warned the staff not to withhold articles in order to publish the growing lists of successful participants, and finally declined to take over financial sponsorship of the program. Soon after, the program faded.[34] The Evergreen Park consistory in Illinois wrote the committee about its unhappiness that Kuiper had suggested editorially that consistories stand the cost of hymnals for the winners. Responding, the committee washed its hands of any responsibility, attributing the project completely to Kuiper, and Kuiper apologized for "having compromised" the committee.[35]

---

[33]   Minutes, Publication Committee, 4/7/1936, art. 5.
[34]   Minutes, Publication Committee, 2/1/1940, art. 7; 5/1/1940, art. 12; 6/5/ 1941, art. 12; 11/6/1941, art. 8.
[35]   Minutes, Publication Committee, 7/3/1941, art. 2.

Another educational venture of longstanding interest to Kuiper was Sunday school lesson material. He had found satisfaction in the synod's decision to develop its own denominational material and in its discouragement of use of International Sunday School lessons. Meanwhile Vande Water's *Sunday School Newsie* was being used in mission-chapel Sunday school programs. The Grand Rapids City Mission board, after significant discussion, dispatched two members to meet with the publication committee to propose making the denominational material more "mission friendly," which would allow phasing out the independent material. After attempting to adjust its regular Sunday school curriculum and materials as requested, the committee proposed to the synod of 1942 that it approve production of a separate curriculum for mission Sunday schools.[36] The synod approved the proposal. It did not follow its advisory committee's recommendation that H.J. Kuiper and Richard Frens, both members of the City Mission board, be named to the committee charged with developing the curriculum. Kuiper was overextended; the publication committee and the Neland consistory were at that time attempting to reduce his load, not increase it. But for a number of years the publication committee produced a Sunday school curriculum and lesson materials tailored specifically for use in mission chapels.

Creating synergies between projects close to his heart was a Kuiper trait. The *Banner* became a platform for city mission work, for equipping believers for evangelism, and for training lay workers through correspondence courses and eventually through the Reformed Bible Institute.

Achievements and Recognition

The success of editors is judged by how widely they are read and how seriously they are taken. By that standard, H.J. Kuiper was a very successful editor. The *Banner* had 11,500 subscribers in January 1929, 38,600 in August 1956. Those numbers represented 50 percent and 82 percent of Christian Reformed families, respectively. More significantly, the magazine was read carefully, almost devoutly. Sabbath patterns and practices in most Christian Reformed homes included reading the *Banner,* often from cover to cover. Sunday recreation and travel were taboo; reading the denominational weekly between services was

[36] Minutes, Publication Committee, 4/3/1942, art. 5. Cf. *1942 Acts of Synod,* Supplement IX, 309-13 for the full proposal.

encouraged. Kuiper's convictions and opinions were well known from his editorials, and they were quoted and discussed regularly, sometimes challenged passionately. In his assessment of Kuiper's life and influence, John H. Kromminga, who had been catechized and made profession of faith at the Neland Avenue church under Kuiper, wrote, "No man in our time has left a deeper imprint on the Christian Reformed Church than Henry J. Kuiper."[37]

Opposition and Critique

But Kuiper also encountered a level of opposition and critique predictable given the positions he held and the forthrightness with which he expressed them. His extended exchanges with John Vander Mey over Christian education the first year of his editorship and the resistance he encountered over the founding of the Reformed Bible Institute a decade later have already been reviewed.[38] "Being editor of a church paper is no task for one who cannot stand criticism," he noted, reflecting on negative reactions he had received for his opinions on singing hymns in worship.[39] He had objected to the theology of some popular hymns and urged organists not to play them as offertories, but he advocated the liturgical use of good hymns reflecting New Testament content. He was caught in the crossfire of those who liked bad hymns and those who tolerated no hymns in worship. "Pity the poor editor," he good naturedly joshed. "For he will now 'get it' from both sides!" He thanked both sets of correspondents for their reactions, allowed them their opinions, and claimed his right to express his. It was a response characteristic of his editorial career. He seldom lost his cool or his civility in the face of opposition.

Most of the reader opposition was contained in letters dissenting from positions he had taken. Some of these Kuiper printed, usually with a rebuttal or clarification. On rarer occasions he acknowledged an error or infelicity in what he had originally written. Ordinarily, the matter went no further. Occasionally, readers who were knowledgeable about the appeal process sought from the publication committee adjudication and redress of alleged editorial injustices. The committee usually supported its editor. It did so not necessarily because the individual members agreed with the position Kuiper had taken, but

---

[37]   *1963 Yearbook,* 338.
[38]   See pp. 96-102, 143-52.
[39]   *Banner,* 64/1683 (5/17/1929), 344.

because it understood and respected the principle of editorial freedom. As long as he expressed his editorial views appropriately and treated dissenters fairly, the committee did not object. On several occasions when he refused to place articles or letters in response to his position and the writer appealed, the publication committee sustained the appeal and directed the editor to print the piece. In his twenty-seven-year tenure these instances were surprisingly infrequent.

The publication committee was consistently noncommittal when he asked its judgment on how to handle an especially sensitive situation. It was not about to take the fall for a decision it was Kuiper's responsibility to make. Sometimes, however, it did. It supported his decision not to run an ad by the Dennis Avenue Christian Reformed Church mission committee announcing an address by Dr. David Otis Fuller—with a collection to be taken for Reformed Bible Institute—since the Baptist Fuller was "actively anti-reformed."[40] Whether the designation of the offering had any bearing on the committee's decision is impossible to say. In general, both the editor and the publication committee showed prudence in dealing with one another and with criticism of the editor.

At times Kuiper incurred criticism that should have been directed at Buiten. He once asked, for example, that a disclaimer of the editor's responsibility for approving ads be drafted and published. The publication committee accommodated his wishes in this regard.[41] At the same time it decided to send a letter of apology to the consistory of the First Chicago Christian Reformed Church, which had objected strenuously to an ad picturing a woman under a shower. At the time Buiten had sole discretion over which ads to run.

The Wezeman Case

The offending ad coincided with the Chicago uproar over the allegedly heretical teachings of the Reverend Dr. Frederick H. Wezeman, the immensely popular principal and Bible teacher at Chicago Christian High School.[42] Wezeman also provided much of the inspiration and leadership for Chicago Christian College, which met afternoons and evenings in the high school building during its short existence, 1931-1937, and of which he was the director. He had been a seminarian from

---

[40]   Minutes, Publication Committee, 10/4/1940, arts. 3 and 4.
[41]   Minutes, Publication Committee, 6/2/1936, art. 4.
[42]   On Wezeman's career in Chicago see Swierenga, *Dutch Chicago*, 397-420.

1918 to 1921 and a supporter of Janssen. For that reason the Chicago-area ministers watched Wezeman closely; scrutinized his creative and extensive, written, Bible curriculum materials; discussed them intensely at their informal *internos* gatherings; and persuaded the high school board to appoint an investigating committee when several troubling positions that appeared to echo Janssen's emphases were detected.

The committee was appointed. It found problems with the material, which Wezeman promised to correct. Wezeman delayed and then did not comply fully with the expected corrections. Meanwhile the school board had reappointed him and continued business as usual.

All this motivated fifteen ministers to sign a 150-page booklet dubbed "The Blue Book" because of its cover. Its primary author was the Reverend Dr. Herman Kuiper, minister of the Fourth Christian Reformed Church in Roseland and brother of R.B. and B.K. Kuiper. The booklet reviewed the unfolding controversy and documented the alleged "higher critical" elements in Wezeman's teaching. The board countered by appointing an outside committee of experts, which included two theologians from Western Theological Seminary in Holland and two from Calvin Theological Seminary in Grand Rapids, to examine the material and render a determinative assessment.

The board expected exoneration of Wezeman. When this committee also found grounds for concern in Wezeman's material, Classis Illinois overtured the synod to deal with the case. Then the high school board printed its own account and defense in the spring of 1936. It became known as "The Orange Book" because of its cover.

At that point H.J. Kuiper, who had been sizing up the developing situation for more than two years, weighed in with two presynod editorials.[43] One appeared four days before the publication committee's disclaimer absolving the editor of responsibility for the controversial shower ad, one three days later. Knowing the explosiveness of "the Chicago situation" and the inevitability of having to speak on it, Kuiper did not need his credibility questioned by the Windy City constituency over Buiten's ad.

Kuiper's two editorials were substantially descriptive. They were based on both the blue and the orange books. Given the acrimony expressed in Chicago church papers for more than two years, the charges and counter-charges, the withholding of financial support for the high

---

[43]   *Banner,* 71/2043 (5/29/1936), 508-10; *Banner,* 71/2044 (6/5/1936), 532-33, 547.

school by several churches, and the open recommendation of more than one minister that people not send their sons and daughters to Chicago Christian High School, Kuiper's editorials were deliberately and wisely restrained. That Edward J. Tanis—the chairman of Wezeman's college board, and one of the only ministerial supporters of the principal—was also a popular department editor of the *Banner*, further illustrated the delicacy of the situation and underscored the need for care. While the editorials attempted to inform the denomination of how the situation had unfolded and what the issues were, they were not entirely objective. Largely even-handed, they tilted toward the concerns expressed by the two investigating committees. Before the month was out, Kuiper found himself presiding over the synodical adjudication of the Wezeman case.

The synod sustained Classis Illinois in its concern over Wezeman's theological views and named a committee to work with Classis Ostfriesland in resolving the matter. Ostfriesland, the German-speaking classis in Iowa and Illinois, had held Wezeman's ministerial credentials since the years he had taught at Grundy College in Grundy Center, Iowa, and was thus ultimately responsible for oversight of his orthodoxy and behavior. The synod's committee was chaired by the Reverend Martin Monsma and included professors Louis Berkhof and Martin Wyngaarden of Calvin Seminary.[44] Wyngaarden was the school's professor of Old Testament. The synod required of Wezeman "that he give a further explanation of his sentiments" and gave its committee a three-part mandate: (1) to present the matter to Classis Ostfriesland on behalf of synod, (2) to assist the classis in interrogating Wezeman, and (3) "to advise it as to a final decision in this case."

Throughout the summer Kuiper restrained himself from editorializing on the Wezeman matter. Then in September, days before Classis Ostfriesland and the synodical committee met with Wezeman in a session scheduled a week earlier but postponed, Kuiper gave his verdict. He stated that when Classis Illinois took action the previous spring, he had resisted expressing his opinion. After the synod met, he had again restrained himself because the synod had found sufficient cause to appoint a committee to work with Classis Ostfriesland in resolving the matter. By the time this editorial appears, he wrote, that

---

[44] *1936 Acts of Synod,* 147. Other members were the Reverends E.B. Pekelder, J. Ehlers, and A. Wassink; Dr. W.H. Rutgers; and the laymen A. Peters and W. Bierma.

committee should have finished its work with classis. He affirmed his objectivity, noting his many Chicago friends who supported Wezeman and that he had not had close contact with any ministers about the matter except G. Hoeksema, pastor of the Third Roseland Christian Reformed Church. He chose not to address the mood in Chicago, which was very tense and complex, he acknowledged. If the issue were resolved, the situation should improve, he believed.

The issue, in his mind, was whether there was modernism in Wezeman's Bible curriculum materials. While he acknowledged procedural faults on both sides, he concluded that the ministers had acted with more integrity than had the high school board. He further concluded that Wezeman had conducted himself in a reprehensible manner, first by signing a document agreeing with the first committee's conclusion that his notes contained modernistic teaching because he felt that doing so would resolve the issue and assure his reappointment; second, by believing that the changes, some made with subsequent resistance and delay, were only cosmetic and not substantive. Kuiper found these attitudes and positions disingenuous and dissembling. He concluded that Wezeman was "unfit to serve as Bible teacher and principal in one of our educational institutions."[45] His editorial hit like an explosion. This was president of the synod, editor of the *Banner*, a founding father of the high school, and a respected former pastor of one of Chicago's more progressive congregations speaking.

Wezeman's response was immediate and forceful. In the Chicago immigrant paper *Onze Toekomst* of September 23, 1936, Wezeman accused Kuiper of attempting to sway "in Hitlerite fashion" the work of the classis and the synodical committee. "Untrue," answered Kuiper less than two weeks later, reminding readers of his deliberate restraint through the summer and claiming that in the recent offending editorial he had not addressed the substance of the case, only procedures.[46] But even if he had chosen to express his opinion earlier, what of it? he asked. Since when are editors of church papers forbidden from attempting to influence ecclesiastical assemblies? He rejected the charge, therefore, that he had been "straining at the leash" to jump into the fray. Maybe he should have written much sooner, since the situation had deteriorated so far that enormous damage had been done. He asked only that the Chicago people consider what he said now "with a clear

45   *Banner*, 71/2058 (9/18/1936), 868-70.
46   *Banner*, 71/2060 (10/2/1936), 916-17.

Dr. Frederick Wezeman, around whom the controversy swirled in the 1930s.

and open mind." Wezeman's positions touch the authority of the Bible, he stated pointedly, and this is the basis for all other true doctrine. But because they do so indirectly, their seriousness eludes lay people. That Wezeman was so well liked and so effective with students made his views all the more pernicious, in Kuiper's opinion, and they should have been challenged years before.

The publication committee was nervous. It decided that no more should be published on the Wezeman controversy until it had been resolved. The classis and the synodical committee met again in November. By then it was apparent that the two bodies were not of one mind. Classis Ostfriesland, while admitting that Wezeman had expressed himself at times in unclear and theologically questionable ways, found him to be loyally Reformed. The committee found him elusive, theologically dangerous, and worthy of deposition. In January an anonymous group called the Christian Reformed Laymen's Association of Chicago, Illinois, disseminated a pamphlet naming Herman Kuiper, G. Hoeksema, W.H. Rutgers, A. Blystra, the ministers of Classis Illinois, H.J. Kuiper, the synod of 1936, and the synodical committee as those who promoted "strife, enmity, and division" rather than "peace, love, and unity." It was a sweeping indictment of a substantial and powerful portion of the ordained establishment. It could not have helped Wezeman's cause. The pamphlet advocated peace and unity by restoring Wezeman's good reputation.

Editor Kuiper may have been restrained from editorializing on the Wezeman case and its proceedings, but he judged that he might speak on the pamphlet. And he did. In an editorial entitled, "Not the Way of Peace and Love," he argued that the anonymity, inflamatory rhetoric, distortions, and accusations contained in it deserved exposure for what they really were.[47] Wezeman and his followers were the real disturbers of peace and unity, not those who came to the defense of truth.

The publication committee of the *Banner* renewed its position of not writing on the controversy before it had been resolved. Classis Ostfriesland and the synodical committee presented the synod of 1937 with conflicting reports. Kuiper was again delegated to represent Classis Grand Rapids East. Once at the synod, he was again elected to preside.

The synod accepted both reports, but it noted that the committee's report contained "implicit charges." It asked the four committee members present at synod, therefore, to formulate these charges explicitly and then to present them to the whole assembly. As their formulations were being considered, Wezeman, sensing the direction in which the tide was flowing, "confessed" that his offending materials were problematic and retracted them. The synod gratefully dropped the matter at that point.

In his post-synod reports in the *Banner*, Kuiper's review spread the Wezeman case over three issues; it had been resolved, and he was now free to express his views editorially. Some thought Wezeman caved and conceded too much. Others thought the synod should have taken punitive action. Kuiper pointed out that synod did not compromise "on the real issue." But it accepted the very minimum necessary, he observed, for "false doctrine is sin, a great sin, and all sin must be confessed with sorrow."[48] The synod did not demand an expression of sorrow. It could have asked whether one so confused is fit for ministry, but it did not. It was "magnanimous." Kuiper expressed his wish for healing and peace.

Wezeman had his ministerial credentials transferred to the Fourth Chicago Christian Reformed Church as its associate pastor. He continued to serve as an effective leader and administrator at Chicago Christian High School until 1951, when he accepted the position of president of Northwestern Junior College in Orange City, Iowa, and resigned from the ministry of the denomination.

That the two successive synods that dealt with the Wezeman controversy turned to Kuiper for leadership is noteworthy. Their choice was likely driven by a combination of factors. He had demonstrated

---

[47]   *Banner,* 72/2076 (1/22/1937), 76-77.
[48]   *Banner,* 72/2100 (7/8/1937), 652.

leadership, good judgment, and dedication in such areas as worship and hymnody, Christian education, city missions and evangelism, worldly amusements, and denominational publications. He had also sounded the note of compassion, hope, and generosity in the Depression years. His reputation as an articulate defender of Reformed orthodoxy was solidly in place. It is impossible to know what factor or combination of factors led delegates to vote for him as president of the synod in 1936 and again in 1937. But Kuiper later noted that he regarded those positions with the greatest sense of satisfaction of any he had been accorded in his ministerial career. If they reflected the high-water mark of esteem for him in the church, as they may well have, his involvement in the Wezeman case also disclosed an undercurrent of opposition and resentment toward his forceful, some thought unloving and judgmental, defense of Reformed orthodoxy. This reaction was felt and expressed most intensely by Wezeman's most ardent supporters. In the coming years, opposition to Kuiper and his views would increase over a widening range of issues.

Tensions with Jacob Buiten

For the most part Kuiper and business manager Jacob Buiten got along well and showed one another mutual respect. Buiten was a fine manager who watched expenses and turned a profit. By 1941, profits from the two church papers had enabled the publishing operation to send more than $64,000 cumulatively to Calvin Seminary, as synodical policy directed.[49] Kuiper, on the other hand, wrote with a Reformed clarity, directness, and conviction that appealed widely to the constituency and that gained readers. More readers meant higher profits. The two men complemented one another well. With regularity Kuiper acknowledged the fine work of the staff, particularly on anniversaries of their employment, singling out Buiten and Van Ess.

Inevitably, there were points of tension. This occurred where Kuiper and Buiten's respective responsibilities overlapped or butted against each other. As the first printings of the *Psalter Hymnal* sold briskly, Buiten endeavored to keep a supply in stock to fill a steady stream of orders. As they began to use the book, musicians and others reacted to some of the music. Kuiper and Daniel Zwier of the *Psalter Hymnal* committee, intent on making improvements, in March of 1938

---

[49]   Minutes, Publication Committee, 2/6/1941, art.15.

Jacob Buiten, business manager, as he appeared toward the end of his long, effective career.

requested a delay in reprinting the book in order to solicit a wider reaction of Grand Rapids organists and other musical experts.[50]

Since the synod of 1937 had not continued the hymnal committee, the two men were operating on ecclesiastical inertia, not an explicit mandate. As holder of the copyright, the publication committee two months later declined the men's pressure to propose a new edition to synod, but it did grant them permission to introduce some modifications in several numbers. The two men retained the services of an expert who changed the music of several chorales that summer.

A year later, Kuiper presented the publication committee with the need for still further revisions. The committee decided this would not be possible, since a new printing was urgent. Furthermore, it had in hand a letter from Calvin College professor Henry Van Andel, who had also been on the *Psalter-Hymnal* committee, objecting to some of the changes that had already been made to "improve" the arrangements

[50]   Minutes, Publication Committee, 3/5/1938, art. 5.

that he and Seymour Swets, a young professor of music, had provided. The galleys for the next printing were on Kuiper's desk for proofreading. His proposal denied, he let them lie there for several months. The music printing company complained about the delay. The publication committee reminded Kuiper in successive months to complete the work and to return the galleys. The usually efficient, prodigious Kuiper took six months to complete a two-week task.[51] Buiten could not have been happy. But Kuiper's passivity was directed less toward his colleague than toward a committee moved more by market forces than by his musicological competence.

However, when Kuiper objected to placing ads for the *Christian Reader's Digest* in the *Banner* on the ground that the magazine advocated premillennialism, the publication committee adjusted policy to require that all ads of a nonbusiness nature were to be reviewed by Kuiper.[52] Buiten had had total control of advertising for twenty-five years. The next year the two men disagreed on the composition of an advisory committee to research agency policy. Then they disagreed over whether to implement a government, war-time directive to reduce paper consumption by shrinking the size of the magazine. Then they argued over whether to run headlines across the entire page.

The dissonance spread. Calvin's executive committee complained to the publication committee that the college and seminary were now being inadequately covered in the *Banner*. Kuiper, with committee consent, had reduced coverage in the effort to save paper. John De Korne was unhappy about how his articles on missions were being trimmed. The constraints of the Second World War obviously affected personal and interagency relationships as the paper was reduced in size and the editor succeeded in strictly limiting the percentage apportioned to advertisements. These pressures, the over-involvement of Kuiper in outside projects in the early 1940s, and the cumulative effect of carrying two full-time jobs took a toll on the editor's health as well as on his relationships.

After Kuiper's hospitalization in the spring of 1944 and in response to the medical directive that he reduce his commitments, Kuiper wrote the publication committee that he would withdraw from the nomination that year if the editorship continued as a part-time

---

[51] See Minutes, Publication Committee, 6/1/1939, art. 4; 10/5/1939, art. 7; 11/2/1939, art. 3.

[52] Minutes, Publication Committee, 4/3/1942, art. 3.

position.[53] In that case, he stated, he preferred to devote his full energies to his pastorate at Neland Avenue. The committee recommended and synod approved the full-time editorship. The decision meant that for the first time Buiten and Kuiper would be working together daily.

That summer Kuiper successfully negotiated with the publication committee that in the future he would determine where departmental materials would be placed, that ads would be limited to eight columns per issue as long as the paper remained reduced to twenty-four pages, and that he would determine which material would be run in a smaller type size.[54] Buiten was unhappy with the curtailing of advertising space, and for the next nine months the two negotiated, with advice from the committee, a more refined, explicit division of labor. By the next February, the committee decided that no articles, advertisements, or announcements were to be placed by the business manager without having been seen and approved by the editor. In effect, full-time editorship moved Kuiper into the concurrent role of managing editor.

The redefined arrangement apparently ran smoothly for three years. Then in a dust-up over secretarial support, Kuiper submitted to the publication committee a lengthy document respectfully asking for action "without delay" on several matters.[55] It asked the committee to stipulate explicitly that the position of editor/managing editor was coordinate with and not subordinate to that of the business manager. It further requested a clear ruling that his own secretary was subject to his "exclusive supervision" and that any redeployment of her time be cleared with him. He also wanted it understood that her tenure would be determined by him and that he would consult with the committee concerning her salary. These had obviously been points of friction between Kuiper and Buiten, further consequences of making the editorship a full-time position. Sensitive to the delicacy of the situation and appreciative of Buiten's managerial competence and success over three decades, the committee heard Kuiper at length in two conversations, twice dismissed him to deliberate, then gave him what he asked.

Jacob Buiten and H.J. Kuiper served well together for another eight years, when both retired with honors and the deep appreciation of the publication committee and the church. Both contributed strong

[53]   Minutes, Publication Committee, 6/1/1944, art. 6.
[54]   Minutes, Publication Committee, 7/7/1944, art. 3.
[55]   Minutes, Publication Committee, 10/7/1948, art. 8.

and gifted leadership, under which the magazine flourished. Each respected the other. It is a tribute to their characters that they resolved their differences through times of change and stress. To his credit, Buiten yielded on more points at issue than did Kuiper.

The Last Decade

After the Second World War the world was changing. So was the *Banner*. In 1946 J.B. Hulst retired from the publication committee, on which he had served since 1914, when the denomination took over the magazine. Since 1930 he had chaired the committee. A banquet was held in his honor in the Neland Avenue church basement. Kuiper paid him considerable tribute.[56] Hulst was seventy-eight at the time. He had been an astute and steadying influence on the publication.

As a full-time editor, Kuiper became more involved with the wider realm of evangelical publication. He had always followed developments in the broader church world through exchange copies of other religious papers, which he read regularly and quoted frequently. Almost fifteen years before, he had expressed his hope editorially that a coalition of evangelical churches could be formed to thwart the ravages of liberalism on American life. When the denomination became involved in the formation of the National Association of Evangelicals (NAE) in the 1940s, and some of its leaders served the new organization in key positions, Kuiper endorsed participation enthusiastically. By 1946 he was serving on its publication commission and was one of five Christian Reformed delegates to its convention that year.[57]

He followed the development of the organization closely in his editorials and defended membership in it stoutly against the rising chorus of voices arguing that the denomination should resign from it. In 1949 he was elected vice president of the Evangelical Press Association, an NAE spin-off, and in 1950 he served as its president.[58] When the denomination did withdraw from the association in 1951, Kuiper expressed his deep regret. For him the premillennialism and Arminianism of many members was eclipsed by their loyalty to the inspired scriptures and by the impact Christian Reformed representatives, including Mark Fakkema, had in fostering commitment to Christian schools among the membership.

---

[56] *Banner*, 81/2558 (6/7/1946), 709.
[57] *Banner*, 81/2557 (5/31/1946), 676-77.
[58] *1950 Agenda for Synod*, 160.

Internally, the most damaging setback experienced by Kuiper in the later years of his editorship was his estrangement from the denomination's academic leadership. This erupted publicly in the Flynn affair. Lester De Koster, a young speech instructor at Calvin College, writing in the *Banner's* "Voices in the Church" column, criticized the NAE's uncritical endorsement of John T. Flynn's book *The Road Ahead*.[59] The book condemned a perceived trend toward socialism in government policy-making and warned against its encroachment on personal freedoms. De Koster identified logical fallacies in the book and exposed its alleged racism. By its NAE membership, the denomination was implicated in the association's endorsement of this bad book, emphasized De Koster. Our Calvinism could and should offer better sociopolitical commentary than Flynn and the NAE did, he argued.

Kuiper promised a response in the next issue of the *Banner*. The book does not deserve "to be disposed of by such disdainful characterizations," he wrote the following week. Socialism was a growing menace, as its infestation in Great Britain displayed. Flynn's book deserved to be widely affirmed in its "general principles," though not necessarily in its details, he stated.[60]

If he had stopped there, the exchange would have attracted only momentary and dispassionate notice. But Kuiper, riled by the assault on the NAE, launched into a homily on the college and its board. Noting that young professors were trained at universities whose faculties were rife with liberals and socialists, he admitted his suspicions. "We wonder just how much attention our board of trustees" pays to the "danger" that college appointees may be influenced by such views. It did not help that De Koster had cited criticism of Flynn by the Methodist bishops, the Federal Council of Churches, and the World Council of Churches. "Frankly we can't quite conceive of anyone reacting so vehemently to Flynn's book without wondering whether he is in sympathy with the socialistic trend in this country. We know where Flynn stands on this issue, and we should like to know where our Calvin teacher stands." Calvin faculty members should not echo the "theories of unbelieving professors," but should construct a Christian social, political, and economic approach based on the principles of the Word.

Kuiper's reaction was not limited to De Koster. He was astounded that a newsletter of the "Youth for Calvinism Group" had not only

[59] *Banner*, 85/2772 (8/18/1950), 1020.
[60] *Banner*, 85/2773 (8/25/1950), 1028-29.

The Road Ahead

AMERICA'S CREEPING REVOLUTION

John T. Flynn

1951

THE DEVIN-ADAIR COMPANY

New York

The title page of Flynn's controversial book.

attacked Flynn and the NAE, but also the Christian Reformed leaders involved in the NAE. It had asked, "Have we been misled by the synodical yea-sayers, or have our men lost their prestige on the NAE board in the last year, or were they out to lunch when these Resolutions were passed?" The newsletter's tone was condescending and cutting. Indignantly, Kuiper rejected the "insolence" reflected in these "smears" of honorable church leaders. He urged readers to buy and to read Flynn's book and to judge for themselves. He even gave them an address where they could obtain a discounted copy.

Reaction was immediate. Eighteen college and seminary professors sent a short letter simply stating their concern that readers would think that "the Flynn line of thought is the Reformed line of contemporary economic-political thought." Kuiper reprinted it over all the signatories' names.[61] While he thanked them for communicating their opinion, he was unhappy with the letter's brevity. "We did not know that so many of them refuse to feel alarmed at the constantly increasing powers of civil government in our country," he taunted. He challenged them to provide a fully developed, Reformed alternative to

[61] *Banner,* 85/2776 (9/15/1950), 1124.

Flynn, observing that the church deserved to know where they stood. "The favorable response to our editorial was without precedent in our twenty-one years of work as an editor," Kuiper added, twisting the journalistic blade.

De Koster's response was as incisive as it was incensed. He rejected emphatically the notion that he was a Socialist, enumerated a list of all-American values he treasured, and promised, "If ever I do endorse [socialism], Mr. Editor, I shall not fear to say so." He schooled the editor on the difference "between argument on a subject and argument aimed at a person." Writers in "Voices" "*should not have to endure* insinuations, however phrased, directed at themselves or their places of employment"[62] (italics De Koster's). He then dissected nine specific instances of Flynn's carelessness, distortions, and bigotry. Kuiper responded each of the following two weeks.

The professors sent their rejoinder within a fortnight. They wrote "in the interest of denominational welfare," because the editor had far exceeded anything they addressed originally. They issued five short, clear affirmations. One, they wanted to remove suspicions he had cast on Calvin faculty members. Two, they stood in the social and economic lineage from Calvin through Colijn, the articulate Dutch Reformed political leader of their generation. Three, they were neither Socialists nor Socialist sympathizers and stood opposed to statism and collectivism. Four, all defenders of freedom were not defenders of Christ, as Voltaire, Rousseau, and Flynn demonstrated. Five, as specialists and nonspecialists, they promised to address these issues in constructive times and places. "For the rest . . . , in view of your kind of editorial writing and comment, no further statement in the *Banner* can be fruitful."[63]

The next month the officers of the Calvin board of trustees addressed a letter to the publication committee expressing regret that the editor had undercut denominational trust in the college and seminary and hope that the committee would not further tolerate such editorial abuse. The letter was published adjacent to a Kuiper editorial reminding the church that the synod of 1912 had judged socialism to be beyond the pale of Christianity and that its adherents, if church members, should be disciplined.[64] Letters of opinion on both sides of

---

[62]   Ibid., 1143.
[63]   *Banner,* 85/2778 (9/29/1950), 1207.
[64]   *Banner,* 85/2781 (10/20/1950), 1284.

the controversy appeared in "Voices" for the next month. Even Richard Postma, Kuiper's ally thirty years earlier on the masthead of the *Witness* and subsequently in fostering Reformed boy's clubs, defended his Young Calvinist writers' critique of Flynn and the NAE. At the end of November, the publication committee decreed a halt to the debate and gave space for a final article by De Koster and a final editorial by Kuiper. They honored De Koster's request that the two pieces be printed in the same issue, which they were. Nonetheless, Kuiper once again gave himself the last word by directing readers to De Koster's article first, since his editorial was written after he had received and read De Koster's and in rebuttal to it.

The exchanges were damaging to both the *Banner* and the college and seminary. The magazine lost credibility among many thoughtful and educated members of the denomination. The academic institutions lived under a shadow of suspicion for a number of years. Neither result was warranted or healthy. To some extent the exchanges reflected the tensions and fears of the early Cold War era. They also were yet another instance of Christian Reformed people and institutions not understanding or addressing the wider culture with uniformity. They certainly mirrored and intensified differences within the church, differences which came to expression the next spring over the accusations seven college students communicated in writing to the board of trustees over the formation of competing religious magazines that year, and over the termination of four seminary professors at the synod of 1952.[65] If H.J. Kuiper is appropriately credited with the many positive contributions he made to Christian Reformed life and institutions, he must also be assigned responsibility for contributing to an unhealthy mood of suspicion and to growing polarization within the denomination.

The last four years of Kuiper's editorship were less eventful. In the summer of 1956, he retired one month after Jacob Buiten did as business manager of the magazine. Both men were appropriately recognized and honored. With their departure a truly remarkable and successful era in the magazine's history came to an end. The *Banner* was received in more than 80 percent of Christian Reformed homes. In the majority of them it was read seriously and thoughtfully. Beneath the dissent and dissatisfaction there prevailed a far deeper denominational identity

---

[65] On these matters see James A. De Jong, "Growing and Changing: the Seminary and the College, 1945-1972," in *Love beyond Knowledge, Grace beyond Limits* (Grand Rapids: Calvin College and Seminary, 2001), 30-33.

Retiring Editor, Rev. H. J. Kuiper, Who Served with Distinction — Photo by Thomas Stob
from 1929 to 1956
TO GOD BE THE GLORY!

Cover of the September 14, 1956, issue of the *Banner*,
recognizing Kuiper's years as editor.

and cohesiveness. In that unity, the church was already initiating new ministries and expanding existing ones. It was loyal and uncommonly generous in these efforts. As a church leader and the editor of its weekly magazine, H.J. Kuiper had contributed significantly to what the Christian Reformed Church had become by its centennial in 1957.

CHAPTER 10

Editorials on Reformed Spirituality

In his editorials in the *Banner* from 1929 through the summer of 1956, H.J. Kuiper ranged as widely as his understanding of Christian faith and life took him. That was a considerable distance, for he believed that all of life is a religious response to God and that God requires faithfulness in every aspect of life. For Kuiper, then, spirituality embraced and was expressed in everything about a person and about the believing community. To organize and review Kuiper's editorial emphases on the subject accurately, therefore, is a challenge. This and the following two chapters endeavor to do so by looking first at his sense of the believer as a person and as involved in the family and in the church; then at his sense of the ecumenical Christian community; then at his insights on the relation of the church to the world.

Personal Spirituality

The life of faith begins with spiritual rebirth, with receiving a new heart through the renewing work of the Holy Spirit. In a typical editorial on the subject entitled "What Is Spiritual Life?" Kuiper answers, "It is the life that is hid with Christ in God.... It is begotten in the heart by the Holy Spirit, on the ground of the atoning work of Christ on the cross." It begins with the work of regeneration, and it grows in resistance to sin and in becoming Christ-like. It "operates through faith and expresses itself in prayer, study of the Bible and loving obedience to God's law. Spiritual life is a life of daily communion with God." It is life in-dwelt by the Holy Spirit. "True spirituality puts its stamp on all the powers and activities of the soul: imagination, judgment, reason, affections and volitions."[1] True spirituality, therefore, is more than human idealism that transcends physical interests and materialism. It is more than the emotions of joy, hope, love, trust, or remorse for sin. It is life with God, in Christ, that expresses itself in continuous adoration of the living God, desire to please and serve him, turning and flight from sin, and delight in fellowship with the Creator and Redeemer. Kuiper followed this editorial with a second piece asking readers to assess whether they were spiritual or carnal Christians. He profiled each. The real strength of a church, he concluded, is not its size or wealth, but the spiritual growth and vitality of its members.

Two years earlier, the editor warned against two extremes in spirituality: "worldliness and otherworldliness, unspirituality and overspirituality." The former is more prevalent, he judged, the latter not the worse of the two. "Lukewarmness is our greatest sin and worldliness the most prevalent spiritual disease," he wrote.[2]

Three years later he stated that "genuine religion" is squeezed out by the preoccupations and superficiality of modern life. A little religion is burdensome and superficial. Genuine religion "is the foundation of all our thinking, the keynote of all our activity." It is supernatural in the sense that it "overarches" and lifts up all of life's endeavors.[3]

A greater danger than worldliness or modernism, he wrote in 1938, is neglect of the life of the soul on the pretext of being too busy. Lack of spirituality is the worst problem faced by the church; a new emphasis on Pentecost is the best antidote. After the Second World War, Kuiper listed many positive signs of Christian Reformed vitality—all programmatic and external. But negatively, he discerned in church members a lack of a vital spiritual life, an absence of sufficient interest in Bible study, anemic religious conversation, and religious formality in Christian Reformed homes.[4]

Subsequent editorials appealed for spiritual renewal and revival in the church and its members. Genuine spirituality remained a fundamental concern of the editor until the end of his career.

Spiritual awakening is fostered by prayer and intensified study of the Word, in that order, Kuiper held. Lack of spirituality is the church's

[1]   *Banner*, 67/1864 (12/2/1932), 1044.
[2]   *Banner*, 65/1734 (5/16/1930), 468-69.
[3]   *Banner*, 70/1971 (1/4/1935), 4.
[4]   *Banner*, 81/2586 (12/27/1946), 1524-25, 1543.

greatest enemy and problem, he reiterated. Its two causes are "the lack of communion with God through prayer and diligent study of the Bible, and the . . . abandonment . . . of the pure gospel." The first fosters the second. Similarly, recapture of the first yields increased emphasis of the second. Prayer and life in the Word are both fruits of the Spirit's work, which is why Kuiper stated in the same context that Pentecost is more important for the church's spiritual life than Christmas or Easter.[5]

"Spiritual awakening" was a preferable term to "revival" for Kuiper, since the latter connoted for him a manmade rather than a Spirit-controlled movement. In American church life he saw too much revivalism with its Arminian emphases. There, religious technique and the subjective human emotions eclipsed the truth of the Word, he believed. But prayer and immersion in the Word were continuous refrains in Kuiper's editorials, since they were for him the twin ingredients of authentic, personal spirituality.

Personal prayer was essential, nonnegotiable, for him. The pattern of family prayer was a Kuiper given. It had to be vital, creative, reflective of actual needs and events and had to avoid the deadening pattern of unthinking repetition. Prayer meetings and prayer days were important, too, as long as they avoided superficiality and religious clichés. Several times in his career Kuiper produced a series of editorials on prayer, emphasizing both its need and its content.

Encouragement to read and study the Bible seriously was an equally sustained theme in his writing. The sin of not reading the Bible is "one of the greatest sins in the church today," he affirmed in 1950. His crusade promoting Reformed Bible Institute training in the denomination and his Know Your Bible League program in the late thirties and early forties have been reviewed already. His editorials recommended aids like the "Daily Manna" calendar,[6] popular biblical meditations, and the writings of Andrew Murray on prayer in the interest of cultivating spirituality among his readers.

Where true spirituality flourishes, Kuiper instructed, one finds a deep conviction of sin, close fellowship or communion with God, strong faith, genuine joy, ardent prayer, and remarkable zeal for God's work. New interest in the study of the Bible and its basic doctrines is another result. Holier, stricter living and less complacency and more

---

[5]   *Banner,* 73/2144 (5/26/1938), 484.
[6]   The "Daily Manna" was edited by the Reverend Martin Monsma for many years and was used widely in the Christian Reformed Church. It consisted of one-page, tear-off devotional meditations for every day of the year.

indignation about sin and evil are other signs of spiritual renewal. So are deeper brotherly love and Christian fellowship, powerful conversions, and transformation in Christian Reformed homes and churches.[7]

The week before he penned these instructions, Kuiper had cited as important instances of spiritual awakening the Reformation, the movements inspired by the great eighteenth-century evangelists, the early nineteenth century European *Reveil*, the 1834 *Afscheiding* in the Netherlands, and the birth of the Christian Reformed Church in 1857. For Kuiper the pursuit of true spirituality was his most important and fundamental editorial theme.

The Covenant Home

The spiritual home was a covenantal requirement for Kuiper. God's covenant with his people promises saving grace to believers and their children. The theme of the covenant was one to which he returned often in his editorials. For him it was a practical doctrine. It formed the basis for Christian marriage, in which husband and wife consecrate their union to the Lord, responding to his saving faithfulness by pledging love and fidelity to God and to one another. As partners, they are spiritual equals who are to encourage, nurture, and support one another in the faith. The family altar is a place of daily shared prayer, reading and discussion of scripture, and even songs of praise.

God intends covenant marriages to produce children. Kuiper opposed deliberate avoidance of conception through the practice of birth control. Intentional childlessness was a form of covenant infidelity. The doctrine of the covenant is the basis for his articulate defense of infant baptism on a number of occasions, none in such detail and eloquence as in his polemic against the theology of the Reverend M.R. De Haan of Calvary Undenominational Church in Grand Rapids.[8]

On the controversial matter of whether adopted children were members of God's covenant, thereby requiring the covenant sign and seal of baptism, in the early 1930s Kuiper recognized good arguments on both sides and considered the issue to be one on which differences were tolerable. By the end of the decade, he supported the denominational decision that such children were members of the covenant and ought to be baptized. He consoled bereaved parents with

---

[7]   *Banner,* 72/2094 (5/27/1937), 508.

[8]   *Banner,* 64/1674 (3/15/1929, 188-89; 64/1675 (3/22/1929), 208-209.

the assurance that their children who died in infancy or before they reached the age of discernment were elect, heirs of heaven. Kuiper's *Banner* editorials often featured appeals to parents to nurture and guide their children in the ways of the Lord. They also showed a keen interest in young peoples' events and the important role of youth in the life of the church. His sense of covenant obligation to children and young people was the foundation of his case for obligatory Christian schools. Covenant spirituality as Kuiper articulated it was a special strength of the Christian Reformed Church during the first half of the twentieth century. For him this emphasis was an important ingredient in denominational cohesiveness.

If spirituality was fundamental to all other issues in Kuiper's editorializing, his emphasis on Christian nurture in its various forms was his most frequently visited editorial theme. Reformed spirituality had to be nurtured—constantly. He wrote on some form of Christian, covenant nurture at least once in every six issues throughout his tenure as editor—more often than he wrote on the work of the synod, on worship, on evangelism, or on organizational issues in the local congregation—all prominent emphases.

His editorials on Christian nurture revolved frequently around family worship and devotions. Kuiper condemned formalism in family devotions: clichés and mindless repetition in prayers, lack of enthusiasm and vitality, inaudible Bible reading and prayer. The father should give thought to making prayers and Bible reading specific, expressive, and connected to events and needs of the day. Both should occur at every meal. Length was less important than meaningfulness. Children's memorized prayers mouthed after the father's prayer detracted from the family character of the father's prayer. Repeating the last word of the scripture reading was a useless device, in his judgment. Having a Bible for every family member, taking turns reading verses, and interjecting explanations or questions were all helpful practices. Comments and brief discussions at the conclusion of devotions were important techniques for making devotions vital.

Family devotions were so important for the well-being of the church and of society, as well as for personal spirituality, that everything possible should be done to "preserve and improve" them, he wrote.[9] Lack of ability in leading family prayers occurs because fathers do not practice serious, disciplined, private prayer and because they do not give

---

[9]   *Banner*, 67/1801 (9/11/1931), 788.

their family prayers thoughtful planning, he suggested at one point. Bible reading must be interesting, and feeding the soul at meals is as important as feeding the body. It would be good, from time to time, for the father to delegate prayer and Bible reading to the mother and to children. On another occasion, Kuiper observed that memorization of scripture is a fine spiritual discipline for both children and adults. It would correct the reality that Christian Reformed people, in his view, were better versed in doctrine than in the knowledge of scripture.

The spirituality of a covenant home included the loving discipline of children, Kuiper believed. He once quoted with approval a University of Michigan professor who, in an address to a civic women's club, advocated discipline and obedience in child-raising. This refreshing alternative to the prevailing approach emphasizing permissiveness, self-expression, and disciplinary restraint is both biblical and necessary for a healthy society, Kuiper judged.[10] In nurture, parents and teachers must take the long view, since neither excessive toleration and permissiveness nor diligent and consistent guidance may produce immediate results.[11]

Kuiper thought the Christian home was imperiled by many modern forces: "breakdown of parental authority, mixed marriages, birth-prevention, the idea of companionate or trial marriage, and the disappearance of the family altar." Modern society's structure contributes to this breakdown, he analyzed. The factory in an industrialized society removes work and livelihood from the home. Feminism renders many young women unfit to run a home, and their employment leaves men unemployed. Removal of the father from the home due to his employment also disengages him as the chief family educator, guide, and disciplinarian. Restlessness caused by the pursuit of leisure and travel militate against family spirituality. The radio and the automobile have made the world much more accessible, therefore more influential in Christian households. The pernicious influence of the daily newspaper is still worse. "Its lurid description of crime, its funnies, its sport and theater pages, its popularization of the theory of evolution, its 'modern' stories, often even its advertisements breathe a worldly spirit which is bound to weaken the Christian character of our homes," Kuiper concluded.[12]

"The Family Circle" page was introduced by the editorial committee of the *Banner* in the early 1930s in an effort to curb the

[10]   *Banner*, 64/1666 (1/18/1929), 41.
[11]   *Banner*, 67/1800 (9/4/1931), 764-65.
[12]   *Banner*, 68/1906 (9/29/1933), 772.

influences undermining the covenant home. It was successively produced by the Reverends B.H. Spalink and Henry Verduin. Kuiper reported at the time of the transition of contributors that many families, including his own, were using the column with great benefit in their family devotions. He recommended that many more families incorporate its use into their devotions.[13] In another editorial he reflected on reports of its wide use and also noted that he promoted using it by his church families when he made family visits. From the outset of marriage, he held, solid spiritual foundations must be laid in covenant homes.

A Reformed World View

For H.J. Kuiper, true spirituality was also expressed in a Reformed world view. He wrote: "A deep piety is of the very essence of true Calvinism because Calvinism magnifies the sovereign grace of God as the power that transforms our entire inward as well as outward life. It teaches that Christianity is not only a creed and a way of life but also an inner experience resulting from personal fellowship with God through the indwelling Spirit."[14] Balanced Calvinism also does justice to all aspects of the Christian life: the intellectual, the emotional, and the volitional, he advocated. It shares the fundamentals of the faith with Fundamentalism without denying the believer's obligation to live and serve responsibly in this present age. At the same time, spiritual separation from the world is essential to this position, he believed, and an overemphasis on common grace dilutes and compromises real Calvinism.

As editor of the *Banner*, Kuiper was convinced that Christian Reformed spirituality was unique on the American scene. He was also aware of how indebted it was to its Dutch sources and how jeopardized it was by its American context. In an editorial entitled, "Derailed, Stalled, or Retarded?" he wrote that forces operating on and within the denomination had impeded the revival of Calvinism for which many, including himself, had hoped and prayed. Americanization, abetted by World War I and the 1921 immigration laws, had discouraged the flow of enthusiastic immigrant proponents of Neo-Calvinist spirituality to American shores. "The era of great prosperity," ending with the market crash in 1929, was characterized by Christian Reformed flirtation

---

[13]   *Banner,* 69/1928 (3/2/1934), 189.
[14]   *Banner,* 86/2804 (3/30/1951), 388-89, 409.

with premillennialism, fostered by "one of our prominent ministers." This theology captured considerable interest in the church and was only thwarted with much effort and discussion. Some advocates of a more evangelical approach to Christian faith and life diminished denominational interest in Calvinism. The common grace controversy sapped energy in the 1920s. Materialism and worldliness distracted us, Kuiper continued. Then the Depression strained our resources and inhibited expansion of our program.

The progressive Calvinistic development had not been derailed, he wrote, but it had been slowed and impeded. "Too few are interested in new projects that are distinctive." The era before the Great War was commonly regarded as the era of "the development of the deaconate," which spawned giving for Christian schools, societies, federations, and city missions. It was the time when the Christian Reformed Church chose not to join wider American parallels but to form its own, distinctive initiatives. In this important, retrospective editorial, Kuiper saw a real danger that the church's unity would fracture and that three groups would emerge, "the one clinging to historic Calvinism, the other espousing a sort of Fundamental evangelicalism, and another inclined to follow in the wake of the liberal, socializing, modernistic churches of our land."[15] He knew that the first represented biblical spirituality, and he aimed to continue articulating and advocating it in his editorials.

Each year Kuiper remembered the Protestant Reformation in late October. "Twentieth Century Reformation" is typical of his Reformation Day editorials. In it he reminded readers that they must not just remember the event and its heroes, but also must emphasize its great doctrines with clarity and zeal.[16] These are fundamental for a Reformed worldview. Today we must stress Protestant doctrines like scripture, creation, and miracles, which were not in dispute in the sixteenth century but are now, Kuiper counseled. Liberal theology is pernicious. It undermines true spirituality. More hope exists for the heathen to come to true conversion than for the liberal Christian, as the writer of Hebrews intimates in dealing with the subject of apostasy. We cannot fraternize with liberals as though they are brothers in Christ, Kuiper stated. Theirs is a different spirituality from ours. Kuiper promoted a life-embracing spirituality grounded in Reformed doctrine as rediscovered and articulated by sixteenth-century Reformed leaders

---

[15]   *Banner,* 75/2227 (1/12/1940), 28-29.
[16]   *Banner,* 78/2423 (10/29/1943), 892.

and as given new life in the *Afscheiding* and *Doleantie* movements of the nineteenth-century Netherlands.

Sabbath Observance

A basic element in Kuiper's approach to spirituality and discipleship was a rigorous but joyful observance of the Sabbath. In one of his earliest and best explanations of the subject, he stressed that the fourth commandment is still in place and is still binding because it is grounded in God resting on the seventh day. "There may be ceremonial elements in the Sabbath command, but its essence and substratum are as unchangeable as God himself."[17] Israel's people forgot the day in Egypt. God reminded them of it at Sinai. Today in Christian countries people are using the day for "carnal pleasure" rather than in God's service. The Sabbath principle remains in place as the Lord's Day for the New Testament church. Kuiper had no sympathy for the Puritan Sabbath, "a day of gloom." For him Sunday ought to be "a day of gladness, of spiritual uplift, inspiration, and service." As Jesus taught, the day was instituted for man, "to supply his human needs" as a divine image-bearer and servant of God. So the positive aspects of keeping the day holy or separate from other days should be stressed: worship, religious instruction, works of mercy, spiritual reading, and self-improvement. If these features are emphasized, the day will not degenerate into a legalistic avoidance of forbidden practices. For Kuiper, modern culture's use of Sunday as a day off to indulge in pleasures, recreation, travel and joy-riding, shopping, or jobs around the house and yard was to miss the Sabbath's intended purpose. By using it to draw closer to God, believers would find that Sabbath blessing would permeate and bless every day of the week.

Kuiper's subsequent editorials on the subject of the Sabbath, which all but disappeared after the Second World War, referenced his positive theology of the day. But they emphasized and belabored the church members' increasing departure from its intended purpose. Summers, with vacations and a more relaxed pace of living, made people especially vulnerable to Sabbath abuse. He complained in 1931 when Holland, Michigan, extended its Tulip Time celebration to Sunday, and the roads into the town were clogged with traffic. Weekend parties at cottages by Christian Reformed young people were often, he thought, "a pernicious evil, an extreme form of worldliness and inimical to the

---

17   *Banner,* 65/1744 (7/25/1930), 692.

welfare of the church."[18] He urged churches to fight for the Sabbath by joining and supporting the Lord's Day Alliance and by every other legal means available. But the most effective antidote to Sabbath erosion was faithful observance of the day by the individual Christian and by covenant families. Half-hearted, formalistic, compromised observance would only undermine this divine institution so essential for spiritual vitality. The Sunday newspaper, Sunday sports, Sunday travel, and attending church only once on Sunday were all tactics of the enemy. For Kuiper, "to take a vacation from public worship merely because one is away from home on Sunday is as inconsistent as it is for a married man to make love to another woman when he is out of the city."[19] His vivid affirmation indicated how seriously he took Sabbath observance. He did not state that all inconsistencies were equally reprehensible!

In the mid and late 1930s Kuiper editorialized on the Sabbath with every Grand Rapids referendum to relax statutes requiring the Sunday closing of grocery stores. He had been very cool toward women's suffrage, he admitted, but now he urged Christian Reformed women to get out and vote in favor of keeping stores closed for the sake of their children's spiritual health. Buying on Sunday compels others to work extensively and is to be avoided in all cases. Working in restaurants or pharmacies were works of necessity and mercy on behalf of those who cannot cook or for those who need medicine in emergency situations. But on Sundays even such places should keep short hours. And, "We do not need the Sunday newspaper. We do not need to purchase gasoline on the Lord's Day. We do not need to purchase food stuffs on the one day of the week which is in a peculiar sense God's own. Much less should we patronize ice cream soda parlors on our day of worship."[20] Such practices are entering wedges for worse compromises to follow.

When readers asked the editor for a ruling on a specific Sunday activity, as they sometimes did, Kuiper usually wisely answered that "border-line" situations had to be faced and answered locally by those who knew the people and the situations involved. He used these questions as opportunities to remind readers of the main principles and to warn them against the dangers of misusing the Sabbath. He thereby avoided being cited as an authority or partisan in local disputes.

Kuiper faced a moral conflict concerning Sunday labor when World War II broke out and President Roosevelt ordered defense

---

[18]   *Banner,* 66/1789 (6/12/1931), 549.
[19]   *Banner,* 67/1834 (4/29/1932), 412.
[20]   *Banner,* 72/2114 (10/21/1937), 989.

factories to operate seven days a week. The synod of 1941 had sent a letter to the president stating that Sunday labor should be avoided. After the bombing of Pearl Harbor, Kuiper modified his views enough to categorize the effort as a work of necessity for supporting American troops. However, the government ought to stipulate work schedules that allow workers to attend church, and it should never force anyone to work against his conscience, he wrote in a two-part piece in January, 1942. As the war progressed, he became increasingly concerned that the pattern of Sunday labor would persist in peacetime. He was less concessive toward Joseph B. Eastman, director of the Office of Defense Transportation, who ruled that to conserve gasoline milk deliveries could be made only every other day, not daily. Because every two weeks the delivery would fall on a Sunday, Kuiper supported the Christian milkmen who skipped one delivery every fortnight and railed against the inflexible bureaucrats who refused to allow a late Saturday delivery instead.[21]

Kuiper restated the bedrock principle for determining Sabbath activity after the war, when he feared that many compromising activities justified by the conflict would continue. "We do believe that only such things are permissible on the Lord's Day which in one way or another contribute to the worship or the service of God on that day."[22] Keeping the day holy was "the first line of defense" against Satan and his forces. The health of the Christian church and home were at stake in this spiritual conflict. The power and proximity of this battle determined that, in the closing years of Kuiper's editorship, most Christian Reformed television sets remained off until after the evening church service. If parental and local application of his principle felt legalistic to children and young people, those who read the *Banner* carefully and took its editorials seriously understood that keeping the Sabbath holy was essential for maintaining spiritual vitality.

That the Sabbath was to be permeated with praise and joyous celebration was not only emphasized in Kuiper's editorials. The emphasis was reinforced by his selection and promotion of good Christian music via the *New Christian Hymnal* and the first edition of the *Psalter Hymnal.*

---

21 *Banner,* 78/2422 (10/22/1943), 868.
22 *Banner,* 80/2530 (11/23/1945), 1116.

Stewardship and Tithing

Stewardship and tithing were also important features of spirituality for Kuiper. He reflected on them periodically and forthrightly in his editorials. Stewardship was the principle, tithing the main practice of it. Stewardship, he thought, was a relatively new theme or doctrine for the Christian church, and he was exhilarated that the church at various points in its history refined and augmented its doctrine.[23] Because the Bible, especially in the teachings of Jesus, was full of stories and sayings about wealth and money, the church should preach about stewardship and tithing regularly. He was afraid that this material was "practically unused," however, even in Reformed preaching.

A misconception that H.J. Kuiper sought to correct was that tithing, like the Sabbath, belonged to the Old Testament era, not the New. It was a practice in place before Moses gave the law, he stressed. And even though it is not directly commanded in the New Testament, Paul calls believers to the higher principle of giving as God has prospered them. Kuiper suggested that tithing is the minimum standard and that the wealthier one is, the higher the percentage of income one should give.[24]

In several editorials in 1935 he expanded on tithing. He deplored the literature that argued for tithing because God rewards such giving with even greater financial blessings. Also, leaders who saw tithing as the solution to a church's financial problems are fostering a "materialistic" attitude toward giving. Often emphasis on it produces legalism, as well. Steady, consistent tithing is far preferable to the emotional techniques, crisis appeals, and contrived events designed to motivate giving in many communions. When stressed for the right motives and in a biblical spirit of gratitude, tithing by everyone in the congregation would yield amazing resources for the Lord's work. If everyone in the Christian Reformed Church had been tithing, he once observed, "streams of money would have been poured into the Lord's coffers and marvelous things would have been accomplished in our various spheres of organized Christian activity."[25]

Contrary to conventional opinion, Kuiper believed that the Depression years were the time to talk about stewardship and giving,

[23]   *Banner,* 65/1756 (10/24/1930), 956.
[24]   *Banner,* 70/1989 (5/10/1935), 436.
[25]   *Banner,* 67/1817 (1/1/1932), 4.

not the time to avoid the subject. Now that prosperous times are past, Kuiper said, we should not "wail about the depression," but examine ourselves and "confess that we have not been faithful stewards" of God's gifts. Some—precious few!—churches have been generous. God judges those who withhold their tithe, as Malachi 3 explains. God is rebuking the country and the church.[26]

In an editorial entitled, "Thinking of Others," he explained that some church budget envelopes had two compartments, one marked "For Ourselves" and the other designated "For Others." He argued that in the Christian Reformed Church the theological school and the emeritus fund belonged in the first category, but that sadly both had been suffering due to denominational financial neglect during the Depression. The synod had cut the emeritus fund for retired pastors and their widows by 20 percent, and it was actually receiving only half of that adjusted amount, which in effect amounted to a 60 percent reduction. Some recipients were living in downright destitution. He thought the denomination should be scandalized, and he appealed for more generous support. Then, to amplify the public embarrassment he had just inflicted, he commended the Reformed Church in America as doing a much better job for its ministerial retirees than did the Christian Reformed Church.[27] On another occasion, when a reader asked whether debtors should contribute to the church, his terse response was that people should not pay off creditors with the Lord's money.

Giving is genuinely spiritual when done in true joy, out of love for God, and sacrificially, Kuiper taught. It is not spiritual when done to win favor or recognition—either from God or others, or when it is attached to some reward, recognition, or pleasurable social activity. Worldly persons cannot give spiritually, but Christians can give "carnally," and many do. "If all members of our churches would practice tithing, they would begin to enjoy giving. And if we should all begin to enjoy giving, none would feel the need of methods of money-raising which are carnal rather than spiritual," he wrote.[28]

During the war, he drove his emphasis on spiritual giving home with the account of Christian Reformed young men at the army base near Alexandra, Louisiana. They met weekly with the Christian Reformed camp pastor in his home. They adopted the practice of

---

[26] Ibid.
[27] *Banner,* 67/1866 (12/16/1932), 1093.
[28] *Banner,* 68/1914 (11/24/1933), 956.

giving a tenth of their meager military wages for that work. Kuiper used the example to inspire young and old alike. He encouraged parents to instill the same value and discipline in their children at an early age. "The sincerity of a man's piety may be measured by his willingness to make material sacrifices for the sake of his religion," he ended.[29]

Spiritual giving is thankful giving, he emphasized. Envy is twice blind: to one's own blessings, and to the struggles and miseries of the person envied. It is an affront to God, since it questions God's wisdom in distributing wealth, and it kills contentment.[30] He added, for good measure, that hoarding food and gasoline in an era of rationing is selfish. Nor should soldiers pilfer German homes, for stealing is sin— even against the vanquished, he wrote at the end of the war. Genuine stewardship and a generous spirit extended that far for H.J. Kuiper.

Canadian Immigration: A Diaconal Opportunity

No twentieth-century development changed the Christian Reformed Church more than Dutch immigration to Canada after the Second World War. At the end of the conflict, no Canadian classis existed in the denomination. The fourteen Christian Reformed congregations in Canada together had fewer than 450 families and were affiliated with three U.S. classes. More than 300 of the families belonged to the nine churches in western Canada, six of which pre-dated the First World War.[31] After World War II, immigrants from the Netherlands surged across the Atlantic, primarily into Canada, where many of them were met and resettled with assistance from Dutch-speaking Christian Reformed pastors.

As editor of the denomination's weekly, Kuiper supported the denomination's creative and timely outreach to the postwar Dutch immigrants. Kuiper had been a dutiful and appreciative student of Dutch church life and theology for decades. He had lobbied editorially for a generous diaconal response to Dutch suffering in the late stages of the war and immediately after it. As destitute immigrants, often

---

[29]   *Banner,* 76/2325 (12/12/1941), 1156.

[30]   *Banner,* 76/2315 (10/3/1941), 916.

[31]   See Tymen E. Hofman, *The Strength of Their Years* (St. Catherines, Ontario: Knight Publishing, 1983) for an account of the earliest settlements, in Alberta. His more recent book, *The Canadian Story of the CRC: Its First Century* (Belleview, Ontario: Guardian Books, 2004), extends the account to all of Canada.

with large and young families, began arriving, he urged support for them. Some immigrants also came to the United States but in smaller numbers. Because they were readily assimilated into well-established Christian Reformed congregations, where they were often sponsored by American relatives or friends, Kuiper did not write about them. His editorial attention was focused, rather, on the larger proportion that arrived in Canada, where the need for all sorts of advice, relocation assistance, and financial support was substantial.

By the fall of 1949, the editor noted that most of the fifteen Christian Reformed churches by then organized in Canada had doubled in size within the past year, due to the influx of immigrants. Many other immigrants were located beyond the orbit of these congregations and needed help to establish new congregations. Kuiper urged an immediate and generous response to the synod's decision approving a campaign to create a $150,000 emergency church building fund for this purpose. It would require seven to ten dollars per family to reach synod's goal. The money would be deployed as grants to build or expand church buildings to accommodate the enormous influx of immigrant members.[32] This was a magnificent commitment, since the total denominational quota approved that year was less than thirty-eight dollars per family, and the money had to be raised within one year. The next week, Kuiper provided news briefs on sites where services were being held—thirty in Ontario alone—a list of ministers dispatched to work among the new arrivals, and pictures of a number of emerging churches. Thereafter, the editor kept the church informed regularly about developments on the Canadian scene.

By December Kuiper reported that the fund had already reached $100,000. The immigrants continued arriving. The fund was soon depleted. In 1951 the synod authorized a second $150,000 infusion. Kuiper again promoted it, noting that the first goal had been exceeded and that he was sure the second one would be too. Some small, indebted U.S. congregations were contributing as much as twelve or fifteen dollars per family. But by the fall of that year, twenty-six groups were still in need of assistance. The editor reminded the denomination that only one-fourth of the $10,000 grants to each group were gifts, and that three-fourths were loans repayable at modest interest rates. The need is "more pressing" than two years ago, he added, since there

---

[32]   *Banner,* 84/2729 (10/14/1949), 1188. Details of the plan are found in *1941 Acts of Synod,* 82-83.

were now sixty-six churches and emerging congregations in Canada. By January, 1953, the number had risen to eighty-nine, a number 600 percent greater than four years before. Kuiper made yet another appeal for help to erect new church buildings, calling the need perhaps "the greatest emergency" the denomination had ever faced.[33] The visionary editor championed efforts to assimilate Dutch-Canadian immigrants into the Christian Reformed Church, remembering no doubt the blessings which the huge infusion of Dutch-American immigrants produced for the church of his childhood. Present sacrifice would yield future blessings. The project both expressed and reinforced the diaconal aspect of Christian Reformed spirituality.

Spirituality and Church Life

A vibrant church was the context in which devotional life, Sabbath celebration, stewardship, and works of mercy were both formed and expressed. Faithful, active membership in a church that exhibited the confessional marks and qualities of the true church was essential for a healthy spiritual life, in H.J. Kuiper's opinion. Understandably then, he editorialized at considerable length on all aspects of church life.

If public worship is the centerpiece of church life and if preaching is at the heart of worship, as Kuiper certainly believed, he devoted proportionately less time to the subject of preaching than to topics like covenant nurture, worldliness, or evangelism and missions. The reason for his relative reticence on the subject was that the importance of preaching and the confessional principles defining it were not in dispute in his era. They were clearly understood and universally embraced in the denomination. So, in his early years as editor, he focused on introducing and defending the new, uniform order of worship and on issues related to hymnody and the *Psalter Hymnal*, projects on which he had labored so intensively during his Broadway and Neland Avenue pastorates.

After World War II his attention to worship ranged wider but was also incidental, due no doubt to the fact that he successfully persuaded the publication committee to introduce a new, regular column entitled, "The Church at Worship." He did advocate good order and form in public worship but warned against formalism. In single editorials he rejected the idea that elements of worship prior to the sermon are mere "preliminaries," defended the Reformed use of the Decalogue in worship, advocated shorter services, and warned against the extremes of

[33]   *Banner,* 88/2894 (1/16/1953), 68-69.

ritualistic formality and casual informality. Worship must be from the heart, an outpouring of adoration of God. Chewing gum or coughing spells or unruly children were all disruptive and had no place in the sanctuary. On one occasion he offered that the word "church" ought to be reserved for God's people and not be used for the building in which they worship. On another he paid tribute to church organists, who are under-appreciated as worship leaders. He characterized the simplistic, jazzy hymns and choruses finding increasing favor among Christian Reformed people as liturgically "infantile." And at the very end of his *Banner* tenure, he advocated a discerning balance between things old and new in public worship.

Some of Kuiper's best, most discerning insight on the spirituality of public worship appeared in the early and mid-forties. Preaching is the "most essential" part of public worship, prayer is second, and congregational singing is a close third, he wrote then.[34] The value of congregational singing, which also is "essential" in public worship, is fortified by the Old and New Testament emphases on praise in worship and on the visions of saints in glory singing God's praises. "Worship without song would lack the inspiration, the fervor, the depth of feeling which should characterize it. Sacred music gives wings to our souls and enables them to soar upward to the throne of God to lay their sacrifices of praise at his feet,"[35] he rhapsodized in statements that provide as penetrating an insight into the heart of H.J. Kuiper as any found in the entire body of his writings. Accordingly, his editorials on public worship give disproportionate space to singing rather than preaching or prayer. The next week he editorialized on "how to improve congregational singing." Members of the congregation must "spiritualize" it by singing thoughtfully, with their hearts and minds as well as with their mouths. They must let the organist dictate the tempo. The minister should select music thoughtfully, to match the message, mixing more familiar and less familiar numbers. He should log the dates when numbers were sung so that he used the whole collection over time and did not repeat favorites to the neglect of others. Consistories should provide fine organs and support good choirs. Finally, Kuiper added, sacred songs should be part of our home life, for this will improve singing in worship.[36]

---

[34]   *Banner*, 77/2341 (4/3/1942), 316-17.
[35]   Ibid., 317.
[36]   *Banner*, 77/2342 (4/10/1942), 340.

Several years later Kuiper reflected on the spirituality of prayer in public worship. Written prayers by renowned ministers he judged too ornate, theological, and discursive for Christian Reformed services. He counseled ministers to read and reflect on the prayers in the Bible. The psalms present "fervent supplications, lofty adorations, ardent thanksgivings, heart-searching confessions." The Lord's Prayer is "terse, almost abrupt," in its "staccato supplications." Let these be the minister's patterns. Petitions should be "direct, concrete, and urgent."[37]

A succeeding editorial stated that ministers must be more "deeply conscious" of their "ministry of intercession" in worship. In Acts 6 the apostles saw their calling as prayer and preaching. "Personally we would rather say that *preaching* and *interceding* are the two most important activities of the officiating minister and that the two are equally important and vital" (italics Kuiper's). If so, then adequate preparation must be made for both. This calls for "the right kind of praying in our study" before mounting the pulpit, private prayer "with minds and hearts steeped in the spirit of devotion."[38] It also requires that ministers have a clear mental outline of the general and specific matters for which they will pray. This approach is much more important than writing out polished literary productions, concluded Kuiper. The last contribution in this, the longest series the editor wrote on prayer in worship, advises congregations to encourage good pulpit prayers by paying attention, commenting to the minister on meaningful prayers he offers, and requesting specific causes for prayer. The minister must always guard against talking to the people instead of to God in prayer—against "preaching with his eyes shut."[39]

Concerning actual preaching, Kuiper identified its spiritual purposes as to "instruct, exhort, and console." This three-fold aim addresses the three functions of the soul: thinking, feeling, and willing, and appeals to the human intellect, emotions, and volition.[40] All three dimensions of humanity have been perverted by sin, and all three are renewed by grace, especially through effective preaching, the "chief means of grace." Preaching that is consoling "is a spiritual art, requiring the unction of the Holy Spirit and a spiritual skill of the highest order.

[37]   *Banner,* 80/2487 (1/19/1945), 52-53.
[38]   *Banner,* 80/2488 (1/26/1945), 76-77.
[39]   *Banner,* 80/2494 (3/9/1945), 220-21.
[40]   *Banner,* 73/2162 (10/6/1938), 916.

It presupposes a tender and sympathetic heart and the ability to live into the trials, fears and sorrows of others."

Kuiper devoted another editorial to "admonitory preaching." This kind rebukes people for their sins, just as the biblical prophets and apostles sometimes did in their sermons. A minister who avoids this responsibility for fear of losing favor is not faithful to his calling or to Christ. Such preaching must not be so mild or general that it is painless or touches no one. Candid but nonabusive and love-driven admonition is needed to shape people spiritually.[41]

Instruction in the faith occurred in every sermon, but it received systematic treatment in faithful preaching of the Heidelberg Catechism, which Kuiper advocated from time to time in his editorials. He made a point of the church order's emphasis on "regular" and "faithful" rather than "weekly" catechism sermons, which schedule was not always "workable." Doctrinally, exegetical rather than topical sermons were most suited to instruction in the faith, for the latter are an open invitation to liberalism. Kuiper's editorials, like his sermons, accented the great doctrines of Christ's person and work on the great Christian holy days. They also warned against secularizing and commercializing Christmas and Easter. The legendary doctrinal depth and precision of Kuiper's own sermons is borne out by an examination of them.[42] His editorials, on the other hand, have less of this flavor, no doubt due to the presence of the "Our Doctrine" column and doctrinal articles produced by others. On issues in dispute in the church, both Kuiper's sermons and his editorials were doctrinally lucid and polemical. He was not one to shy away from defending the faith entrusted to him.

If Reformed spirituality was formed and expressed substantially through the preaching, praying, and singing of public worship, it was reinforced by other dimensions of congregational life for Kuiper. He wrote from time to time on all features of congregational life, from orderly congregational meetings to church architecture to relatives serving together on the consistory. Public profession of faith by young

---

[41] *Banner,* 73/2165 (10/27/1938), 988-89.

[42] An extensive collection of some 2,500 of Kuiper's manuscript sermons, dating from the last part of his Englewood pastorate through his ministry at Neland Avenue, illustrates his three-fold emphasis in preaching. It is located in the Henry J. Kuiper Collection, Collection 153, boxes 2-4, Archives, CRC. The early sermons are written at length in small booklets; the later ones are typed, single-spaced, on both sides of one 8 ½ by 11-inch sheet. His sermons are lucid, didactic, and at times incisively practical.

people and faithful church attendance are important, but they can be deceptive, he warned in a short series on "fallacies regarding church life." The first fallacy is that the number of young people making profession of faith is a measure of the Spirit's work in a congregation. "It is more important to weigh our church members than to count them," he counseled. We should not expect an unrealistic level of spiritual maturity from young people, nor should we lower the standards so low that no statement of authentic spiritual experience or solid knowledge of the Reformed faith is required.[43] Several weeks later he exposed as false the notion that a full house on Sunday nights equals "a good attendance."[44]

As an editor, Kuiper demonstrated the same love for the church's children and young people that he did as a pastor. He devoted himself pastorally to their nurture in the faith, and a measure of his rapport with them was his active leadership in the American Federation of Reformed Young Men's Societies and the offices he held in that organization. But, among all the activities and programs a church has for its youth, nothing is as vital and necessary as catechetical instruction, he believed. Editorially he praised good Sunday school programs and welcomed young men's and women's societies as important components of congregational life. But he "insisted" on catechism instruction for nonprofessing youth. "The American church began to fall when it began to shift the emphasis from teaching to inspiration, from steady educational effort to spasmodic emotional campaigns, to revivalistic spurts and jerks," he wrote early in his editorship.[45] Providentially, he went on, the Christian Reformed Church still has a deep, widespread commitment to indoctrination. Knowing the teaching of scripture is important for a strong, grounded faith and for Christian life. Our commitment to the covenant obligates us to it, for the catechism program is the spiritual nursery for our youth. Parents must support the program. Consistories must admonish parents to this. So must the pulpit. Ministers must make classes dynamic and interesting. The catechism season should be lengthened to nine months.

Two years passed, and in a moment of editorial candor Kuiper admitted that, compared with twenty years earlier, catechism in the Christian Reformed Church had improved. He acknowledged that as an instructor of youth in the faith he had made many mistakes,

[43]   *Banner,* 76/2295 (5/9/1941), 436.
[44]   *Banner,* 76/2298 (5/30/1941), 508-509.
[45]   *Banner,* 64/1701 (9/27/1929), 668-69.

and he stated that that could have been avoided if the *curatorium* had insisted on providing a good teaching methods course in the seminary curriculum.[46] He argued that good facilities are needed for effective catechetical instruction: desks or chairs with a surface for writing, maps, a blackboard, and a musical instrument. Also, ministers should not be expected to handle all the classes, but the church should provide a competent assistant for teaching younger children and for grading papers. Classes should not be larger than thirty-five students.

In the mid-1940s he still believed that catechism instruction was the most important youth work in the church. The disappearance of catechism classes "would be the worst of all calamities which could befall our denomination."[47] We would lose much, he wrote: a grip on the "cardinal truths" of the gospel, an understanding of God's redemptive plan, zeal for pure doctrine, doctrinal preaching, and discernment of the Reformed faith from run-of-the-mill evangelicalism. Vulnerability to religious error, ensuing lukewarm spirituality, and apostasy would follow. "Feed my lambs" is "the very first task" of the church, and it is performed in the catechism class. But to keep it, we must "improve" it, Kuiper argued, and he used five ensuing editorials to define what he meant by "improvement." In 1947 and again in 1955 he produced discerning editorials on the church's catechism program. He urged parents and consistories to put "catechism first" in their churches— before any other weekday activities. The Reformed strength and spiritual vitality of the church depended on this.[48]

As adamant as Kuiper was on the necessity of the catechism program for nurturing Reformed spirituality, so was he skeptical about the Sunday school program as implemented in two hundred Christian Reformed congregations that employed the International Sunday School lesson materials. He once reviewed Christian Reformed unhappiness with the lessons, going back to his childhood at the First Christian Reformed Church in Grand Rapids, where J.B. Hulst had refused to use the material in his own class. Kuiper lamented the synod's inability to cut through the divided opinion in the denomination on Sunday school materials.[49]

---

[46] *Banner,* 66/1768 (1/16/1931), 44-45.
[47] *Banner,* 80/2519 (9/7/1945) 820.
[48] *Banner,* 90/3032 (10/21/1955), 1252. See also *Banner,* 82/2595 (2/28/1947), 260 and 283.
[49] *Banner,* 70/2020 (12/20/1935), 1156-57.

In "A Dangerous Series of Lessons" he had earlier detailed his reservations. There he reported introducing and reviewing International Sunday School materials on Friday evenings for the Neland Avenue Sunday school teachers with increasing alarm. The lessons present "the social gospel," ignore the main themes and organic unity of scripture, and consistently distort the biblical passages adduced, he alleged. These lessons are "a standing menace to the purity and welfare of our church and of every church which uses them," he stated in his opening paragraph.[50] "We confess frankly," he concluded, "that we are up in arms against this lesson system. It is a menace to our Sunday schools, our children and our churches." Kuyper was therefore delighted to report in December 1936, the year he had first presided over the synod, that, after eighteen years and several unsuccessful requests, the synod had finally decided that the denomination should develop its own, Reformed, Sunday school materials. He believed that a sinister force against Reformed spirituality had been turned away from the doors of Christian Reformed congregations.

In each of his congregations, Kuiper promoted spiritual vitality by leading a variety of societies for both men and women, by organizing and leading choral societies, and by advocating distinctive youth groups for boys and for girls. He promoted fellowship though young men's and young women's societies. Shortly before he became editor, the Federation of Reformed Men's Societies had been formed, emulating the association for young men's societies, and Kuiper acknowledged one of his own elders, Henry Hekman, as president of the fledgling organization and predicted that soon many more churches would organize groups that would join the movement. This will, he predicted, "bring about a revival of interest in our Reformed principles among the men of our churches."[51] He lauded the early meetings of the American Calvinistic Conference on a more academic level in the late thirties and early forties. His encouragement of Bible study through correspondence courses and his Know Your Bible League program was designed to foster deeper spirituality in the Christian Reformed Church. From time to time he urged the development, maintenance, and regular use of well-stocked church libraries. Late in his editorial career Kuiper advocated creating reading clubs in local congregations; he hoped to see twenty or so such circles in larger congregations, where good and important contemporary books would be discussed, for this

[50]   *Banner*, 64/1713 (12/20/1929), 956-57.
[51]   *Banner*, 64/1706 (11/1/1929), 789.

would yield articulate and discerning Christians.[52] He also applauded the appearance of summer camps and conventions for Christian Reformed children and young people after the Great Depression. All of these societies, organizations, and programs reinforced the means of grace entrusted to the organized church. They contributed to the spiritual formation of a cohesive, dedicated, doctrinally informed, and confident body of Christ.

Crucial to the well-being of the local congregation and its effectiveness in producing spiritual growth and development was leadership. Kuiper often wrote on ministerial issues and on the duties of local office bearers. In late 1939 and the first half of 1940, he produced at least a dozen editorials on ministers.

Finding the right match between a minister and a congregation was important. Kuiper liked the Reformed system of calling pastors, for it involved the congregation. Congregational participation in calling a pastor is a privilege only a few Christian traditions accord their members, he noted. It is conducive to better pastor-church relations than in other systems, even if sometimes ministers overstay their effectiveness. But consistories must nominate prospective ministers carefully, as no minister is suited to every congregation. He sanctioned prior consultation with trusted seminary professors and other ministers concerning a candidate's suitability.[53]

Matters to consider in calling, he wrote, are ability as a preacher, pastor, and teacher; Christian character; and the sociability of the man, his wife, and his family. Youth, advanced degrees, and availability should not be the primary requisites.[54] In fact, Kuiper regularly lamented the fact that churches were more inclined to call younger than older men, whose wisdom and experience were too often overlooked.

A call to serve another church must be followed by a man's spiritual conviction to accept that call before it can be considered as a compelling call of God. Four implications of a spiritual approach to the calling process are: (1) that church politics have no place in the process; (2) that patience is required by both parties if the match turns out to be less than ideal; (3) that devotion and zeal in ministry flow from the spiritual conviction of a true call; and (4) that a proper spiritual disposition is required in the calling process.[55]

---

[52] *Banner*, 84/2691 (1/14/1949), 4.
[53] *Banner*, 73/2172 (12/15/1938), 1157.
[54] *Banner*, 73/2174 (12/29/1938), 1208-1209.
[55] *Banner*, 74/2175 (1/5/1939), 4-5.

For a minister, soliciting calls by whatever means is an illicit running ahead of God. The initiatives found in business and politics are inappropriate in the church, Kuiper held.[56] Kuiper considered it advisable, although not obligatory, for a minister to consult his present consistory in considering another call. Requesting an extension in the pursuit of clarity in responding to a call is legitimate. Usefulness in the kingdom of God should be the determining consideration, not salary, which is what people in the pew often mistakenly think tips the scales in making a decision on a call received. Ministers are under no obligation to give reasons for their decision regarding a call, and in fact this may be counterproductive. Ministry is a lifetime calling, he believed, and "emeritus" is not a word found in scripture; ministerial status should be retained after retirement and men should continue to exercise their calling in more limited, strategic ways as long as strength and health permit.[57]

Kuiper concluded the lengthy series by addressing the problem of ministers staying too long in a charge, losing their effectiveness, and causing strained relations with their churches. It is a problem not easily resolved, he admitted. The church needs to devise a way for pastors to relocate after five years or so, since very few are capable of sustaining a successful long-term ministry. He recognized that not all can be excellent preachers. So he argued for specialized ministries: pastoral workers, evangelists, youth pastors, and catechists. So far the church has not been motivated or creative enough to provide for such specialization, he admitted.[58] The problem of achieving the right fit between minister and congregation continued to vex the editor throughout his career, and he produced another series on the subject in the 1950s.[59]

Kuiper's sense of the importance of church leadership for fostering healthy spirituality is further illustrated by a two-part editorial he produced just three weeks into his work as *Banner* editor. In it he first addressed the church's attitude toward elders and deacons. The congregation should pray for them; respect them for the sake of Christ and their offices, not their personalities or abilities; and trust and support them. Second, he had a word for the office-bearers: wrestle

---

56   *Banner,* 74/2177 (1/19/1939), 52-53.
57   *Banner,* 74/2181 (2/16/1939), 148-49.
58   *Banner,* 74/2204 (7/27/1939), 700-701.
59   See *Banner,* 87/2875 (9/5/1952), 1086; 87/2887 (11/28/1952), 1444-45, 1469; 87/2888 (12/5/1952), 1476-77, 1501.

in prayer over those people entrusted to your spiritual care; become thoroughly informed on the church order and your duties; meditate on the mysteries of the faith; be diligent and diplomatic in your pastoral contacts; devote all the time necessary to meetings and careful deliberation; and protect confidences.[60] Another time Kuiper noted the uniqueness of the Reformed elder, who was a spiritual caregiver and defender of biblical truth, unlike in hierarchical traditions that did not know the office, or in churches that functioned only with trustees. "Strong elders," he said, are second only to strong pastors as the leadership needed for healthy churches. They must be people who not only possess the required biblical qualities for the office, but also people who are theologically well-read in order to discern error and to give spiritual counsel.[61] Family visits, often endured by the membership as an "affliction," are the main work of elders. To be effective in nurturing spiritual growth, these visits must be conducted as conversations rather than religious inquisitions. They should meet the immediate needs of the family visited by bringing encouragement, support, praise, counsel, admonition, or instruction—but always from the Word. An effective family visit will be enjoyable for both parties, Kuiper emphasized.[62]

Kuiper had equally high regard for the office of deacon. He championed the formation of diaconal conferences after World War II and lamented the fact that Christian Reformed deacons had been overlooked initially by the synod in providing relief for the distressed in the Netherlands immediately following the Allied victory. The office shows Christ's compassion for all in distress—for those in the household of faith, but also for others. Galatians 6:9-10 admonishes us not to be weary in doing good to all people, he pointed out. Deacons model generosity and stewardship for the congregation. Deacons that hoard resources, protecting large fund balances, stifle benevolent giving, he believed.[63] In a column years earlier, he had stressed that the historic Reformed emphasis on caring for their indigent through the diaconate had given Reformed churches a solid reputation with local government and social agencies. It also had deterred the Christian Reformed Church from slipping into the social gospel by way of reaction to an overly spiritualized Christianity, as had happened in some churches without

60 *Banner,* 64/1666 (1/18/1929), 40-41.
61 *Banner,* 73/2152 (7/21/1938), 676.
62 *Banner,* 75/2245 (5/17/1940), 460-61.
63 *Banner,* 84/2706 (4/29/1949), 516.

this office.[64] Kuiper offered practical ideas from time to time on the effective conduct of the offices of elder and deacon. He maintained that through both offices Christ ministered to his people and helped them mature as believers.

Denominational identity and loyalty were also important dimensions of Reformed spirituality for Kuiper. He once made a long, impassioned plea for more denominational loyalty and unity, emphasizing the distinctive strengths of the Christian Reformed Church. These strengths were eroding, compared to a generation ago, he lamented. Then the church was more central in the lives of people. Subsequently, individualism and independent attitudes had gained ground, and people found it too easy to transfer to other denominations. Even our people are infected with the disease of "church unionism," he observed. While denominational pride and self-satisfaction are wrong and should be discouraged, denominational cohesion is important for preserving wholesome spirituality.[65]

For Kuiper the denomination was more than "a loose aggregate of local churches" that are independent and meet occasionally in "conferences." Rather, the denomination was a "church." He regarded the Christian Reformed Church as "one spiritual body, one organizational entity." He elaborated that the Reformed idea of denominational unity requires "*authoritative* major assemblies," but only in those limited matters that concern all the congregations and on issues that could not be resolved at the minor assemblies (italics Kuiper's). Consistories are bound by the assemblies' decisions. Independentism and "synodocracy" were both dangers to be guarded against, in Kuiper's opinion. "The worst threat" to the Christian Reformed Church, living in an individualistic and free society, however, is not the latter, but "consistorial and congregational unconcern about synodical decisions."[66]

Not surprisingly, therefore, Kuiper used the pages of the *Banner* to foster strong identity with the denomination and its ministries. The college and the seminary received considerable attention, and Kuiper was ever vigilant concerning their Reformed loyalty. He reinforced the importance of denominational mission activity, stressed in the department edited successively by Henry Beets and John De Korne. He kept readers informed on the emerging broadcast ministry of the

[64]   *Banner*, 65/1763 (12/12/1930), 1116.
[65]   *Banner*, 73/2163 (10/13/1938), 940-41.
[66]   *Banner*, 84/2725 (9/16/1949), 1084-85.

denomination. He answered many questions on issues of church polity, thereby helping church members understand how the denomination operated. He provided a steady diet of local church news and often featured church buildings on the front cover. This practice not only gave local congregations visibility and importance, it reinforced their connection with the denomination. He stressed the necessity and privilege of supporting denominational efforts financially and in prayer. But Kuiper's most sustained editorial attention denominationally was given to synods.

By late April or early May he had begun reviewing the forthcoming synod's agenda. Once the synod concluded, he reported on its proceedings and decisions. In the early years of his work as editor, he provided summaries of crucial debates, paraphrasing and summarizing key speeches by delegates, whom he named. His reports were largely objective and factual, although he did not hesitate to offer his opinion on matters about which he held deep convictions. The wrap-ups extended into August, even September, until the publication committee urged more restraint and brevity. But what Kuiper's coverage of synodical proceedings achieved was a sense of their importance and a denominationally informed and engaged constituency. His extensive reviews invested readers in denominational ownership. During his editorship, Christian Reformed people who read the *Banner* faithfully—and that included a remarkably large percentage of the membership—had a clear sense of who they were and where they stood as a church. Denominational loyalty was a substantial and resulting component of their spirituality.

Conclusion

While he never said so, Henry J. Kuiper's paramount objective as editor of the *Banner* was to enhance the spiritual health of his readers. The way he handled church news, covered synods, confronted challenges to the faith, reflected on political developments and cultural trends, responded to readers' questions, rallied support for a new endeavor, admonished greater faithfulness, defined the church's stand on an issue, or celebrated God's faithfulness demonstrated his fervent desire that his readers walk with the Lord. His editorial tone made the *Banner* more than a promotional tool for denominational ministries. It was more than an instructional manual in Reformed orthodoxy. The magazine aimed to form people in the Reformed faith, until they matured in Christ and were shaped for service to the glory of God. To the degree that there was a correlation between the editor's unspoken, inferred purpose and the prevailing spirit in the denomination, the Christian Reformed Church was blessed and effective as a living church of Christ.

CHAPTER 11

Perspectives on Wider Christian Fellowship

Kuiper's years as editor of the *Banner* spanned the most optimistically ecumenical part of the twentieth century. This was an era of major reunion movements in mainline Protestantism, the birth of the World Council of Churches (WCC) and the Reformed Ecumenical Synod (RES), and the emergence of the National Association of Evangelicals (NAE) as an alternative to the Federal Council of Churches (FCC).

The *Calvin Forum* began publication in the early 1930s and was edited ably by Calvin Seminary professor Clarence Bouma. It ceased appearing about the time Kuiper retired as *Banner* editor. The magazine headlined Reformed correspondents from around the world and was widely read by Christian Reformed ministers and leaders in higher education. Neither before nor since were these groups more knowledgeable about Reformed Christianity worldwide than during the second quarter of the century. As one of them,[1] Kuiper also tracked ecumenical discussions and developments in his *Banner* editorials, and they were featured in other columns as well. His views on ecumenicity are important for understanding the Christian Reformed Church's sense of its place in the wider Reformed communion of his time.

---

[1] Kuiper himself only contributed one or two articles to the magazine in its almost twenty-five-year history.

Years of Turmoil

Kuiper's first several years as editor were characterized by ecclesiastical upheaval and opportunity. He paid close attention to both. Whether it was the Federal Council, the Reformed Church in America (RCA), the Northern Presbyterian Church, the emergence of Westminster Seminary, or the popularity of the nondenominational movement led in Grand Rapids by the Reverend M.R. De Haan, developments in the wider church elicited his early comment.

Six weeks after assuming his position, Kuiper noted that the new president of the Federal Council was the Methodist bishop Francis J. McConnell, a thoroughgoing modernist whose election had also been lamented in the *Presbyterian*. Kuiper wondered why it had not "dawned on" orthodox people and leaders in member denominations that they had nothing in common with such people and should not participate with them in the same organizations and denominations.[2] To him the McConnell appointment was confirmation that the Christian Reformed Church (CRC) had made the correct decision in 1924 to terminate its council membership. He neglected to remind his readers that the overture to terminate had originated in his Broadway consistory.

Some people in the Reformed Church were by now also questioning their church's membership in the FCC. Later that spring, Kuiper commiserated editorially with a Mr. Hamstra from New York, who had written him that an RCA pastor who had recently been buried as a Mason with Masonic rites may have been permitted to preach in Christian Reformed congregations.[3] Kuiper warned of the dangers inherent in some church unions under consideration, including one that included the Northern Presbyterian Church, the Reformed Church, and the United Presbyterian Church.[4] He quoted approvingly and at some length two Reformed Church ministers who had publicly opposed the proposed union.

Simultaneously, the Northern Presbyterian Church and Princeton Seminary, which were experiencing even greater dissonance, attracted Kuiper's analysis. He deplored how the Princeton Seminary administration and board had achieved a reorganization that put modernists in control and marginalized the orthodox element on the faculty. The merger discussions in that communion, if successful,

[2]   *Banner*, 64/1671 (2/22/29), 133.
[3]   *Banner*, 64/1683 (5/17/1929), 345; and 64/1684 (5/24/1929), 365.
[4]   *Banner*, 64/1686 (6/7/1929), 400-401.

would unite that church with others at odds with it confessionally. He articulated how the church union movement was predicated on the modernistic doctrine of the Fatherhood of God and the brotherhood of all men, that it hated the antithesis between believer and unbeliever, and that it would not be satisfied with one visible Christian church, but that it would not rest until all people of all religions were united organizationally.[5]

Two months after he had reflected enthusiastically on the commencement address at Calvin College and Seminary delivered by the brilliant young Cornelius Van Til, he again wrote about Princeton Seminary in the editorial, "A Gloomy Situation." Van Til, who had just been appointed to the Princeton faculty and was due to commence teaching in September, and several other "aggressive conservatives," had resigned because of the organizational changes at Princeton. Kuiper called this "the death knell" of conservative, orthodox, Westminster confessional theology in the Northern Presbyterian Church. A new seminary could not reclaim the denomination, he felt. The "middle-of-the-roaders" would stay on the faculty and in the denomination, though disaffected. The church would henceforth be controlled by the modernists. Since it was too late in the day for reform, the only alternative was for those still faithful to secede, as the faithful had done in the Reformation and in the *Afscheiding*.

Before long, however, Kuiper reported that two Christian Reformed ministers—R.B. Kuiper and Van Til—had resigned their pastorates to teach at the newly formed Westminster Seminary in Philadelphia. Kuiper characterized the new school as a continuation of the true and faithful Princeton, where so many Christian Reformed ministers over the previous forty years had completed their theological education. Both men had first declined their appointments, then agreed to serve for one year. Kuiper congratulated them. The Christian Reformed Church is still small, strong, and pure, he continued. But in time it will face "the same dangers and evils" to which the Northern Presbyterian Church has capitulated.[6] While it would be preferable to retain "our very best men" to face these threats, both professors will almost certainly find it impossible to leave the school after one year, as planned. Time proved him right.

[5] Ibid.
[6] *Banner,* 64/1700 (9/20/1929), 645.

Closer to home, the growing nondenominational movement in western Michigan was causing Kuiper alarm. M.R. De Haan had recently broken with the RCA and was attracting a large following among Reformed and Christian Reformed members. The Reverend J.P. Battema had just left the Wyoming Park Christian Reformed Church with a contingent of members, after falling under the censure of his consistory and the church visitors. He gravitated toward the De Haan movement. Kuiper observed that these two recent congregations were part of a wider national development, and that J. Bennink's secession group from the Unity Reformed Church in Muskegon and his own brother-in-law J. Bultema's earlier withdrawal from the First Christian Reformed Church in the same city all supported and identified with one another in the publication, *Grace and Glory*. To counteract the movement, Kuiper published an article by Louis Berkhof demonstrating how these movements denied the long, fruitful, theological work in the confessional traditions down through the centuries. Kuiper also wrote an editorial entitled, "Undenominational Creeds," in which he analyzed at length the creedal statement of De Haan's church.[7] He judged that its defense of the fundamentals and explicit warnings against worldliness were good. But he missed anything on election, original guilt, sanctification as the Spirit's work, regeneration as prior to faith, the covenant of grace, the distinction between visible and invisible church, the Lordship of Christ, and good works as contributing to the assurance of salvation. His conclusion was that the De Haan movement was un-Reformed and that its doctrinal stance paled in comparison with the three forms of unity.

Yet, Kuiper admitted candidly that the movement had something to "teach us."[8] First, because our people leave our denomination so easily, we have to do a better job of indoctrinating them, he said. They leave either because they do not agree with our teachings, want other doctrines, or because our doctrinal teaching is dry and lacks spiritual warmth. Good catechism preaching will never drive people away, he added. The catechism is "so thoroughly evangelical and so eminently practical" that it is conducive to the kind of preaching that will hold as well as inspire people and inoculate them against doctrinal error. Such preaching needs the foundation of good catechism teaching, instruction of the youth that is both interesting and practical, in congenial facilities, with good instructional books, and with adequate

[7]   *Banner*, 65/1724 (3/7/1930), 220-21.
[8]   *Banner*, 65/1725 (3/14/1930), 244.

help and reinforcement for the minister. Why should the minister carry the full load, with huge classes, while the Sunday school has one teacher for every ten or twelve students? he asked. We should also learn from this nondenominational movement that we should be more urgently and earnestly evangelistic. Fervor and passion for souls need not compromise our intellectual strength. These nondenominational churches are "the unpaid debts" of denominations, he acknowledged.

Later in 1930 Kuiper endorsed the suggestion of the Reformed Churches of the Netherlands (GKN), whose proceedings he watched more closely than those of any other church, that a Reformed ecumenical synod be created.[9] He also strenuously opposed a proposal by a committee of the Grand Rapids ministers' conference to form a local council of Protestant, evangelical churches, whose president would be the voice of Protestantism in the city.[10] Believing that this pseudoecumenism was increasing nationally, he editorialized on the local proposal. "Evangelical" is a vacuous word, he asserted. When biblically examined, it can apply fully only to Reformed, creedal Christianity. He also judged that the directive for ministers to read and vote on the matter soon, before churches could consider the proposal, smacked of "clericalism." Kuiper retched at the thought of the Christian Reformed Church being part of a council with churches that compromised the gospel. He would be in favor, if the need could be demonstrated, of a truly evangelical council, one which could be a counterweight to a consistently liberal council.

When the RCA's paper, the *Leader*, reopened the issue of membership in the Federal Council, Kuiper praised the Reverend Dr. Winfield Burggraaf, the recently appointed editor, for courageously making the case for his denomination to terminate its membership in the FCC.[11] Burggraaf admitted that he had once been in favor of membership and that he remained grateful for all that the Reformed Church had both received and contributed through its membership. But he now conceded that the dominant modernism controlling the organization led him to call for withdrawal. He supported the sentiment to this end, strong in the Chicago Reformed churches, and instructed other readers on how to craft effective overtures. Kuiper congratulated this "brother," who, a few years later in 1934, resigned

9   *Banner*, 65/1758 (11/7/1930), 1004-1005.
10   *Banner*, 65/1761 (11/28/1930), 1076-77.
11   *Banner*, 66/1781 (4/17/1931), 356.

Winfield Burggraaf,
editor of the *Leader*,
whom Kuiper praised
for his stance on the
Reformed Church in
America's membership
in the Federal Council.

as professor of systematic theology at Western Seminary after serving only three years.

Also in 1930, Kuiper reported on the acrimonious debate in the *Leader* between Professor Albertus Pieters of Western Seminary, who used a series of FCC Lenten meditations to document the council's modernism and to argue for RCA withdrawal, and Professor Milton Hoffman of New Brunswick Seminary, who accused his western colleague of "character assassination" and urged the church to stay the FCC course.[12] When the RCA's general synod "side-stepped" the membership issue that year, Kuiper offered Pieters and his supporters encouragement and support and counseled them to persistence and endurance.

Whether it was precipitated by the Reformed Church's debate and decision that June, a pointed exchange with Samuel McCrea Cavert, general secretary of the FCC, over the meaning of the word "evangelical,"[13] or the accumulation of ecumenical issues over the previous two years, Kuiper embarked on a thoughtful series of editorials stating his position on the Christian Reformed Church's "external relations." Alongside the six-month series, he exposed the fallacy of the nondenominational claim to follow no creed but the Bible, rebutted

12   *Banner*, 66/1791 (6/26/1931), 596.
13   *Banner*, 66/1789 (6/12/1931), 548.

Albertus Pieters,
Western Seminary
professor of systematic
theology, a champion
of orthodoxy in Kuiper's
opinion.

De Haan's pamphlet rejecting infant baptism, and responded testily to the Reverend Dr. Evert J. Blekkink's characterization in the *Leader* of the Christian Reformed Church as "isolationistic." By then retired, Blekkink had edited the paper for a time after 1906 and joined the Western Seminary faculty six years later. The wonder is not that the CRC withdrew from the FCC, chided the seasoned Reformed Church leader, but that it had joined in the first place.

If Blekkink had been following my series thoughtfully, Kuiper retorted, he would understand how "groundless" his charge was.[14] It comes to this, said Kuiper. The Christian Reformed Church believes that the Head of the church commands us to have no fellowship with unbelievers, which is what liberals and modernists are. The Reformed Church in America has a prevailing toleration of such association. That is a substantial difference between the two denominations, but it does not make the CRC an advocate of "isolation." Furthermore, Blekkink maligns the denomination when he asserts that the CRC does not permit Reformed Church members at its communion tables or its ministers in its pulpits. If a Christian Reformed consistory does due diligence and satisfies itself on their faithfulness, RCA members are heartily welcome at Christian Reformed Communion and RCA

---

[14]   *Banner,* 67/1809 (11/6/1931), 980-81.

Evert J. Blekkink, earlier editor of the *Leader*, who considered the Christian Reformed Church "isolationistic."

pastors may certainly be invited to preach in CRC churches. Kuiper noted that Blekkink's attacks were not helpful. Open acknowledgment of differences was honest. But more important is to be "genuinely concerned about [one another's] welfare and progress."

Kuiper's exchange with Blekkink was uncharacteristic of his editorial style. This was one of only several occasions on which he disagreed pointedly with a Reformed Church in America leader in print. When he did, it was in ecclesiastical self-defense, in response to a direct attack, and not at his initiative.

Series on Ecumenicity

Kuiper's series of editorials on ecumenical relations articulated the position that he held for the rest of his life. Entitled "The Problem of Our External Relations," it ran intermittently from July through November of 1931. This problem is a major one for us, he began. It will become especially acute in the next decade, as we move away from the Dutch language and face increasing engagement with other Christian groups. The problem comes to this: "How shall we in a practical way recognize our oneness with the church universal without surrendering our Reformed heritage and without in the least weakening our stand for the distinctive principles of our denomination?"[15] This issue, he

---

[15]   *Banner,* 66/1793 (7/10/1931), 644.

said, touches our fellowship with other denominations, church union proposals, councils of churches, missionary cooperation, post-graduate programs for seminary graduates, policy on calling ministers from other denominations, seminarians at other seminaries who want to serve the Christian Reformed Church, and support for special organizations like the Lord's Day Alliance, tract societies, and Bible societies, among others. It is a problem that needs to be fully and carefully addressed, and there needs to be definition of principles to guide the church in its external relations.

Kuiper believed that the educated leadership of the church, especially its ministers, would determine the shape of ecumenical relations. They must articulate and defend the denomination's unique, distinctive convictions to avoid their dilution and loss.[16] Mixed marriages across denominational lines and the welcoming of members from outside Christian Reformed ranks without proper indoctrination would weaken the church, he stated. The popularity of recent inventions like the car and the radio were certain to contribute to greater exposure to society in general and to other denominations in particular.

The first guiding principle Kuiper developed in his series was that of the universality of the church.[17] He stated that the great Dutch Reformed theologian of the previous era, Herman Bavinck, had shown that this principle is not at odds with the church's rich diversity or pluriformity. The invisible church permeates many visible churches and is spiritual. This does not mean that all churches are equally faithful or good, but it does call us to discernment in our church relations and it disallows isolation from other denominations. On the other hand, Kuiper expanded, it also undercuts the virtual return to the Roman Catholic error made by those in the popular church union movement, since they equate the visible with the invisible church.

The editor's second principle is that of denominational loyalty, which he believed calls each denomination to cultivate and protect its unique gifts and strengths. This confessional and denominational variation is beautiful, like the variety of flowers in Kuiper's garden. Here he described the unique beauty of the Christian Reformed flower in God's ecclesiastical garden. "It is Calvinistic in doctrine, Presbyterian in government and strict in its moral emphasis. Its outstanding virtue is that it presents a full-orbed gospel. It is very serious when it claims

---

16   *Banner,* 66/1795 (7/24/1931), 676.
17   *Banner,* 66/1797 (8/7/1931), 708.

to have the purest, deepest and truest interpretation of the Word of God."[18] Each denomination finds a meaningful place in the church universal when it develops its peculiar strengths and qualities, while avoiding extremism and sympathetically and discerningly appreciating those of other denominations. "There seems to be a prevailing opinion among Christian people and among church leaders that by stressing its distinctive features, a denomination restricts and impairs its usefulness." The result had been such a "discoloration and fading away of boundary lines" so that many churches had become monotonously indistinguishable and had even blurred a clear-cut line between what is Christian and what is non-Christian. Many tolerated any and all, even conflicting, views and practices. This, Kuiper believed, was the tolerant, communal spirit of the times, in which a church bold in its uniqueness was "an oddity." The danger to the Christian Reformed Church was not that it would remain distinctive, but that it would *gradually yield to the leveling spirit in the world*" (italics Kuiper's).[19]

In his fourth editorial in the series, Kuiper observed that while no one would dispute the principles he had developed, their application might be more controversial. He believed that Article 85 of the church order compelled the denomination to have its strongest external relations with Reformed churches faithful to their calling.[20] For Kuiper that meant especially the Reformed Churches in the Netherlands, the old Reformed Church in Bentheim and Eastfriesland, and the Reformed Church in South Africa. Exchange of delegates at one another's assemblies and correspondence for the purposes of counsel, correction, and approbation for confessional and liturgical changes was the shape this contact ought to take. American sister churches less closely related, but with whom the denomination exchanged greetings on a less intimate basis, were the Reformed Church in America, the United Presbyterian Church, the General Synod of the Reformed Presbyterian Church, and the Associate Presbyterian Church. He felt that more frankness and mutual correction should be part of these exchanges. He was especially concerned that the Christian Reformed Church retain the Dutch language in its college and in its grammar and high schools in order to maintain contact with the Calvinistic revival

---

[18]   Ibid.
[19]   Ibid.
[20]   *Banner*, 66/1799 (8/28/1931), 740. Article 85 of the church order then in force states that "churches whose usages differ from ours merely in non-essentials shall not be rejected."

underway in the Netherlands. Unless we do, he predicted, "it will be practically impossible to preserve the faith of our fathers."

Writing in the early 1930s, Kuiper stated that the denomination should also develop official, external relations with other evangelical churches. Presently it was impossible, he noted, since no local or national councils of evangelical churches and no associations for foreign and domestic missions existed where this could occur. His opposition to membership in the Federal Council of Churches and the practice of local councils in admitting modernists and liberals only heightened his wish that such a body existed for churches that hold to the fundamentals of the Christian faith. Kuiper's vision would be realized a decade later, when the National Association of Evangelicals was born. Meanwhile, he consoled himself and his readers with the assurance that unofficial relations existed among evangelical believers and churches through the reading of one another's theological and devotional books and magazines, through attendance at conferences together, and in other spiritually fortifying ways. Kuiper pointed to this contact to demonstrate that the charge of Christian Reformed "isolationism" is unfounded.[21] His next editorial in the series was devoted entirely to his refutation of Blekkink's essay in the *Leader*.

Two extremes are to be avoided in external relations, Kuiper believed. Isolation out of complacency and self-satisfaction would cause "spiritual petrefaction" [*sic*], or the inability and unwillingness to change.[22] This would eventually cause denominational death. But dismissing denominational loyalty and strengths, as though emphasizing them is Pharisaism, would produce blandness and relativism. Progressive, vital conservatism was Kuiper's recommended path. Let us build on and extend that which we have received, he urged. Let us insist on meaningful contact with other churches, but without apologizing for or hiding who we are. By any and all means, we should have no ecclesiastical or spiritual fellowship with modernists.

The perspective that Kuiper articulated in this early series of editorials is one that he maintained throughout his ministry. He cherished, emphasized, promoted, and defended the unique strengths of the Christian Reformed Church. He was unapologetic about denominational differences, but he considered them to be testimonies to the Spirit's unique work in different contexts. From them,

---

[21]   *Banner,* 67/1802 (9/18/1931), 812.
[22]   *Banner,* 67/1811 (11/20/1931),1028-29.

denominations could learn from one another. In a later editorial, "The Good of Denominationalism," he explained that appreciating one's denominational uniqueness "is conducive to ecclesiastical harmony, purity and variety" internally and enhances one's witness externally.[23] He developed each point. Kuiper from the outset of his work as editor criticized and warned against "the church union movement" that defined liberal and mainline ecumenicity. He was convinced that invariably it produced a lowest-common-denominator brand of Protestantism that was not equal to meeting the spiritual demands of the modern era.

Legitimate Associations

Kuiper's articulated position on ecumenicity was applied to a variety of subsequent issues. He noted with approval several times in the 1930s the fellowship fostered by the League of Evangelical Students, also on the Calvin campus, and endorsed the organization for church offerings. He promoted the first and second meetings of the American Calvinistic Conference in 1939 and 1942, respectively. The topics at the latter gathering show the breadth of the Calvinistic world-and-life view and the Reformed interest in matters civic and cultural, he observed.[24] He was pleased that orthodox Reformed speakers from the Reformed, Christian Reformed, Congregational, and a number of Presbyterian denominations participated.

He was unhappy when Klaas Schilder, a caustic Dutch minister calling for reform in his own church, visited Grand Rapids in 1939 and arrogantly invited Christian Reformed and Protestant Reformed leaders to a meeting to consider his theological resolution of the common grace controversy and his promised facilitation of the reunion of the two churches. Dominated by disquisitions by Schilder and Herman Hoeksema and an absence of serious interchange, the attempt failed. Berkhof and Kuiper were happy they had not attended the ecclesiastically unofficial event.

In the summer of 1943, Kuiper used two editorials to express frustration with the unilateral initiative of the young Orthodox Presbyterian Church to start a Christian university, with its reticence in taking a clear stand against lodge membership, and with its disapproval of the Christian Reformed Church's decision to join the

---

[23] *Banner,* 81/2572 (9/20/1946), 1076.
[24] *Banner,* 77/2343 (4/17/1942), 364-65.

NAE.[25] Relations were more constructive and cordial between the two churches when Machen was still alive, he observed.

Toward the end of the Second World War and immediately thereafter, he informed readers with sadness about the split in the Reformed Churches in the Netherlands and provided an incisive analysis of the theological differences on the doctrine of the covenant which contributed to the breach.[26] He commended the balanced statements of the Conclusions of Utrecht on these matters, as they had been approved by the Christian Reformed synod in 1908, and he regretted that Schilder's unwillingness to cooperate with the synodical process in the GKN had aggravated the situation. He drew a lesson on the importance of open and respectful interchange for his own denomination.

Kuiper's aversion to the Christian Reformed Church's membership in theologically compromised ecumenical organizations did not stop him from watching developments in them closely or from critiquing their initiatives in the *Banner*. His commitment to catholicity based on biblical fidelity compelled him to promote trans-denominational contacts and projects wherever he believed Christ was truly known and honored.

---

[25]   *Banner,* 78/2413 (8/20/1943), 685; and 78/2415 (9/3/1943), 716-17.
[26]   *Banner,* 81/2545 (3/8/1946), 292.

CHAPTER 12

The Believer and Society

For all of H.J. Kuiper's emphasis on spirituality, personal piety, and the church, he had a fairly robust and well-formed Kuyperian view of the Christian's place in society. When parishioner and Neland Avenue predecessor H. Henry Meeter published his book *Fundamental Principles of Calvinism,* which reflected that tradition, Kuiper wrote, "It belongs to the class of books whose appearance we hail with delight because it is the kind we need most."[1] It was early in his role as editor of the denominational weekly. Good books in polemics and devotions were necessary, he wrote, but Reformed Americans need books on Calvinism "more than all others." Let some say what they wanted about "unduly stressing our distinctive world-and-life view," that was what was needed because both laymen and leaders were rapidly losing their ability to imbibe this perspective from Dutch materials. Kuyper, Bavinck, and those around them produced "a wonderfully rich literature" which was "gradually becoming inaccessible to our people." It was the church's task "not only to develop the master thoughts of these great men of God, but also to popularize them," he wrote. That is why Meeter's book was so important and why Kuiper believed the church needed many more like it.

---

[1]   *Banner,* 66/1774 (2/27/1931), 189. That his esteem for Abraham Kuyper only "amounted to lip service" is questionable, given this editorial and many other calls H.J. Kuiper issued for social engagement and transformation. See Bratt, *Dutch Calvinism,* 126.

Tilt toward the Antithesis

The world-and-life view developed by Abraham Kuyper, Herman Bavinck, and their disciples revolved around the ideas of the antithesis and common grace. How one accented and balanced these two ideas determined how believers in the Christian Reformed Church perceived and took their places in human society. The antithesis, according to Kuiper, meant "contrast" and it stressed that the regenerate, believing community was radically, spiritually different from the world, or from unbelieving people. That contrast ought to come to expression in every sector of human society, in every dimension of human life. The idea of common grace emphasized that God was at work in the unbelieving community as well as among believers, accomplishing his purposes without changing peoples' hearts but guiding them by his Spirit to realize a measure of civic, public good. The antithesis had been operative in human history since the fall of Adam and Eve, and it pitted the seed of the serpent (unbelievers, the devil's followers) against the seed of the woman (believers, the Lord's people). The two groups were engaged in spiritual warfare that came to expression in every area of human endeavor. Common grace had been restraining evil as long as humanity had been sinful, and it explained why common cultural ground and a measure of cooperation could occur between believers and unbelievers.

Thus, the two ideas do not contradict each other, but they balance each other. Denial of the former ends in liberalism; denial of the latter ends in Anabaptism, Kuiper explained.[2] He injected both ideas into his editorials regularly, so consistently that his regular readers—the majority in the denomination—developed clear convictions about where they stood and why on a whole range of social issues and about which organizations in society to join or not join.

H.J. Kuiper once stated that believers must understand that the idea of the antithesis is the more important and strategic of the two ideas for guiding them through life on earth and into glory.[3] He

---

[2]   *Banner*, 69/1925 (2/9/1934), 116.

[3]   *Banner*, 74/2214 (10/12/1935), 940. Years later Henry Stob articulated what he and like-minded others had long believed when he challenged the idea of antithesis as it functioned for H.J. Kuiper and his side of the church. See Stob, "Observations on the Concept of the Antithesis," in De Klerk and De Ridder, *Perspectives*, 241-60. Denominational dynamics from 1880 through 1980 can be understood essentially in terms of the interplay and application of these two ideas.

acknowledged that the antithesis was also present within the believer and within the church, as the people of God struggled against the flesh. But—and this is highly significant—that is not how the idea was used in Kuiper's editorials. There it basically pitted the church against the world, believers against unbelievers, Dutch Reformed institutions against the main institutions and prevailing values of American society. In 1951, toward the end of his career, when he felt the second generation of his readers was becoming too comfortable and accommodated to North American society, Kuiper devoted three editorials to a biblical-theological survey of the idea of the antithesis, then five to the challenge of the antithesis. In the second set he spelled out the implications of the antithesis for every sphere or sector of human life.

Human Associations

Christians may, even must, associate with non-Christians or nominal Christians in human society, said Kuiper. But they may not be friends with them. One of "the most dangerous forms of worldliness" is forming friendships with worldly people, as both Paul and James warn in the New Testament. This has been the route out of the church and away from God for many of our young people, Kuiper once warned.[4] Christian high schools and colleges have the essential consequence of fostering Christian friendships, and for that reason they ought to admit only committed, orthodox Christian students into the student body. A person can have only one or at most several very close friends in a lifetime. Life without such a friend is lonely and contributes to many suicides. We are created as social creatures, needing the interchange of friendships, as the holy Trinity itself models. Openness, unshakable trust, durability, and giving and receiving wholesome criticism are all traits of true friendship.[5] We obviously must find friends among God's people, therefore, with those of like-minded values and convictions. Making friends is more difficult as we become older, and one of life's greatest losses is the death of a real friend. In an editorial specifically for young people, Kuiper urged them not to mistake spiritual separation from the world for clannishness. The latter is more pronounced among other ethnic-immigrant groups than among the Dutch, he contended.[6]

---

[4]   *Banner*, 70/2016 (11/22/1935), 1060.
[5]   *Banner*, 67/1865 (12/9/1932), 1068.
[6]   *Banner*, 70/2015 (11/15/1935), 1036.

"Mixed marriages" received frequent attention by the editor as a consequence of his theological perspective. Mixed marriages ethnically, nationally, denominationally, and racially were "inadvisable" because of the complications they produce for people who lack common ground. But mixed marriages spiritually are clearly forbidden by scripture. The latter kind weaken the church, Kuiper pointed out. On the other hand, spiritually strong marriages strengthen the church, society, couples, and their children. Spiritually renewed hearts are required for solid marriages, where devotions at the family altar are vibrant, always observed, and led by both spouses. The first few years of marriage are especially crucial, for then the patterns for the rest of the marriage are established and the potential for clashes are greatest. Differences are inevitable, but when they degenerate into quarrels, especially unresolved quarrels, bitterness develops and marital tragedy is invited. Forgiveness must be asked and granted, admonished Kuiper.[7] When the synod of 1944 received thirteen overtures concerning a proposal to change the church's position on admitting people divorced on unbiblical grounds and remarried, Kuiper protested, noting that it would be harmful to both the church and to society.[8] He admitted that early in his ministry he had favored relenting on this historic position, believing in the power of repentance and forgiveness, but that the sorry state of marriage in American society compelled him to change his mind. That December, following the synod's reaffirmation of its position, Kuiper pleaded with young people to avoid mixed marriages.

The idea of the antithesis governed choices not only concerning friendship and marriage for Kuiper, but he gave it weight in advocating Christian as opposed to public schools, in rejecting lodge membership, and in assessing whether one could join a secular labor union. Any organizations that required an oath of allegiance upon joining, operated in secrecy, employed quasireligious rituals, or articulated humanistic goals or values exhibited features of the kingdom of darkness and were at odds with the kingdom of light, in his opinion. Christians ought not to be associated with them, lest their Christian witness be compromised.

---

[7]   *Banner,* 74/2194 (5/18/1939), 460.

[8]   *Banner,* 79/2456 (6/16/1944), 556-57. At the time he wrote, the only "biblical ground" for divorce recognized by the Christian Reformed Church was adultery. After more than a century of intense, sustained debate on divorce and remarriage, the denomination adopted a more lenient position in 1980. See *1980 Agenda for Synod,* 310-28, for the report, *1980 Acts of Synod,* 40-41, for the decisions.

Two organizations above American reproach that were problematic for Kuiper and serve as examples of how he applied the idea of antithesis were the Boy Scouts and the Girl Scouts. During his first year as editor, he stated his reasons for opposing membership in the former. In 1937 he wrote a series of three editorials that articulated in more depth his opposition to the Boy Scout movement.

He had been favorably disposed to membership during his Englewood pastorate, he admitted, but then he studied its literature carefully. The *Handbook for Scoutmasters, A Manual of Leadership* was especially enlightening. Aiming at the physical, mental, and moral development of the boy, the movement advocated religious grounding of the young man without specifying a denominational preference. But the scout oath and the scout law suggested to Kuiper that the movement disseminated a form of modernism because these elements suggested that the young man is inherently capable of keeping the oath and following the law. This "doctrine of being good and doing good" was the essence of "scout religion," he stated. The law listed a number of virtues to be cultivated, but omitted honesty, truthfulness, and keeping the Sabbath. The handbook stated that scouting ideals were consistent with the values of "the modern church," and thus promoted the religion of modernism, Kuiper extrapolated.[9]

The second editorial in the series argued that the movement had features of the lodge. The third reviewed his own history with the movement, including discussions at ministerial *internos* meetings and a visit with two Boy Scout leaders that year at the Pantlind Hotel in Grand Rapids. In this editorial he reported that the outcome of that meeting was that he and several others formed a committee for proposing to the Young Men's Federation an alternative Christian boys' organization. Four years later he reported that a number of clubs had been formed and were doing well, even though they had no mechanism for staying in touch with one another. E.R. Post, principal of Grand Rapids Christian High School, the Reverend W. Kok, and Kuiper were on the original committee. They had met a number of times, developed the organizational model, drafted a manual, and recently decided to expand the group. Richard Postma, president of the American Federation of Young Men's Societies, two federation board members, and several others had been added.[10] It was the inception of the Calvinist Cadet Corps and its sister organization, Calvinettes,

9 *Banner,* 72/2116 (11/4/1937), 1036-37.
10 *Banner,* 76/2277 (1/3/1941), 4.

both of which were formally launched a decade later and subsequently adopted several name changes.

To those on the outside and some on the inside, separate organizations gave the appearance of "clannishness," denominational judgmentalism, and aloofness, despite Kuiper's usually studied examination of possible associations with the wider culture and his clear articulation of the Reformed principles on which his proposed alternatives were founded.

Race Relations

In the context of condemning the intolerance of Europe's fascist and socialist states, particularly Hitler's policy toward the Jews, Kuiper also condemned the intolerance of the Ku Klux Klan in North America.[11] That it was virtually his only comment on American race relations before the end of the Second World War is as much a commentary on society's racial complacency as on Kuiper's acceptance of the status quo. When he did begin to reflect editorially on the subject, he was consistent with his earlier reflections on mixed marriage. In 1945 he wrote two "In Brief" paragraphs on the matter.[12] The first, entitled "Nazis in America," recounted an American bishop's reaction to the ticket agent who inquired, when he called to book a train reservation, whether he was white or black. The bishop wrote that anyone who discriminates against blacks or Jews is a Nazi at heart. Kuiper admitted "an important element of truth" here, for "racial pride and race hatred" are wrong, unbiblical. He referenced Galatians 3:28. In the next piece, "No Distinctions at All?" he questioned the idea of "*absolute* equality between whites and negroes." The obvious differences between the "endowments" of individuals cannot be applied to races or to classes of people. But if there exist cultural differences, do they not "justify maintaining *certain* barriers?" he asked (italics Kuiper's). Kuiper defended integration of public places, full participation in public privileges, and equal access to public positions of leadership. But he advocated a miscegenation policy for "intimate social contacts" and marriage. He acknowledged that it was difficult to know "just where to draw the lines of distinction," but he was certain they existed. Hatred and disparagement of those who are racially different, however, is sinful, he stated.

[11]   *Banner,* 73/2172 (12/15/1938), 1156.
[12]   *Banner,* 80/2525 (10/19/1945), 965.

Eugene Callender (right) welcomed by Herman Bel, president of the Synod of 1952, after it approved his candidacy for ordination.

In 1951 the home missions board called the Reverend Eugene Callender, a black American and a graduate of Westminster Seminary, for evangelism in Haarlem. The appointment received considerable interest in the church and by the synod. A committee of leaders drafted a series of resolutions on race relations that were considered and approved at the Young Calvinist convention that summer. In that context, Kuiper again commented on the subject of race—in the fall of 1951 and the first half of 1952. When he wrote that hiring Callender to plant Negro churches was preferable to assimilating a handful of Negro families into white congregations, Harry Boer wrote that that position was tantamount to segregation. Kuiper responded that the synod had not expressed itself on which strategy was preferable. He also observed that intellectuals influenced by liberal presuppositions posited the inherent equality of the races but minimized the inequalities. Kuiper maintained the *de facto* inequality of the black and white races culturally, not soteriologically, spoke appreciatively of the social and economic "gains" recently made by blacks, and called for a careful, biblical study of this "complicated" subject.[13] His was a patronizing position and was out of step with the more progressive and enlightened position in the church and in society.

[13] *Banner,* 86/2831 (10/19/1951), 1252, 1277.

The next spring, in April and May, Kuiper analyzed the Young Calvinist resolutions on race relations in six editorials. He applauded and affirmed the early ones, which explained the Reformed position on creation, fall, and salvation without regard to racial difference. When Kuiper again challenged the notion of cultural equality and proposed that wealthy investors create modern and acceptable housing developments exclusively for blacks, he crossed a social line and incurred a firestorm of reaction. Even his personal association with and praise for George Washington Carver, his admiration for Booker T. Washington as "one of the greatest orators" he had ever heard, and his condemnation of Southern Jim Crow laws did not offset his offense.[14]

Callender, who had been deluged with apologies from embarrassed members of the denomination, wrote a temperate and irenic response, noting that racism was the most "stubborn social sin in the world today" and the greatest "hindrance to evangelism."[15] He did not accuse Kuiper of racism but expressed his deep concern and "annoyance" that Kuiper's views might be taken as the views of the denomination, which he knew they were not.

Kuiper assured readers and Callender that his positions were his own and not the church's, although he noted that he had received considerable support for his opinions. In the end, he said that prejudice had nothing to do with the patterns he proposed for race relations, and he said no one had taken the trouble to refute his arguments on them. He still believed what he had written, therefore, concerning separate housing and churches. They were views which he never retracted. But he never again addressed the issue of race relations in his *Banner* editorials and regrettably never mounted an attack against racial injustice in North America or against the emerging *apartheid* in Reformed South Africa.

Worldliness

H.J. Kuiper's pastoral and synodical attention to worldliness, which reflected his deep conviction that the antithesis called for defining and living a distinctively Reformed world-and-life view, naturally found expression editorially in the *Banner*.[16] He wrote what he preached and

---

[14]   *Banner*, 87/2852 (3/14/1952), 324-25, 348.
[15]   *Banner*, 87/2863 (5/30/1952), 700.
[16]   For his pastoral and synodical attention to this issue, see chapters 3, pp. 00, and 4, pp. 59-63, 71-74.

what he applied to "problem cases" at Broadway and Neland Avenue. In his editorials he broadened the range of associations and the number of activities that he branded "worldly."

Not just social dancing, card-playing, and theater attendance came under withering editorial attack. He wrestled in print with the propriety of laborers joining unions whose tactics were biblically problematic and that were governed by a spirit of self-interest. He regularly attacked gambling as a spiritual menace. Even raffles were not benign, but a form of gambling. Boxing was an especially offensive American pastime inappropriate for God's children; following it or attending matches was, he said mid-way through his first year as editor, "a sinful worldly amusement." Any game of chance trifled with God's providence, whereas games of skill were appropriate pastimes; caroms, checkers, chess, and quorts received editorial imprimatur. Frequenting bars and saloons did not pass muster, but Kuiper believed that ratifying the 18th Amendment to the U.S. Constitution had been a mistake and ought to be repealed. Liquor ought to be politically regulated, not forbidden. When Grand Rapids women began forming bridge clubs, Kuiper wrote that the activity was contrary to the spirit of 1928. A circus was a worldly place, undoubtedly because of scanty dress and risk to performers rather than any concern for animal rights. The Chicago Exposition might be attended with discernment, but patronizing county fairs, especially the midway, was discouraged. He warned farmers against joining the Grange because of its similarities to secret societies. He approved of attending professional baseball games, but when the Detroit Tigers played in the World Series of 1934, he wrote that tickets were too expensive for a responsible Christian. Listening to broadcasts of Sunday games was wholly inappropriate. Kuiper was uneasy about dramatic presentations, but he tolerated college and high school and even young peoples' society plays as long as they were approved by responsible and spiritually mature authority figures. Immodest dress and preoccupation with the latest fashions were spiritual danger signals. Annually he warned against the secularism and materialism of Christmas celebrations. And he wished Halloween, which was an American holiday of pagan derivation, had never been conceived. He applauded several initiatives to eliminate political corruption in Grand Rapids, to curb the sale of pornographic materials, and to stop prostitution. When television became a feature of American life, he applauded the potential of the invention but predicted that its undisciplined use would "test our faith" as believers. Kuiper's attention to worldliness was broad, practical, and continuous; but it usually focused on personal morality and behavior and seldom addressed the more complex issues of political and economic policy.

In 1929 W. Burggraaf reviewed a new book by R.B. Kuiper in the *Leader*. He praised R. B. as being wiser than some of his colleagues and their synod for defining Christian action "by a set of rules." H.J. Kuiper was quick to enlighten his Reformed Church counterpart. He noted that R.B. had signed the 1928 synodical report against worldly amusements as one of the committee members and that he had served on the synodical advisory committee that had recommended it to the churches.[17] Despite the correction and clarification, H.J. Kuiper became identified as the Christian Reformed crusader against worldliness. His repeated editorializing on the theme warrants this identity.

The publication committee reported in 1930 that it had not carried out its mandate to reprint the worldly amusements report in the two church papers and in pamphlet form. Consistories had been directed to send orders for the pamphlet to the committee secretary. Heyns reported that, by the spring of 1930, he had received none. The synod received the committee's report for information and defeated an overture from Classis Grand Rapids West to print and to distribute the pamphlet to every church at synodical expense.[18] This stirred the Reverend John De Haan, Sr., Christian Reformed minister in Lamont, Michigan, to undertake the project himself and at his own expense. A year later, H.J. Kuiper reported that the eight thousand copies originally printed by De Haan were already sold out, which thoroughly disproved those synodical voices that had said the demand for the brochure would be minimal.[19] He admitted that some orders had been cancelled because of the Depression, but Kuiper was confident that there would be future demand for it. In the years ahead, he fueled that demand by editorializing on worldliness as he saw it, referencing the report regularly, and resisting subsequent overtures to modify its prohibitions.

Kuiper's resistance to worldliness was motivated by a fear of losing healthy spirituality. When values and practices deflected the believer's love and attention from God and his kingdom and fastened the affections of the soul on the things of this age, worldliness was

---

[17]   *Banner*, 64/1692 (7/19/1929), 500.
[18]   *1930 Acts of Synod*, 14-15.
[19]   *Banner*, 66/1784 (5/8/1931), 428-29.

present. Worldliness was understandably congenial to liberal thinking and theology. The state of the heart and condition of the soul were Kuiper's basic concerns.

He allowed that Christian organizations could legitimately show good, prescreened educational films. Dr. Wyngaarden of the seminary had been doing so. The objection was not to movies as such. They are nothing more than a series of rapidly flashed still photos, he argued. But a film entitled *Zimba*, sponsored by the Christian Ex-servicemen's Club and advertised in the *Banner*, contained some objectionable language and a scene of half-naked African women dancing. He clearly disapproved of Buiten's latitude in accepting the ad and acknowledged, "Personally, we would be ready to support any movement sponsored by Christian people to produce pictures which could safely be shown in any reputable place adapted for the purpose."[20] It was not wrong to provide good movies for the entertainment of our young people in the proper setting. But the theater and Hollywood films were worldly, unfit for Christians.

A month later he followed up with an editorial giving a long quote from someone who had been involved with the theater for four decades and who emphasized that it was virtually impossible for a woman engaged in the acting profession to maintain her moral integrity and sexual purity. Life in that culture inevitably coarsened morals, and Kuiper stated categorically that Christians should shun it and have no part in supporting it for that reason. In 1933 he cited a book by a Pennsylvania public official arguing that the movie industry, which thrived on sex and violence, corroded the nation's morality and contributed to crime. In 1937 he produced a series of five editorials parsing Christian Reformed attitudes and practices regarding Hollywood films and reported gratefully that the denomination's majority still abstained totally from movie attendance.

In 1938, in the second of two editorials on dancing, Kuiper admitted that the Bible does not condemn "the promiscuous dance," but only because it was unknown in Bible times.[21] However, the Bible has much to say about sexual arousal, lust, and putting oneself in a position of vulnerability to impure thoughts and actual sexual immorality. The dance, even folk and square dancing, invite such ideas and are stepping stones to more intimate forms of dancing, he argued.

---

[20] *Banner*, 67/1813 (12/4/1931), 189.
[21] *Banner*, 73/2134 (11/4/1938), 244.

In the late 1940s and early 1950s, when efforts were again made to temper the language of 1928, Kuiper's editorials lobbied against them. He summarized, explained, and defended the report in great detail for a new generation. The denominational position on worldly amusements remained unchanged, but certainly not unchallenged or untested, during his tenure as editor. For H.J. Kuiper and his generation, to combat worldliness was an important dimension of fostering godliness and living completely to the glory of the Heavenly Father.

Politics and Government

Kuiper upheld the Reformed doctrine that government was ordained by God to restrain sin in human society, to maintain justice, to defend borders against aggression, and to promote the peace and order in which life can flourish. Government, then, was fundamentally God's tool for holding in check the dark side of the antithesis; as such it was a gift of common grace. If government officials were instruments of God who deserve respect and support, as he believed, Kuiper did not advocate Christians entering politics. He encouraged his readers repeatedly and strongly to intercede for government leaders.

Kuiper held that democracy or a republican form of government has so many advantages that people would never choose autocracy or dictatorship over it, though sometimes those forms are forced on them. Lethargy of voters, either by not exercising their duty to vote or by not informing themselves of the issues, was the biggest problem with this form of government, in his view. Christians should lead the way by doing their civic duty and by being informed voters, though it is not a sin not to vote. He did not favor compulsory voting, as was the law in the Netherlands. Generally, modest politicians made the most honest and effective leaders. Be suspicious of candidates who trade politically on their church membership, he warned.[22]

Common grace makes the participation of Christians in the political process possible. Healthy nationalism and patriotism are natural instincts created by God. Christians should express both loyalties without the guilt imposed by pacifists or those working for a global dictatorship of the proletariat, he wrote in the 1930s. Christians,

[22] *Banner,* 65/1728 (4/4/1930), 317. Zwaanstra, *Reformed Thought and Experience,* 233-34, documents that years earlier, in Holland, Kuiper advocated local option on the issue of both prohibition and the formation of a Christian political party.

in fact, make the best patriots and citizens, for their political faithfulness includes intercession for their country, confession to God of their nation's failures, support of Christian institutions, healthy home life, sending their children to Christian schools, and obedience to the laws of the land. All this contributes to a healthier, stronger country, Kuiper wrote.[23] It is as natural for a Christian citizen to love and support his country as it is for a father to love and protect his children.

As he watched the weak democracies of Europe crumble and be replaced by dictatorships, Kuiper celebrated the freedoms of the United States, including the freedom of religion. He cautioned that the greatest threat to freedom was the irresponsible and unrestrained abuse of freedom, for this compelled society to impose limits and restraints.[24]

Kuiper's position on the place of the church in society was clear. He contended that there is no such thing as a social gospel, only social implications of the gospel. The church is called to preach the gospel, not "social regeneration."

> The church that preaches on all kinds of social themes and spends its time in working for human betterment has forsaken its heavenly calling. Its glory has departed. Jesus did not command his disciples to go into all the world to clear the slums, abolish slavery, bring capital and labor together or work for world-peace. That may be the business of the Christian, but it is not the calling of the institutional church.[25]

Kuiper penned this opinion in the mid-thirties. Two months later he amplified the individual Christian's responsibility: It "is not sound Calvinism" for the individual Christian to ignore social evils or not to work hard to challenge and remove them. Christians are to fight sin "in every sphere" of life in which they are engaged.[26]

The next year, he allowed some room for social issues on the pulpit. He instructed that ministers who attempt to let the gospel light shine on social issues should be guided by several principles.[27] First, they should recognize that there are many social policies on which Christians can legitimately differ; ministers should never preach their personal opinions on these matters as though they are God's

---

23 *Banner*, 66/1792 (7/3/1931), 620-21.
24 *Banner*, 68/1884 (4/21/1933), 364-65.
25 *Banner*, 69/1927 (2/23/1934), 164.
26 *Banner*, 69/1933 (4/6/1934), 292.
27 *Banner*, 70/1990 (5/17/1935), 460.

will. Second, ministers should, when speaking on these matters, be thoroughly informed, since many of these issues are very complex. Third, when doing so, one should be sure he and his church members are above reproach on social matters like paying fair wages and providing decent working conditions. Upon occasion he reminded readers that ministers, and especially Christian school teachers, were underpaid.

Kuiper was in something of a quandary as an editor and a preacher. He wanted no part of the social gospel, but he felt compelled to apply the gospel to social issues. And he did, with limitations and restraint. When President Roosevelt proposed and promoted the National Recovery Act in an attempt to overcome unemployment during the Depression and appealed to the churches and their leaders to endorse the idea, Kuiper compromised. He did not participate in the Sunday stipulated for promoting the initiative or use the liturgical suggestions and materials provided for it, but noted that most Christian Reformed people admired and supported the president's efforts and that ministers should definitely pray for God's blessing on the National Recovery Act.[28] Kuiper believed that the United States should not have gotten involved in the First World War, and as the Second World War approached, he advocated the isolationist position taken by Senator Vanden Berg of Grand Rapids.[29] He went so far as to write that he opposed the sale of weapons overseas, even if it gave the advantage to Germany, and he urged people to write their representatives in Washington to vote for that position. In early 1941, he was still editorializing that America had "no right" to go to war with either Germany or Japan. But he changed his editorial tune after the bombing of Pearl Harbor. He bristled at the War Department's directive to keep the defense industry working around the clock, seven days a week, but conceded as already noted that this was "work of necessity," advocated lobbying the department to give time off for people to attend church, and feared that Sunday labor would continue after the war.

Whenever during his career a local referendum was held on instituting a lottery or allowing Sunday commerce, Kuiper told readers to vote against it. He also advocated capital punishment, unemployment insurance, and fair wages. He opposed a closed shop but railed against the sins of unregulated capitalism that exploited workers. Following several editorial announcements on House Bill

[28]   *Banner,* 68/1903 (9/8/1933), 724.
[29]   *Banner,* 74/2211 (9/21/1939), 868-69.

4264 proposing that Christian school tuition be deductible from gross income for tax purposes, Kuiper reported that the young congressman Gerald Ford had assured him that it was still under study in committee and that he would support it when it came to the floor. Kuiper urged people to write their own congressmen, urging them to support the legislation.[30] Where it affected the Christian's personal values, religious practices, and public morality, Kuiper did not hesitate as preacher or editor to advocate a political position.

After he wrote his major paper on socialism in college and contended with a professed Socialist in his second congregation, Kuiper was consistently and emphatically opposed to socialism. His position became more thoughtful and nuanced during the Great Depression. Two years into the Roosevelt Administration, he wrote that America was experiencing "a definite trend toward socialistic thinking," as seen in administration policies.[31] He agreed with the political columnist Walter Lippman, however, that these policies did not amount to "genuine socialism," for the Socialist Party was dissatisfied with them. In the directed economies of both communism and fascism, little room was accorded individual initiative and rights; this is not the case with Roosevelt's programs, Kuiper noted. In directed economies, "censorship, espionage, and terrorism" are required for them to function and survive. They cannot tolerate allegiance to any higher power than the supreme political authority, hence they are inherently antireligious and anti-Christian. "Christian socialism is a misnomer, a contradiction in terms," he wrote. With all its faults, capitalism encourages individual initiative and freedom. Lippman pointed out that the United States under Roosevelt had found ways to mitigate socialist distortions, and Kuiper concurred.

In another editorial of the same vintage, Kuiper admitted that formerly he had favored government ownership of utilities and natural resources. Mismanagement under the National Industrial Relations Act and rigid control of agricultural production had cured him, however. These and other initiatives threaten to "wreck" the New Deal, he ventured. Those clamoring for more government involvement and control were "drifting away from a Christian philosophy of the state."[32]

[30] *Banner*, 89/2952 (3/12/1954), 325, 349.
[31] *Banner*, 69/1942 (6/8/1934), 509.
[32] *Banner*, 70/1980 (3/8/1935), 220-21. Bratt finds that Kuiper's suppport for the New Deal "declined rapidly" between 1934 and 1936. Bratt, *Dutch Calvinism*, 148.

Dean Henry Ryskamp of Calvin College protested when Kuiper invoked him and the Dutch theological ethicist at the Free University, Gerhard Geesink, since both took a less restricted view of government initiatives than the editor had taken. Fifteen years later, the gulf between Kuiper and faculty leaders at the college was even deeper, as the exchanges over Flynn's book show.

Peace and War

During the early years of his editorship, Kuiper resisted the strongly outspoken pacifist movement. Liberal churches and the Federal Council of Churches promoted it. Kuiper observed that if the United States had been more prepared militarily, Germany might have been deterred from attacking its shipping in the First World War, a war entered against the will of a majority of the American public, including himself. The peace movement errs when it says that war is never justified, he offered in the early thirties. Most times it is not, but sometimes it is both essential and righteous. But, a warring spirit is never acceptable to God. Christians should celebrate efforts to promote peace. Sometimes, however, nations must band together in warfare against rogue nations to maintain world order. At the same time, Kuiper was not naive about expecting a long era of global peace and tranquility at the end of history.[33] Two years later he wrote a long series exposing pacifism as biblically unwarranted and as practically dangerous. Human nature being as depraved as it is requires maintaining a strong military force as a deterrent to aggression.

Ironically, Kuiper commenced the series in March 1934, the month that Frederick Wezeman began publishing his socially and politically progressive *Chicago Messenger*, a regular contributor to which was John J. De Boer, Wezeman's nephew and a professor of education at Chicago Normal College.[34] Kuiper's stance infuriated De Boer, who accused the *Banner* editor of placing a "sentimental halo" on militarism. "Step down from your high horse, and let's reason together," implored Kuiper. Show me where my interpretation and application of scripture are wrong. Emotional outbursts are tantamount to a concession of defeat, he needled. "A pacifistic God would not avenge sin, give up his only-begotten Son for the satisfaction of his justice in order to make salvation possible, or cast the impenitent into hell."[35] The exchange

---

[33] *Banner,* 67/1821 (1/29/1932), 100.
[34] Swierenga, *Dutch Chicago*, 413-14.
[35] *Banner,* 69/1938 (5/11/1934), 412-13.

happened two years before Kuiper would express his theological mistrust of Wezeman and his unhappiness with his supporters, but the estrangement between the more progressive Chicago leaders in Christian education and Kuiper and the ministerial establishment was already evident on issues like pacifism and militarism.

During the late thirties, Kuiper wrote often on political and military developments. He deplored Mussolini's invasion of Ethiopia. Glad that the United States was not a member, he regarded the League of Nations as weak, vacillating, and unwilling to enforce its sanctions against Italy for its aggression. He deplored Hitler's militarism, secularism, and policy toward the Jews. At the end of the decade he wrote that the loss of freedom in European nations followed the loss of Christianity; the latter invited and caused the former, he believed. As much as he deplored Germany's aggression against its neighbors, he believed Hitler was a modern Cyrus whom God was using to judge Europe for turning away from him. Yet, he remained steadfastly isolationist until the United States itself was attacked. On the other hand, in the early months of World War II he deplored as "misguided" the opposition in liberal seminaries and liberal ministerial associations to the military draft and the public advocacy in those quarters of claiming conscientious objector status. The tragedy was that these positions gave the church the appearance of a fifth column entity. Unfortunately, it had the most to lose should godless totalitarianism prevail, he analyzed.[36]

Once the United States entered the conflict, Kuiper supported the effort completely and advocated unwavering patriotism. He was especially concerned about the spiritual welfare of Christian Reformed young men and women in military service. Early on he promoted the use of camp pastors near large bases where soldiers were in training. He ran news articles that followed the work of Christian Reformed chaplains in all branches of military service. He began a program of sending the *Banner* at no cost to young people in the service. He urged pastors and families to pray fervently for their physical and spiritual protection. He voiced his concerns about the impact that heavy work schedules, women in the workforce, Sunday labor, spousal separation, increased wealth from high wages and overtime, and other wartime realities would have on the moral and spiritual lives of church members. In 1942 he critiqued the thirteen articles contained in, "Bases of a Just and Durable Peace," a statement formulated by a commission

[36] *Banner,* 75/2274 (12/13/1940), 1156.

of the Federal Council of Churches as not being explicitly Christian. In 1943 he translated and ran a dozen installments from a fine book by Dr. H. Colijn articulating a Reformed position on citizenship and national identity, one embraced by Colijn's Antirevolutionary Party in the Netherlands.

In 1944 Kuiper began to think about the role of the church in the post-war world. First, it should be realistic, he advised, for interest in religion will not increase after the war. Also, the church had no right "to demand a place at the peace table" of political resolution, as liberal churchmen expected. It should influence policies through the preaching of the Word. It should "deal with fundamental moral principles, not with policies . . . ." The church should be concerned about service personnel by ministering to them faithfully while they were still in uniform, and by cultivating a deeper spirituality herself.[37] This was the most significant contribution the church could make to rebuilding life after the war.

At the end of the war, Kuiper celebrated victory but grieved for those who had been killed, maimed, or dispossessed. He observed that neither the United States nor Germany had repented of the sins that had precipitated the conflict: evolutionism, hatred of the Jews, intolerance of true religion, and class hatred. In an editorial entitled, "The Moral Aspect of Atomic Bombing," Kuiper was aghast at the destruction of Hiroshima and echoed the dread of the Vatican and the *New York Times* in response. Convinced that wars would not cease, he wondered which nations would use the atom bomb next, against whom, and how long it would be before it would be deployed against American cities. "We must be sure that our cause, which in the beginning was a righteous one, does not become unrighteous because of the use of inhumane methods in fighting our enemy."[38] He stopped short of condemning the bombing of Hiroshima, and he never considered pacifism as an alternative. Seven years later Kuiper barely mentioned the Korean War.

Conclusion

In the sixteen years of his editorial life through the Second World War, H.J. Kuiper displayed an informed, wide-ranging engagement with social issues. He thought about the world and its condition as a neo-Calvinist, one persuaded that he had been called to claim every aspect

[37]   *Banner,* 79/2461 (7/21/1944), 676-77.
[38]   *Banner,* 80/1931 (8/18/1945), 748.

Kuiper toward the end
of his tenure at the
Banner.

of human life and endeavor for the glory of God and in obedience to the Lordship of Christ. He read widely. He critiqued responsibly for the most part. He drew out the social implications of the gospel where application was obvious, and he allowed for varying opinion where they were not. But his social commentary was always embedded in the categories of the gospel. It was never a substitute for them. He showed a measure of toleration for federal social programs that in less desperate times he would have resisted. He was honest about changes in his political and social thinking made during his career. He had not been inflexible, but the changes he made were definitely in a more conservative direction. That shift reflected his deepening conviction about the radical, desperate sinfulness of human nature and human institutions.

By contrast, the last decade of Kuiper's editorship showed comparatively less attention to social and political issues. The one exception was his rather regular editorializing on labor unions for several years. He appreciated the corrective that unions had brought to the exploitation of workers by unchecked, unregulated capitalism. But by mid-century he deplored the corruption, the methods, and the naked self-interest of several of the most powerful American labor unions. He urged support of the Christian Labor Association as an alternative. His attention now was focused more exclusively on the church, personal morality, and American evangelicalism. These were themes prominent during the early phase of his editorship as well. But now his editorial interests narrowed somewhat. The shift was not a reversal. He merely, but definitely, tacked with the shifting cultural winds of a new era. Kuiper had always believed and written that this age is ultimately unredeemable. In his final years he concentrated on the family of the redeemed and what he thought they needed to hear "to live and die happily."

By then the times were beginning to pass him by. Kuiper's clash with emerging attitudes on race relations coincided with his intense disagreement with academic leaders over Flynn's book and the National Association of Evangelicals. It also overlapped with the turbulence within the college and seminary over allegedly liberal sympathies. His long-defended position against worldliness was being more openly and emphatically tested. The appearance of the *Reformed Journal* and *Torch and Trumpet* in this setting is simply an indication that positions were crystallizing as a new phase of Christian Reformed cultural engagement began. The restraint so clearly articulated and forcefully promoted by the earlier Kuiper was increasingly difficult to maintain. Whether "safety" was the chief concern or a caricature of a deeper spirituality became the dominating issue. Because matters of the heart are subject, ultimately, only to divine scrutiny and judgment, debate about them is irresolvable and, if persistent, inevitably fractious.

Epilogue

When H.J. Kuiper died in December 1962, three weeks short of his seventy-seventh birthday, the Christian Reformed Church had not yet entered the years of cultural turmoil that would redefine the world and to a significant extent also the church. The racial polarization that left inner cities in Los Angeles and Newark and Detroit in ashes was still just over the horizon. John F. Kennedy's Camelot prevailed. Vietnam was a remote, largely unheard of former French colony to which the U.S. government had assigned military advisors to equip an emerging democracy against encroaching communism; war clouds were still only the size of a man's fist. The sexual revolution, inaugurated with "the pill" and accelerated by women's liberation and abortion on demand, was barely underway and substantially undetected. The Christian Reformed Church remained tied theologically to the apron strings of the mother church in the Netherlands. Vatican II had been announced, but it was still the era of Protestant-Catholic, and Protestant denominational, balkanization. The Third World independence movement was in its infancy, and Western power and values retained control globally.

Kuiper belonged to and died within the middle years of the Christian Reformed Church's existence, when the world was still relatively stable and intelligible from a Euro-American and Protestant perspective. As a pastor and an editor he brought the gospel in and for a world whose foundations, while shaken by the world's two hot wars and its subsequent cold war, looked as though they might hold. But whether they would hold, as he had contended consistently throughout his long ministry, would depend on constant spiritual vigilance and uncompromised defense of the faith. He maintained to the last the essential calling of the Christian pulpit in maintaining social order through preaching conversion to Christ and to the norms of Christ's kingdom.

Kuiper was persuaded that the Reformed view of the world and the believer's place in it transcended in excellence all other religious or ideological options. He devoted a lifetime to defining and defending that position. With others, he led the church out of its immigrant infancy into an era of religious confidence marked by a disciplined, loyal, and generous devotion to denominational enterprises. The church became American, but only warily and certainly not fully so. Religious leaders continued to remind it, though with increasingly less force and clarity, that the religious antithesis placed it fundamentally at odds with "the world." H.J. Kuiper and leaders like him hedged it about with separate organizations and projects designed to protect and propagate Reformed distinctiveness.

The years of his ministry were in many ways years of growth and spiritual prosperity. Throughout his career he was ever mindful of how quickly a religious establishment could lose its first loves, its theological moorings and its spiritual vitality. His energies were devoted to preventing such an occurrence, even until the month of his unexpected death. His commitment to this calling never wavered, although after 1950 his capacity to discern the complexities of new times and issues and to lead effectively were diminished. Nonetheless, Kuiper played a very significant part in shaping the Christian Reformed Church in the years of his ministry.

Within a decade—certainly two—after Kuiper's death, both the world and the church would confront new challenges that would test a new generation of church leaders. They would not—could not—do so without drawing heavily on the legacy of his generation or without contending with its limitations.

Appendix

Ministerial Service

Henry J. Kuiper: Representative Positions of Ministerial Service

(The following list was compiled from material in the annual Yearbook *of the CRC, the annual* Acts of Synod, *and various other records. It undoubtedly is not exhaustive, and it does not include leadership positions held in the congregations Kuiper served, nor ad hoc classical assignments. Some positions were held for many years, others only briefly; only the year in which the particular service commenced is given. Nomenclature in the sources is not always consistent.)*

1907   Ordained, pastor, Luctor CRC, Luctor, Kansas
1908   Alternate, CRC home missions committee
        Teacher, Luctor Christian School
1909   Alternate, CRC heathen missions committee
        Delegate to synod, Classis Iowa; advisory committee on church
          order, varia
1910   Minister, Prospect Park CRC, Holland, Michigan
1911   Finance committee, Classis Holland
1912   Alternate, emeritus committee
1913   Minister, Second Englewood CRC, Chicago, Illinois
1914   *Ex bonis publicis* committee, Classis Illinois
        Sunday school rooster committee, Classis Illinois
1915   Deputy for Jewish evangelism, Classis Illinois
        Delegate to synod, Classis Illinois; committee on appointments;
          advisory committee on protests, reporter;
        Board, Chicago Christian High School

1916   Sunday school committee, Classis Illinois
         Committee to contact Chicago Tract Society, Classis Illinois
1917   Student fund committee, Classis Illinois
         Chicago-area Young People's League, president
1918   CRC committee for a uniform order of worship
         Tract committee, Classis Illinois
         Minister, Broadway CRC, Grand Rapids, Michigan
1919   Domestic missions committee, Classis Grand Rapids West;
1920   CRC tract committee
1921   Board, Grand Rapids Christian High School, chair
         Associate and education department editor, the *Witness*
1922   Delegate to synod, Classis Grand Rapids West; advisory
         committee on the Janssen matter, reporter
1923   Stated clerk, Classis Grand Rapids West
         Alternate, Calvin College and Seminary board
         CRC committee for the alliance of Reformed churches
1924   Delegate to synod, Classis Grand Rapids West; reception
         committee; advisory committee on protests re the Janssen
         matter, reporter
         Calvin College and Seminary board CRC committee on
         divorce
c. 1925 *New Christian Hymnal* committee, de facto editor
1927   Alternate, CRC board of foreign missions
         Alternate, synodical deputy, Classis Grand Rapids West CRC
         committee on worldly amusements
1928   Calvin College and Seminary board, vice president, supervisory
         committee,
         Associate editor, the *Young Calvinist*
         Delegate to synod, Classis Grand Rapids West; vice president;
         committee on appointments, chair; advisory committee on
         publications and education
         Editor-elect, the *Banner*
         CRC committee on introducing hymns
         Grand Rapids City Mission Board, president
1929   Alternate, classical committee, Classis Grand Rapids West
         Calvin College and Seminary board, secretary, supervisory
         committee
         Editor-in-chief, the *Banner*
         Minister, Neland Avenue CRC, Grand Rapids, Michigan

1930   Delegate to synod, Classis Grand Rapids East; advisory committee on introducing hymns

1932   Classical committee, Classis Grand Rapids East

Delegate to synod, Classis Grand Rapids East; vice president; advisory committee on psalms and hymns

CRC committee on principles of evangelism

CRC emergency committee for fields, workers, and funds, chair

1934   Convenes synod, preaches synodical sermon; Neland Avenue, convening church

CRC *Psalter Hymnal* committee, chair

1936   CRC emergency committee

Delegate to synod, Classis Grand Rapids East; president

Editor, five-volume Heidelberg Catechism sermon series

1937   Alternate, synodical deputy, Classis Grand Rapids East

Delegate to synod, Classis Grand Rapids East; president

1938   Opens synod; delivers welcoming speech

Alternate, synodical deputy, Classis Grand Rapids East

1939   Reformed Bible Institute board, president

1941   Synodical deputy, Classis Grand Rapids East

1942   Delivered commencement address, Calvin College and Seminary

1943   Alternate delegate to synod, Classis Grand Rapids East (cf. *1943 AOS*, 144)

1945   CRC committee for publication of Reformed tracts

1946   Delegate to the National Association of Evangelicals convention

Publication committee, National Association of Evangelicals

CRC committee to investigate the views of D. H. Kromminga, chair

1949   CRC committee to review synodical decisions on worldly amusements

Vice-president, Evangelical Press Association

1950   President, Evangelical Press Association

1957   Editorial committee, *Torch and Trumpet*; managing editor

Bibliography

Primary Sources

Acts of Synod of the Christian Reformed Church
Agenda for Synod of the Christian Reformed Church
Annuary of the Theological School, 1901-1902
The *Banner*
The *Calvin Forum*
The *Grand Rapids Herald*
The *Grand Rapids Press*
Jaarboekje voor de Hollandsche Chr. Ger. Kerk, in Noord Amerika
Minutes:
> Broadway Christian Reformed Church consistory
> Calvin College and Seminary board of curators
> Classis Grand Rapids East of the Christian Reformed Church
> Classis Grand Rapids West of the Christian Reformed Church
> Classis Holland of the Christian Reformed Church
> Classis Illinois of the Christian Reformed Church
> Joint Home Missions Committee, Classes Grand Rapids East and West
> Luctor Christian Reformed Church consistory
> Neland Avenue Christian Reformed Church consistory
> Prospect Park Christian Reformed Church consistory
> Publication Committee of the Christian Reformed Church
> Reformed Bible Institute board of trustees

Second Englewood Christian Reformed Church consistory
The *Reformed Journal*
Religion and Culture
Torch and Trumpet/Outlook
The *Witness*
Yearbook of the Christian Reformed Church

Secondary Sources

Beets, Henry. *The Christian Reformed Church*. Grand Rapids: Baker, 1946.

Berkhof, Dena. "The Story of My Life." Grand Rapids: mimeographed, n.d.

Berkhof, Louis, et al. "Waar het in de Zaak Janssen Omgaat." Grand Rapids: n.p., 1921.

Boer, Harry R. "Ralph Janssen: The 1922 Loaded Court." *Reformed Journal*, 23 (January, 1973), 22-28.

Boonstra, Harry. *Our School: Calvin College and the Christian Reformed Church*, The Historical Series of the Reformed Church in America, no. 39. Grand Rapids: Eerdmans, 2001.

Bratt, James D. *Dutch Calvinism in Modern America: A History of a Conservative Subculture*. Grand Rapids: Eerdmans, 1984.

Bratt, James D. "Lambert J. Hulst: The Pastor as Leader in an Immigrant Community," in *The Dutch- American Experience: Essays in Honor of Robert P. Swierenga*, ed. Hans Krabbendam and Larry J. Wagenaar, VU Studies on Protestant History, no.5. Amsterdam: VU Uitgeverij, 2000, 209-21.

Brink, J.W. "Personal Reminiscences of the Late Rev. J.H. Vos." *Banner*, 48/856 (3/16/1913): 155.

Bruggink, Donald J., and Kim N. Baker, ed. *By Grace Alone, Stories of the Reformed Church in America*. Grand Rapids: Eerdmans, 2004.

Bultema, Harry. *Valiant and Diligent for Truth: The Autobiography of Harry Bultema*, with a foreword by Daniel C. Bultema. Grand Rapids: Grace Publications, 1986.

Centennial, 1857-1957: First Christian Reformed Church, Grand Rapids, Michigan. Grand Rapids: First Christian Reformed Church, 1957.

De Jong, James A. "Growing and Changing: the Seminary and the College, 1945-1972," in *Love beyond Knowledge, Grace beyond Limits*, ed. Richard H. Harms. Grand Rapids: Calvin College and Seminary, 2001, 23-33.

De Jong, James A. "Henricus Beuker and *De Vrije Kerk* on Abraham Kuyper and the Free University," in *Building the House: Essays on Christian Education*, ed. James A. De Jong and Louis Y. Van Dyke. Sioux Center, Iowa: Dordt College Press, 1981, 27-46.

Harinck, George. "Geerhardus Vos as Introducer of Kuyper in America," in *The Dutch-American Experience: Essays in Honor of Robert P. Swierenga*, ed. Hans Krabbendam and Larry J. Wagenaar, VU Studies on Protestant History, no. 5. Amsterdam: VU Uitgeverij, 2000, 243-61.

Heerema, Edward. *R.B.: A Prophet in the Land.* Jordan Station, Ontario: Paideia, 1986.

Heerema, Edward. "The Reverend Henry J. Kuiper, 1885-1962." *Torch and Trumpet,* 13/1 (January, 1963): 5-6.

Hoeksema, Herman. "Calvin, Berkhof and H.J. Kuiper: A Comparison." Grand Rapids: n.p., n.d.

Hoeksema, Herman. *The Protestant Reformed Churches in America,* 2nd ed. Grand Rapids: First Protestant Reformed Church, 1947.

Hofman, Tymen E. *The Canadian Story of the CRC: Its First Century.* Belleview, Ontario: Guardian, 2004.

Hofman, Tymen E. *The Strength of Their Years.* St. Catherines, Ontario: Knight, 1983.

Holwerda, David E. "Hermeneutical Issues Then and Now: The Janssen Case Revisited." *Calvin Theological Journal,* 24/1 (April, 1989): 7-34.

Knight, John. *Echoes of Mercy, Whispers of Love: A Century of Community Outreach by the Christian Reformed Churches in the Greater Grand Rapids Area.* Grand Rapids: Grand Rapids Area Ministries, 1989.

Kromminga, Carl G. "A History of the Efforts toward a Uniform Order of Worship in the Christian Reformed Church, 1916-1932." Grand Rapids: mimeographed by Calvin Theological Seminary, 1972.

Kromminga, D.H. *The Christian Reformed Tradition.* Grand Rapids: Eerdmans, 1943.

Kromminga, John H. *The Christian Reformed Church: A Study in Orthodoxy.* Grand Rapids: Baker, 1949.

Kuiper, Henry J., ed. *New Christian Hymnal.* Grand Rapids: Eerdmans, 1929.

Kuiper, Henry J., ed. *Sermons on Sin and Grace: Lord's Days I—VII.* Grand Rapids: Zondervan, 1936.

Kuiper, Henry J., ed. *Sermons on the Apostles' Creed: Lord's Days VIII–XXIV.* Grand Rapids: Zondervan, 1937.

Kuiper, Henry J., ed. *Sermons on Baptism and the Lord's Supper: Lord's Days XXV–XXXI.* Grand Rapids: Zondervan, 1938.

Kuiper, Henry J., ed. *Sermons on the Ten Commandments: Lord's Days XXXIV–XLIV.* Grand Rapids: Zondervan, 1951.

Kuiper, Henry J., ed. *Sermons on the Lord's Prayer: Lord's Days XLV–LII.* Grand Rapids: Zondervan, 1956.

Kuiper, Henry J. "The Three Points of Common Grace." Grand Rapids: Eerdmans, 1925.

Kuiper, R.B. *"Not of the World:" Discourses on the Christian's Relation to the World.* Grand Rapids: Eerdmans, 1929.

Marsden, George. "Our Present Task in the American Setting." *Reformed Journal* 31 (September, 1981): 14-17.

Ryskamp, Henry. *Offering Hearts, Shaping Lives: A History of Calvin College, 1876-1966,* ed. Harry Boonstra. Grand Rapids: Calvin Alumni Association, 2000.

Schaap, James C. *Our Family Album: The Unfinished Story of the Christian Reformed Church.* Grand Rapids: CRC Publications, 1998.

Semi-Centennial Volume: Theological School and Calvin College, 1876-1926. Grand Rapids: Semi-Centennial Committee, 1926.

Smit, Harvey A. "Mission Zeal in the Christian Reformed Church: 1857-1915," *Perspectives in the Christian Reformed Church: Studies in Its History, Theology and Ecumenicity,* ed. Peter De Klerk and Richard R. De Ridder. Grand Rapids: Baker, 1983, 225-40.

Stob, Henry J. "Observations on the Concept of the Antithesis," *Perspectives in the Christian Reformed Church: Studies in Its History, Theology and Ecumenicity,* ed. Peter De Klerk and Richard R. De Ridder. Grand Rapids: Baker, 1983, 241-60.

Stob, Henry J. *Summoning Up Remembrance.* Grand Rapids: Eerdmans, 1995.

Stokvis, Pieter R.D. "Socialist Immigrants and the American Dream," in *The Dutch-American Experience: Essays in Honor of Robert P. Swierenga,* ed. Hans Krabbendam and Larry J. Wagenaar, VU Studies on Protestant History, no.5. Amsterdam: VU Uitgeverij, 2000, 91-101.

Swierenga, Robert P. *Dutch Chicago: A History of the Hollanders in the Windy City,* The Historical Series of the Reformed Church in America, no. 42. Grand Rapids: Eerdmans, 2002.

Swierenga, Robert P. "Dutch Immigrants in U.S. Ship Passenger Lists, Port of New York, 1881-1882: an Alphabetical Listing, I, Aalbers—Lefferdink." Photoduplicated.

Swierenga, Robert P., and Elton J. Bruins. *Family Quarrels in the Dutch Reformed Churches of the 19th Century*, The Historical Series of the Reformed Church in America, no. 32. Grand Rapids: Eerdmans, 1999.

Taylor, Marvin J., ed. *Religious Education: A Comprehensive Survey.* New York and Nashville: Abingdon, 1960.

Trotter, Melvin E. *These Forty Years*, introduction by G. Campbell Morgan and endorsement by Dr. Harry Ironside. London and Grand Rapids: Marshall, Morgan, and Scott; Zondervan, 1939.

Tuuk, Edward J. *As to Being Worldly* 2nd ed. Grand Rapids: Eerdmans, 1925.

Vande Water, John. *Miracles in Forgotten Streets.* Grand Rapids: Eerdmans, 1936.

Vande Water, John. *The Street of Forgotten Men.* Grand Rapids: Eerdmans, n.d.

Van Wyk, William P. "Stadsevangelisatie, waarom en hoe?" Grand Rapids: Eerdmans and Sevensma, 1913.

Zwaanstra, Henry. *Reformed Thought and Experience in a New World.* Kampen: J.H. Kok, B.V., 1973.

Zwaanstra, Henry. "Something about B.K." Grand Rapids: Calvin Theological Seminary, 1977.

Zylstra, Carl E. "God-Centered Preaching in a Human-Centered Age." Ph.D. Diss. Ann Arbor: University Microfilms, 1983.

Index